THE OXFORD INTERNATIONAL RELATIONS IN SOUTH ASIA SERIES

SERIES EDITORS
Sumit Ganguly and E. Sridharan

After a long period of relative isolation during the Cold War years, contemporary South Asia has grown immensely in its significance in the global political and economic order. This ascendancy has two key dimensions. First, the emergence of India as a potential economic and political power that follows its acquisition of nuclear weapons and its fitful embrace of economic liberalization. Second, the persistent instability along India's borders continues to undermine any attempts at achieving political harmony in the region: fellow nuclear-armed state Pakistan is beset with chronic domestic political upheavals; Afghanistan is paralysed and trapped with internecine warfare and weak political institutions; Sri Lanka is confronted by an uncertain future with a disenchanted Tamil minority; Nepal is caught in a vortex of political and legal uncertainty as it forges a new constitution; and Bangladesh is overwhelmed by a tumultuous political climate.

India's rising position as an important player in global economic and political affairs warrants extra-regional and international attention. The rapidly evolving strategic role and importance of South Asia in the world demands focused analyses of foreign and security policies within and towards the region. The present series addresses these concerns. It consists of original, theoretically grounded, empirically rich, timely, and topical volumes oriented towards contemporary and future developments in one of the most populous and diverse corners of the world.

Sumit Ganguly is professor of political science and Rabindranath Tagore Chair in Indian Cultures and Civilizations, Indiana University, Bloomington, USA.

E. Sridharan is academic director, University of Pennsylvania Institute for the Advanced Study of India, New Delhi.

THE OXFORD INTERNATIONAL RELATIONS IN SOUTH ASIA SERIES

India's Spatial Imaginations of South Asia

Power, Commerce, and Community

Shibashis Chatterjee

OXFORD
UNIVERSITY PRESS

Oxford University Press is a department of the University of Oxford.
It furthers the University's objective of excellence in research, scholarship,
and education by publishing worldwide. Oxford is a registered trademark of
Oxford University Press in the UK and in certain other countries.

Published in India by
Oxford University Press
2/11 Ground Floor, Ansari Road, Daryaganj, New Delhi 110 002, India

ISBN-13 (printed edition): 978-0-19-948988-6
ISBN-10 (printed edition): 0-19-948988-2

ISBN-13 (eBook): 978-0-19-909549-0
ISBN-10 (eBook): 0-19-909549-3

Typeset Adobe Jenson Pro 10/13
by Tranistics Data Technologies, New Delhi 110 044
Printed and bound in India at Repro India Ltd., Mumbai

Contents

Preface

THIS BOOK IS A result of two very different interests that I have carried for a very long time. While I have taught political theory for over two decades, I have researched primarily on Indian foreign policy. To many, this would appear an impossible combination. My position, however, is uncomplicated. I have merely tried to conceptualize Indian foreign policy by using metaphors of space. I have tried to make sense of India's foreign policy in the subcontinent through concepts like sovereignty, nationalism, citizenship, and territoriality—ideas that are primarily driven by political theory. However, this is not a book on political theory. It is unambiguously an argument on foreign policy. It is my explanation of how India spatializes its foreign policy in South Asia, a theatre that is crucial not only for its ascension as a great power, but even more significant for what kind of a power it wishes to become. I was intrigued by the sad binary that writings on India's policy towards South Asia are afflicted with. Scholarship remained divided by realist readings that shy away from any serious conceptual audit, and post-colonial interventions that theorized without any attentive concern for empirical realities. I do not believe that a *via media* exists between the two. However, I find something useful in both. I have sought, therefore, to distil them in my own ways.

I offer an account of how India understands South Asia as a space of power rather than that of market or community, and attempt to validate my arguments by evidence. Foreign policy choices are hard and real. They are made by political elites aided by a small coterie of bureaucrats and policy intellectuals. It is their imagination that matters. I have thus attempted to read their imagination and offer an explanation. I have not extended a normative case of whether the spatial basis of India's imagination of its neighbourhood has been constraining or liberating, static or dynamic, progressive or regressive, located in a paradigm of control or communication. Further, my book does not find any alteration in India's spatial imagination of South Asia, no matter what domestic configuration of political forces ruled the state. My reading of South Asia has convinced me that liberal or radical imaginations will work only if political forces strong enough to catapult these into ruling coalitions can be generated—no politics, no transformation. This may not be a very exciting argument to make. However, a scholar's task is not only to indulge in discursive analyses, but also to remain grounded in reality. At least my academic training taught me to look at empirical reality critically, but seriously. My book is a humble effort in this direction.

While I had written along these lines for a long time and in unrelated ways, I needed to bring my arguments together in one cover. While I tried to do this for a long time, I could not make much progress due to a variety of reasons. The Fulbright Professional Excellence Fellowship finally afforded me an opportunity to anchor at Yale University for six months between August 2016 to February 2017, and I made the most of Yale's amazing resources to put together the chapters. My first institutional debt goes to the South Asia Council and the Macmillan Centre at Yale. I am particularly indebted to the warm hospitality of the then Director of the South Asia Council, Professor Karuna Mantena, who was kind enough to affiliate me at the South Asia Centre. The entire staff at the SAC and Macmillan, Kasturi Gupta, Amaar Al-Hayder, and Whitney Doel, among others, made me feel at home and shared responsibilities that allowed me to write without hassles. Professor Steve Wilkinson, chair at the Department of Political Science at Yale, was extremely generous in granting me a state-of-the-art office, and extended all support during my stay at Yale, which was vital in ways more than one. Members of staff at the Department of Political Science, particularly Mary Sue, Thomas Hallihan, and Lani Colianna, were unbelievably generous in creating an environment conducive for my work. The material basis of the book was largely was laid at Yale. I also benefited from conversing with a number of scholars there, on a wide spectrum of issues, which helped me come to grips with my argument more effectively.

I have been exceedingly fortunate to have struck friendship with a number of outstanding minds, from whom I have constantly derived ideas and received unstinted support. Professor Rajen Harshe has been a beacon of my intellectual life despite not being a direct teacher at any stage. I have agreed more with him than anyone else, on a wide range of social and political issues that have a direct bearing on this work. My debt to Professor Kanti Bajpai is too enormous to mention. In fact, the central theoretical category that I use in this book is adapted from his work. He allowed me to virtually raid his personal collection of books on International Relations theory that I could not have obtained otherwise. I have learnt something new every time I have interacted with him. My friendship with Professor Rajesh Basrur has helped me in upgrading my readings in several areas and his faith in me, my limited productivity notwithstanding, has never wavered over these years. Professor T.V. Paul gave me several important opportunities in my academic life for which I can never thank him enough. He invited me as a fellow at the Center for International Peace and Security Studies (CIPSS), McGill University, Montreal, for a month in 2014. In fact, it was at McGill that I first seriously thought about writing this book. I am also thankful to Navnita Behera and Siddharth Mallavarapu, my old friends, attached to Delhi University and JNU, respectively, who have been integral to my work in IR theory over these years. While both would possibly have more disagreement with my take in this book, I would welcome their critique. Their camaraderie has kept me going over these years. Two other scholars deserve a special mention. From Professor Sanjay Chaturvedi, I have learned more on space and territoriality than anyone else. I may have my healthy scepticism towards his radical brand of critical geopolitics, but he encouraged me to read a genre of literature that was absolutely essential to my work. I have likewise unabashedly derived ideas, and had been an excellent listener in my numerous interactions with Professor Samir Kumar Das on themes like citizenship, identity, nationalism, and sovereignty, that are reflected in many of my references. Professor Rahul Mukherjee has also been a constant source of encouragement and support.

Two scholars have had the most direct impact on my research outreach. To Professor Sumit Ganguly, I owe more than anyone else in my professional career. His contribution is so multifarious and all-encompassing that I dare not even try to put them to words. His friendship is one of the most treasured relations of my life, while his sharp criticism always comes handy. Likewise, Professor E. Sridharan has given me a number of pivotal opportunities to do theoretical research in areas that are by no means popular in India. I remain genuinely grateful to both of them, for having placed this title under their series.

As an alumnus of the Department of International Relations at Jadavpur University, I was fortunate to be mentored by Professor

Jayantanuja Bandyopadhyaya. It is a personal tragedy that he will not be there to read this book. I have over the years been pampered by my teachers, who later became dependable colleagues, on whom I will inflict this one without a second thought. I thank my teachers, Professor Purusottam Bhattacharya, Professor Rabindra Sen, Professor Sanjukta Bhattacharya, and Professor Arun Banerji for believing in me. I am also grateful to two senior academics, Professor Radharaman Chakrabarti and Professor Rakhahari Chatterjee for their constant encouragement and affection.

I have talked on different facets that have gone into this book on different occasions in Kolkata. I have benefited from the responses of Partha Pratim Basu and Anindya Jyoti Majumdar, my closest friends at Jadavpur University, though I could not make them read my manuscript due to the paucity of time. I have also shared my views and collaborated with Sulagna Maitra, a former student and now a faculty at Dublin College, for which I remain thankful to her forever. I must also record the help I have received from Krishnendu Mukhopadhyay, who researches with me, on many points related to the work. My former student, Rumela Sen, a doctorate from Cornell and now a post-doctoral scholar at Columbia, invited me to Soka University, where I bounced off my central arguments and benefited from the interactions. She, like many of my students who are in the West, has constantly provided me with research articles in quick time that I needed for my work. This was particularly helpful post-Yale, when I was modifying my draft in response to the referee reports that required me to consult readings I had missed out originally. I am also thankful to my former student, Mr Udayan Das, for helping me with copyediting issues. I also express my heartfelt thanks to the editors at Oxford University Press for their manifold contributions.

I had presented some of my ideas that culminate in this book at different universities like Hull, McGill, Yale, Dhaka, and Makerere. The responses and criticisms that I received were genuinely beneficial for me. I have also benefited a lot from two anonymous referees who read my manuscript. I must also acknowledge my heartfelt thanks to the dedicated team of Oxford University Press, without whose manifold contributions the book would not be what it is.

This book would not have seen the light of day had it not been for the contributions of two of my former students. Without the numerous contributions of Sreya Maitra, my former research student and now a teacher of political science, I could not have completed this book. She had virtually single-handedly done the hard work—reading the chapters meticulously, finding errors and correcting them, completing references, lining up the bibliography, and helping me with ideas when I got bogged down in the text. To Anurag Sinha, the most gifted mind I have come across in my teaching career, I owe the debt of unparalleled hospitality at New Haven and for facilitating my affiliation at Yale, without which this book would not have happened. I have, therefore, decided to dedicate the book to both of them.

No intellectual work happens outside the family. I lost my parents between 2013 and 2017. My twin sister, Manisha, as an extended part of myself, shared responsibilities of parental care that allowed me time to work at a very difficult period of my life. We had wonderful parents who socialized us into a culture of freedom. Rather than basking in unreflective affection, I am thankful for their abiding faith in me. My wife, Nandini, as a fellow academic and friend, has borne all the trouble during my sabbaticals and had performed all her tasks with her characteristic perfection that allowed me to read and work freely. I was away before the most important public examination of my daughter's life. Nandini covered for me and guaranteed that our daughter did not suffer from my long absence. Without her support, this book would not have happened for sure. My daughter, Meghna, grew up when the book was underway. She enabled me to have peace of mind that contributed significantly towards wrapping up of the project in time. I can never thank them enough.

Finally, I remain solely responsible for all mistakes and errors that may have escaped multiple revisions and close scrutiny of the manuscript.

Shibashis Chatterjee
Department of International Relations, Jadavpur University
October 2018

List of Abbreviations

ARF	ASEAN Regional Forum
ASEAN	Association of Southeast Asian Nations
BBIN	Bangladesh, Bhutan, India, and Nepal
BCIM	Bangladesh–China–India–Myanmar
BCIM-EC	Bangladesh–China–India–Myanmar-Economic Corridor
BIMSTEC	Bengal Initiative for Multi-Sectoral Technical and Economic Corporation
BJP	Bharatiya Janata Party
BNP	Bangladesh Nationalist Party
BOBCOM	Bay of Bengal Community
BRI	Belt and Road Initiative
BSA	Bilateral Security Agreement
CPEC	China–Pakistan Economic Corridor
CSCAP	Council for Security Cooperation in Asia Pacific
EU	European Union
FDI	Foreign Direct Investment
FTA	Free Trade Agreement
GDP	Gross Domestic Product
IOR	Indian Ocean Region
IPKF	Indian Peace Keeping Force
IR	International Relations
ISI	Inter-Services Intelligence
LDC	Least Developed Countries
LTTE	Liberation Tigers of Tamil Eelam
MFN	Most Favoured Nation
MPAT	Multinational Planning Augmentation Team
MSS	Maritime Safety and Security
NATO	North Atlantic Treaty Organization
NDA	National Democratic Alliance

NER	North Eastern Region
NWFP	North West Frontier Province
OBOR	One Belt One Road
ODA	Official Development Assistance
PLOTE	People's Liberation Organization of Tamil Eelam
PNG	Papua New Guinea
PRC	People's Republic of China
RAW	Research and Analysis Wing
RCEP	Regional Comprehensive Economic Partnership
RECCA	Regional Economic Cooperation Conference on Afghanistan
RSS	Rashtriya Swayamesvak Sangh
SAARC	South Asian Association of Regional Cooperation
SACU	South Asian Customs Union
SAEU	South Asian Economic Union
SAFTA	South Asian Free Trade Area
SAPTA	South Asian Preferential Trade Area
SATP	South Asia Terrorism Portal
SCO	Shanghai Cooperation Organization
SF	Security Forces
SGEP	SAARC Group of Eminent Persons
TDR	Territorialization, Deterritorialization, Reterritorialization
ULFA	United Liberation Front of Assam
UNCTAD	United Nations Conference on Trade and Development
UPA	United Progressive Alliance
WTO	World Trade Organization

Introduction

D O SPATIAL IMAGINATIONS MATTER in India's foreign policy towards South Asia? I argue that India's understanding of its neighbourhood is informed by a certain version of realism, as South Asia remains a space defined in terms of power and sovereign territoriality, in contrast to alternative imaginations based on the market or community.[1] I also claim that this understanding is one held by India's ruling elite—consisting of politicians cutting across party lines, key bureaucrats, army chiefs, and influential policy intellectuals. While the nature of India's nationalism remains contested, the frame of territorialized India is widely accepted, and apart from secessionist outfits in states like Kashmir and a few northeastern states which have challenged this cartographic inevitability from time to time, there are no major political fault lines in the territories and borders of India. However, realism is not the only spatial imagination at work. There are indeed alternative spatial imaginations of India's policy vis-à-vis South Asia. My argument is that while alternative imagination/s of South Asia are indeed ideationally possible, the kind of politics necessary to make this happen is weak, if not virtually non-existent, among political elites in South Asia as a whole. The argument is based on the abiding relevance of sovereign territoriality as the defining tenet of modern South Asia that almost naturally selects realist foreign policies over other alternatives. It intends to show that despite significant changes in domestic configurations in India, both regarding ideological commitments and intricacies of the federal structure, its imagination of foreign policy in South Asia has remained remarkably constant. While relations with neighbours have varied with changing regimes over time, these have moved between fixed points of references, created by India's imagination of South Asia as space marked by sovereign territoriality. In brief, the book asks three questions: first, what conception of space underlies India's vision of its neighbourhood? Second, who articulates this vision? Third, what are the consequences of the dominant imagination?

The book both builds on the existing literature and departs from it. While India's search for great power status and the general drift of its foreign policy in contemporary times has attracted much academic attention, relatively little has been written about India's *constructions* of South Asia. The common view is that India remains fundamentally challenged in its backyard, and therefore, its claim to a major power status hinges largely on how it negotiates these difficulties in its immediate neighbourhood. Admittedly, there is a body of literature that looks at specific issues, such as India's conflicts with Pakistan and China. There are standalone works on other bilateral relations between India and its smaller neighbours, like Bangladesh, Sri Lanka, and Nepal. However, there is a paucity of literature that looks at India's approach to the 'region' conceptually, trying to identify broader trends that induce some sanity into an enormous amount of data that gets produced every day. More crucially, one can divide the writings on India's neighbourhood broadly into two mutually opposed genres that hardly see eye to eye with each other: first, some works describe India's foreign policy in conventional system-friendly terms and follow the lines suggested by the Indian state. These include recent works by scholars like Stephen Cohen, C. Raja Mohan, Sumit Ganguly, David Malone, Rohan Mukherjee, Harsh Panth, Sandy Gordon, and others.[2] This does not mean that these works are in any way rationalizations of India's foreign policy. In contrast, most of this literature is very critical of the foreign policy of the Indian state on specific issues. However, they take India's understanding of the neighbourhood as more or less granted and work their analyses from this baseline assumption. In contrast, we can describe the works by scholars like Itty Abraham, Priya Chacko, Sanjay Chaturvedi, Navnita Behera, and Ranabir Samaddar, among others, as offering a critical, post-colonial reading of India's engagement with its neighbourhood. These works, in their own ways, question the very categories that the other group takes for granted. Hence, on issues like borders, territories, frontiers, and identities, the post-colonial or critical scholars question the very category of 'South Asia'. In a way, a rich body of work on Indian citizenship, immigration, and the diaspora by writers like Neerja Jayal, Anupama Roy, Samir K. Das, Paula Banerjee, and others has strengthened the critical/post-colonial project substantively. These works have drawn attention to questions of identity and imagination more carefully in making sense of how India deals with itself and outsiders. There is also much discussion on the Hindu nationalist project in India and its impact on foreign policy, particularly in the works of Chris Ogden and Christophe Jaffrelot, which has drawn attention to link the domestic and the international closer. Scholars like T.V. Paul and Kanti Bajpai, in their very different ways, have reflected upon India's grand strategy making and sought to engage with both material and ideational factors. Rajesh Basrur's research on India's nuclear policy, though firmly ensconced in the realist school, has occasionally looked beyond narrow considerations of military power in examining New Delhi's ambiguities and vacillations over nuclear decision making.

I acknowledge in particular a recent book by Sandy Gordon (2015) that explores whether India will fulfil its potential as a rising power, or remain bogged down in poverty and corruption and give in to a mélange of deep social, economic, and political flaws, the manacles of domestic segregation and a distressed neighbourhood.

What does this book add here? While I take issue with realist scholarship that does not plumb deep enough or explore sociological spacing at all, I do not find the alternative post-colonial/leftist/critical scholarship offering anything substantive other than nuanced critiques of state and national security discourses. I address security as a legitimate concern for states. Further, I recognize the complex relations between the domestic and the external domains that territorial spacing creates. I am advancing two arguments here. First, I argue that it is essential that we come to terms with how India imagines South Asia. This exercise, however, has to begin in the 'domestic'. In other words, we need to discuss the nature of political community in India. But a region cannot be a mechanical extension of the domestic attributes of the state. Territorial differentiation must be accounted for in any understanding of what a region *means*. All South Asian states are real entities with exceptionally high claims of sovereign entitlements that make them ultra-sensitive to territoriality and borders. Indian foreign policy reflects this commitment to hard borders and remains firmly anchored in territoriality to articulate its South Asian policies. Second, the subcontinent is not merely a collection of states. It is also a society of states. This dual constitution of modern South Asia, both as a body of sovereign states and as a meta-community of shared cultures, identities, and norms, is at the root of India's ambivalence towards and difficulties with its neighbours. I argue that this sovereign imagination is real inasmuch as it guides India's actions in its neighbourhood. The book uses available official sources like briefs and declarations of the ministry of external affairs, party documents, interviews, and press reports as evidence. It uses the standard analytical method to establish its arguments. This is an exegetical analysis that does not attempt any testing of hypothesis.

The book is a valuable addition to the literature that looks at India's rise as a significant power, and in that context, delves into issues of domestic governance and neighbourly and regional relations of New Delhi. The book readily cautions us against coming to any easy conclusions and drives home the point that unless India puts its house in order and faces up to its regional challenges more boldly, its promise to mature into a major power may not materialize. The book is not about India's rise as a great power per se; *it is about India's fraught and complicated ties to its immediate neighbourhood that I read in its cast iron post-colonial commitment to sovereign territoriality.* India's inability to meet its challenges near home cannot be understood unless we view South Asia as a political as well as sociological space. While Gordon's text has a lot on the material aspects of the problem, my book is more focused on *meanings*. I do not discuss India's various neighbourly and domestic challenges related either to governance or security, which keep India under shackles. Rather, I examine why India has *little choice* given its present material and ideational parameters to *reorient* its policies in its neighbourhood altogether. India's foreign policy thus can be read in many registers, and their mutual incompatibility is increasing.

The book contains five main chapters and a conclusion. The first chapter explains the chosen conceptual categories, clarifies the tropes of their deployment, and stitches together the dual narratives of India's domestic and external imaginations. I review tracts on territory and space in political theory, sociology, critical geopolitics, and international relations (IR) theory. The modern subcontinent got territorialized through the colonial experience, which set up India's post-colonial destiny in these terms. Indian leaders were aware of the challenges and problems the country faced. However, their approach to deal with these issues could not transcend the given categories of territoriality, sovereignty, and a sense of difference. I go on to show that India's transforming models of nation-building have evolved within the framework of sovereign territoriality. I also argue that while the use of domestic/international divide is inappropriate to make sense of India's negotiations in South Asia, it is equally facile to see the region as an extension of India's domestic contests. Independence was as real for the other South Asian states as it was for India. However, the fact that the lines of peoplehood and territorial nationalism never coincided in South Asia meant that there will always be tension in working out national projects predicated upon sovereignty. These states embarked on different projects of difference that were crucial to the making of modern South Asia. This chapter shows how India has framed its project and negotiated with others in its neighbourhood.

The second chapter deals with three transformative theses and their possible impact and consequences in South Asia. I examine the impacts of globalization, democratic peace, and human security to find whether these have changed elite mind-sets in the subcontinent. Globalization in the subcontinent is explored to show how the intertwining of the global, regional, national, and local took place through the agency of the state rather than against it. This chapter argues the following: first, globalization has divided the subcontinent along economic lines that complicate India's neighbourhood policies further. Second, the dynamic of globalization has unfolded within the given geopolitical parameters of South Asia, and therefore, no liberal order has grown within the region. This episode brings out the disjuncture of economic and political dynamics in this region despite two decades of globalization. Third, democratic peace has no credibility in South Asia given the intense geopolitical competition between India and Pakistan that also affects the foreign policies of smaller states. The nature of the regime in Pakistan (democratic or military) has had no manifest impact upon the quality of India–Pakistan relations. This rivalry is overlaid by the brooding presence of China that militarizes the space even further. Fourth, while there is a broad realization that human security cannot be tackled effectively through a paradigm of sovereign territoriality, the South Asian states have failed to craft an alternative discourse of security. The state has dominated the agenda of non-traditional security and defined it. South Asian states continue to suffer from fears and tensions since most of these insecurities stem from within and are the products of the state.

The third chapter accounts for the growth of territorial nationalism and realism undergirding India's security thinking in South Asia. I concentrate here on the political and security narratives of Indian elites and show how they have thought about India's security primarily in realist, geopolitical terms. I also show that while the perspectives differ on certain issues across India's major political parties, when entrusted with actual policymaking, these differences lessen quite remarkably. The chapter also discusses the perspectives of the strategic elites in India who legitimize the narrative of space as power. While these experts are not a part of the 'ruling elite', their role in package legitimatization of a realist or power-centric reading of the neighbourhood influences the official narratives to a great extent. The accessibility and privileging of certain discourses over others is an excellent indicator of the spatial thinking of the state.

The fourth chapter is about how spatial imagination steeped in sovereign territoriality bedevilled local efforts to achieve a viable regional political community in South Asia. I invoke functional, security, community, and post-colonial perspectives to interrogate regionalism in South Asia. This chapter shows that despite all South Asian states agreeing upon the virtues of regional cooperation, their underlying expectations are very different, which frustrates regional cooperation among countries. The chapter explains why spatial imagination is cardinal to this failing. It puts in bold relief how India has addressed regionalism in its immediate surroundings and achieved little in the process. I show that the civil society has failed to have any impact in reversing this trend. South Asian regionalism has not paid attention to 'other modes of representation' by non-state actors despite the inability of states to address many pressing issues that affect all the countries of the region. While a few states have found sub-regional cooperation more convenient, the net result has not been very exciting so far, given that such sub-regional cooperation is also subject to the familiar geopolitical dynamics unleashed by territoriality. The limited record of collaboration among India, Bangladesh, Myanmar, Nepal, Bhutan, and China in some sub-regional efforts gives an excellent account of this process.

Spatial imaginations evolve. Frustrations in its immediate neighbourhood encouraged India to broaden its spatial imagination in geographical terms. One such major spatial experiment has been India's 'Look East'/'Act East' policy that is the subject of the fifth chapter. This chapter reads the genesis of India's 'Look East' policy in two spatial registers. First, this policy was reflected in India's urge to redefine its neighbourhood as it finds itself bogged down in its immediate vicinity. This is, therefore, an attempt to transcend geographical limits as India's growing naval and economic capacities make it possible to extend its neighbourhood. 'Look East', therefore, is the exemplar of a new spatial imagination. The second register has to do with India's efforts to find a solution to the chronic economic underdevelopment of India's turbulent and fraught northeastern region by bringing the advantages of scale to this geographically locked-in area. The northeastern states are joined tenderly to the rest of the country by the precarious Chicken's Neck—a narrow stretch of land across the northern part of the province of West Bengal. This region has also not integrated properly with the rest of the country due to some historical, political, and cultural reasons, despite many attempts by the Indian state to reverse this trend. This chapter shows how this experiment has not produced desired results as it stands at variance with the expectations of most groups in India's Northeast. The 'Look East' policy increasingly veers towards the new articulation of the 'Indo-Pacific' as a geopolitical theatre for a rising power that needs to balance against China. In this new great game, the strategic imperatives have come to dominate India's spatial thinking that has moved it even further from a possible radical continental thrust in its 'Look East' policy.

The book, to sum up, tells a story of spatial imaginations of a region, with its attendant achievements and despair, and shows how the differentiated cartography of territorial nationalism still looms large on our shared ontology of social space, thereby making substantive peace and lasting cooperation difficult to achieve in the subcontinent.

Notes

1. This idea was originally suggested by Professor Kanti Bajpai (1995).
2. More recent works by Shyam Saran (2017), Aparna Pande (2017), and Shivshankar Menon (2016) have been explored in Chapter 1 in this volume.

1 Territoriality, Sovereignty, and the State

South Asia and the Politics of Space

TERRITORIALITY IS OFTEN REGARDED as a blind spot in social inquiry. However, there is a major body of literature that interrogates the notion from various vantage points, along with a host of related ideas like nationalism, citizenship, and ethnicity. The relationship between territoriality and space too, though exceedingly complex, has attracted a fair degree of attention in recent years.

This chapter is organized into two parts. In the first section, we look into various tracts on territoriality. We begin with the concerns of political theory, go through the sociological works by Henri Lefebvre, engage briefly with few interventions by critical geographers, and then culminate by looking closely at certain perspectives of international relations (IR hereafter) scholars. In the second part, our focus shifts to India's spatial imaginations of South Asia. This part lays out the primary arguments of the text and fixes the conceptual categories that are to be deployed in the chapters to follow.

The Argument and Scope

This book is about India's spatial imagination of South Asia as a neighbourhood. By India's imagination, I mean to denote the elite visions that are reflected in foreign policy discourses of the Indian state.[1] The idea of a neighbourhood is always a spatial imagery, anchored in some metaphor or the other. The imaginations have two sources. First, they are rooted in India's self-identity as a nation-state. All imaginations are discursive in nature and are intersubjectively constituted. However, the Indian state has objective preferences that it seeks to realize in the neighbourhood. The character of the state, or what may be called 'state identity', conditions these preferences. But a state, no matter how dominant within a given region, cannot imagine the region through its own identity alone. Strategic, economic, and cultural considerations provide the second source of its imagination of the neighbourhood. This indicates a subtext, or a larger narrative, that underpins their idea of a region.

Space and place are related but not identical. According to Yi-Fu Tuan, a space can be accessed intimately through our senses or discursively through our ideas and imagination, mediated, invariably, by symbols and representations. He found space empty in the sense of lacking human values but having the properties of demarcation. Demarcation leads to holding of a space as defensible against intrusions. Space, therefore, seemed abstract rather than social (Tuan 1977: 6). Place, by contrast, was a location marked by intimate contact resulting from human experiences. In a way, spaces became places when humans filled it with meaning and purpose. A place is therefore existential and cannot be tied to observable geographies or time. In a comparable vein, the human geographer Edward Relph contrasted space with a more experientially-based understanding of place, and arranged these on a continuum that had direct experience at one end, and abstract ideas at the other (Relph 1976: 9). In this book, I use the concept of space by being mindful of its distinction from place. I do not claim that all spaces are places. Since I do not write here of an anthropological account of place-making, the central concept that I use is space understood as political territoriality. The spatial vision of a state is a discursive subtext that provides meaning and substance to a state's foreign policy vis-à-vis its neighbours.

India's understanding of South Asia thus involves a two-level exploration. The first deals with the contestations of India's self-identity as a nation-state, and the identity selected by the dominant official elite to condition the state's foreign policy preferences in the neighbourhood. The second relates to the deployment of spatial metaphors that explain India's policy choices as preferences born out of domestic identity considerations, and which cannot automatically be projected on to others. The conjugation of selfhood and the deployment of spatial metaphors answer some of the intriguing questions that plague foreign policy analysis. It explains why a state holds particular interests as vital by arguing that this is a deliberate process of selection by the dominant elite, which renders alternative definitions of benefits invalid, draws attention to the justificatory discourses that are invariably deployed to achieve legitimacy, and shows why alternative spatial imaginations are emasculated in the process.

This book is an attempt to explain how Indian foreign and security policy elites understand its neighbourhood in spatial terms. My central argument is that this understanding is an unmistakably realist one, one that prioritizes a geopolitical conception of space over those of commerce and community. However, this is not an endorsement of political realism. I am also not arguing that the geopolitical reading is the ideal way to look at South Asia in spatial terms. Instead, I posit that since independence, its espousal of a non-aligned foreign policy notwithstanding, the Indian state has leveraged its geopolitical or power imagination. No matter which political party came to power, this spatial imagination has remained unchanged. I intend to showcase the major strands or dimensions of this imagination and argue that neither economic prosperity nor community have succeeded in guiding India's neighbourhood policies. This does not mean that the alternative conceptions are meaningless. The attractions of commerce have certainly affected India's foreign policy choices, and the need for rapid economic development as a precondition to emerge as a major power has been a constant refrain in New Delhi's foreign policy discourses. However, geo-economics has remained subservient to geopolitical concerns, and considerations of strategic interests have, when required, prevailed over the demands of international business, trade, and commerce. The weak domestic basis of commercial liberalism has further accentuated this tendency. The Indian business class has gone global; however, they have not attempted to redirect the goals of Indian foreign policy in South Asia. Likewise, the idea of community is not determinant to India's spatial imagination. Cultural borders are certainly as pertinent to South Asia as anywhere else. Such borders are also more permeable. However, the state has shown little interest in experimenting with cultural borders. The communities living near or at the border certainly have a more anthropological reading of territory and space. However, the state has not subscribed to such a vision. In fact, the state has become more paranoid about surveillance and protection of its borders, which is visible in erection of physical impediments of various kinds in spite of investment in the idea of infrastructural connectivity across international borders. Here, as elsewhere, the state space is distinctly geopolitical and there is no evidence of any alternative cartography of trust, or a humane geography of a region sans hard borders. This account, however, is not a normative statement. I argue that space-making is an intensely political act. Unless political forces, wedded to a radically different or critical ontology of borders and territorial spacing, come to power, there is no possibility of the geopolitical understanding retreating. Hence, my arguments are different from those made by both realists and critical geographers. Unlike realists, I take the alternative spatial imaginations as legitimate. I agree with critical geographers in that post-colonial borders are not natural. However, I differ in recognizing that while borders are artificial (non-natural), they are, nonetheless, and potent and real.

The Theoretical Issues

Borders and Boundaries

Borders, boundaries, and territoriality are distinctive concepts. Before moving on to territoriality, which is the primary concept of this study, a few preliminary observations on borders and boundaries are in order. First, borders make identifications of various kinds and give meaning to the shape of a society. Hence, as David Newman (2010) argued, territory and borders travel together.[2] Second, borders can be of various kinds and these cartographies do not coincide. Particularly, political borders are not cultural borders. Political borders are the result of space making strategies of modern nation-states that do not coincide with cultural spaces. In fact, whether one can invoke the concept of borders to culture at all is contestable. Cultures vary; however, they do not vary according to set rules or patterns. Between the extremes of universalism and irreducible specificities, cultures show a wide variety of patterns. Cultural processes mutate, cultures often communicate and learn from each other, and while some cultures are hostile to change, others are more receptive to transformation. This fungibility of cultural landscapes is not reproduced in the political space-making processes that result in the drawing of the international borders.

It is germane to go back to the writings of Agnew, whose work remains critical in this context (Agnew 1994, 1998, 2008). Agnew showed us that borders must be understood in dual senses. First, viewed physically, borders were regulators of movement of people and commodities; second, the border is also an idea that gets us into thinking and acting in territorial terms, as they 'limit the exercise of intellect, imagination, and political will' (Agnew 2008: 176). In other words, the functions of the physical border can hardly be accounted for unless we recognize the borders of our minds. Borders may be materially constituted with different degrees of physical impediments raised to control movements of people, or they may also represent symbolic processing of differentiation and othering that defines who belongs and who does not—the naturalized insider and the alien outsider. Of course, such meanings are variable and borders are therefore never uniform. Every border is a constraint; hence, they compromise the freedom of subjects. However, the constraint varies from one actor to another and some are invariably more affected than others. More significantly, a border may provide security to many subjects but may adversely affect the material and cultural interests of many others. It is futile to see borders as set functions. Their fluidity and variability is essential to the functions they perform.

Two points follow from this. First, while the materiality of physical borders may be altered both architecturally and as a mode of regulation, the mental borders may not make a corresponding shift. Second, the salience of borders is a deeply normative but political question. The geopolitical reading is thus one of the many readings of borders and territoriality and if the statist meaning is privileged over those of the anthropological, historical, and cultural ones, it reflects a set of mental processes predicated on a certain conception of spatial imagination that is both time bound and limited. Agnew made the famous distinction between borders as national space and as sites of dwelling, which is indicative of the normative presuppositions underlying critical geopolitical thinking that wants to go beyond given borders in the interest of creating a more democratic and humane world.[3]

Second, the meaning of borders varies according to subjects. The national elites who frame foreign and security policies see borders as closed spaces that need to be protected through surveillance, military installations, and check-posts of various kinds. People living in the borderlands, in contrast, see borders as permeable and negotiable, and they need to transcend borders in certain ways, despite the attempts by the state to close such movements. Traders, businessmen, tourists, and pilgrims have their own understanding of borders. It is not that they dispute the lines; however, they do not necessarily give in to the bordering processes of the state and negotiates with the geopolitical meaning privileged by the state. Even states are not universally committed to seeing borders in geopolitical terms. European borders in the era of the European Union (EU hereafter) were after all the natural laboratory of border studies that sought to highlight the multiple meanings of borders and their consequences. However, post-colonial states have high sensitivity to political borders, and even in Europe in recent years, as waves of migration posed major challenges to their underlying demographic contours, tight border control has made a strong return to politics.[4] Similar dynamics can be seen in post-Trump USA and in Australia, among several other states, highlighting the tension between borders of various kinds. The US–Mexican border is possibly one of the most well researched terrains that shows an amazing intertwining of perspectives.[5]

Ranabir Samaddar, Willem van Schendel, Paula Banerjee, and Samir Das, among others, have challenged the national security reading of borders and counterposed to it an anthropological and living account of flows, dreams, passions, and livelihoods, which both recognize and go beyond the statist cast iron frames. Drawing upon the work of Balibar, who saw borders as polysemic, heterogeneous, and a storehouse of many meanings, these scholars espouse many affinities and divergences of the national and social connotations underlying these lines of separation. Their work dwells on the polyvalent nature of borderlands, which are not passive margins, but receptacles of social and cultural space constituting a no man's land among the national, local, and international boundaries (Banerjee 2010: xiv–xvi).

Borders under Globalization

Third, borders have assumed a new meaning in the context of globalization and geo-economics. To begin with, their difference is cardinal. Globalization has prompted a number of scholars to claim that borders were on the retreat, and focus on their porosity and movements. This coincided neatly with the rise of post-structural and postmodern perspectives on identities. This led to new definitions of the political that sought to privilege identities understood as signs and representations that underplayed the centrality of the state's role as the order-producing institution of life. While scholars differ on the nature of the impact of the globalizing processes on borders and territoriality, there are broadly two perspectives. The first is perhaps most graphically represented by Claude Raffestin, who problematizes the notion of space taken as an absolute unit in conventional geography. He alternatively proposes a conceptualization of space that is deeply embedded in human subjectivity.[6] Space is a mental construction, produced and transformed into territory through the projection of human labour qua energy and information. The role of manual and intellectual labour is central to the transformation, conservation, or maintenance of ecosystems and their representations that stand altered by globalization. The forces of globalization have generated a profound reshuffling of old systems of relations and human needs. This eventually has led to the construction or reconfiguration of territorialities and set in motion the TDR (territorialization, deterritorialization, reterritorialization) process. The transformative agenda of globalization has fundamentally challenged all the fixities that were considered to be sacrosanct in traditional geography. 'All our geographical education was based on the "durability" of the visible, as if the places and names of things on the earth were fixed once and for all. The ephemeral and the unstable have taken the place of the durable by the eruption and intrusion of fluidity into territories and territorialities' (Raffestin 2012: 139).

While the new processes of border transcendence were indeed exciting departures, the role that the state continued to play in conditioning those dynamics seemed equally significant. As Passi puts it, 'Borders, border-crossings, and security became deeply intertwined and led scholars to consider such issues as transnationalism or cosmopolitanism, which force us to look beyond ostensibly "separate" spatial scales to connections across them' (Paasi 2013: 480). While globalization has certainly caused an institutional crumbling of borders, a compaction of cross-border social relationships, an increased interdependence of cross-border activities, and an intensification of flows, the scalar model of identity and society remains primarily anchored in national space, both at the theoretical and popular levels (Laine 2016: 468). Scholars like Paasi and Laine, among several others, make it clear that while state borders retain their centrality, their conventional meaning has changed. Borders are not simple constructs; they are always 'complex, multiscalar, multidimensional', and these are fluid, capable of yielding both 'symbolic and material forms', perform novel tasks and shift locations, if required (Laine 2016: 468–9).

Fourth, a number of scholars belonging to critical geopolitics (Ó Tuathail and Dalby 1998), drawing upon post-structuralist thinking, have claimed that attention needed to shift to 'boundary-producing practices rather than to borders per se' (Passi 2013).[7] Their work was critical in explaining how bordering was essential to the discourses of US foreign policy that produced the narratives of othering in the politics of the Cold War. In other words, borders are not mere separations of space; borders also create binaries of national political projects that are essential to make people recognize and accept the lines that did not exist in the past. Scholars of critical geopolitics have given us new tools to interrogate borders, boundaries, orders, and identities. They have also created an interdisciplinary body of knowledge on border studies that draws upon the works of anthropologists, geographers, IR experts, historians, and practitioners of humanities. While anthropologists studied multi-scalar symbolic and cultural meanings of borders (Wilson and Donnan 1998), geographers brought the cultural and political readings together. They were pivotal in explaining the cultural permeability of borders, the way people living at borders adjusted to the narratives of political differences that political borders create, and the rigidity of some states to resist, if not prevent, the processes that sought to escape these lines. In addition, a body of work came to existence on various forms of popular geopolitics based on a discursive usage of novels, comics, and movies as their research materials (Dittmer and Gray 2010).

Territoriality

Territoriality, claims of political authority by the state, the democratic determination of the condition and extent of authority by the people as an attribute of popular sovereignty, and the various justifications of political space are deeply contested in political philosophy. The view of territoriality has gradually shifted from that of property to jurisdiction, though, as Margaret Moore's path-breaking work has brilliantly demonstrated, practices underlying modern IR continue to invoke hybrid forms (Moore 2015). The proprietorial view lingers on in the jurisdictional imagination of territory. The discourse of territory under jurisdictional authority has come to signify the domain in which people deliberate on democratic projects through legitimate institutions. However, Moore has authoritatively shown that this jurisdictional view has a number of different 'justificatory arguments' on territorial rule: it can be justified through claims of collective self-determination of the people, through cultural nationalist arguments of upholding and protecting certain cultural values and institutions, or through a statist theory that defends territorial control as essential to fulfil its tasks, which can either be more Hobbesian (public order and stability) or Kantian (justice based) in nature (Moore 2015: 27–8). In all such accounts, however, the relationship of the state and its people to territory remains open. The democratic view privileges the people as the locus of popular sovereignty, while the statists argue that people 'come into existence *as a people*, as a collective entity, through the state' (2015: 28; emphasis in original). In addition, we need to recognize that democratic decision-making requires boundaries. However, theorists are divided as to what such determination means, particularly on the delicate relationship between existence and control, and perhaps most crucially, who has the power to decide on controlling borders.[8] While Abizadeh (2008) thinks that the state cannot control borders if popular sovereignty is properly mandated, statists like Michael Walzer (1983) and David Miller (2010) draw on a distinction between coercion and prevention to justify the state. However, the fact remains that there is hardly any independent moral audit or ethical justification for bounded sovereignty. Political philosophers either take bounded spaces as given, or they deny them as morally indefensible artefacts. In other words, political theory remains divided over the legitimacy of the state and the existence of territorial rights.

In one of the path-breaking texts on territoriality, Robert David Sack defined the concept as 'the attempt by an individual and group to affect, influence, or control people, phenomena, and relationships by delimiting and asserting control over a geographic area' (Sack 1986: 19). Sack says, 'Territoriality is a strategy to establish different degrees of access to people, things, and relationships' (1986: 20). For Sack, territoriality was a mode of area classification. While it marked off an area where others could not enter, it also communicated symbolically by combining a sense of direction in space and about its possession or exclusion (1986: 21). However, territoriality is not only about regulating the population within and restraining the demographics without. It is about a specific mode of regulation of space that restraints both the inside and the outside at the same time. In contrast to scholars like Sack, who saw territoriality as a mode of spatial delimiting, Stuart Elden broadened it to refer to a mode of contingent form of political organization and theory (Elden 2009).[9]

The French sociologist Henri Lefebvre's work on territoriality and state theory has assumed increasing importance in this conjuncture. Lefebvre articulated a mutually constitutive, three-way relation between state, space, and territory. In one of the most quoted chapters in the final volume of *De l'État* (1976), Lefebvre argued:

> As the product, the child, of a space, the so-called national territory, the State turns back towards its own historical conditions and antecedents, and transforms them. Subsequently, the State engenders social relations in space; it reaches still further as it unfurls; it produces a support, its own space, which is itself complex. This space regulates and organizes a disintegrating national space at the heart of a consolidating worldwide space (*l'espace mondial*). (Quoted in Brenner and Elden 2009: 358)

Lefebvre showed the centrality of territoriality as state space, and how deterministic Marxism and abstract liberal political theory have both neglected its effects. According to Brenner and Elden, for Lefebvre, 'the national territory results from an historically specific, mutually transformative articulation between the state, the continually contested processes within it, and the land or soil that it inhabits, owns, controls and exploits' (Brenner and Elden 2009: 352). Conceived as a strategic and tactical function, a territory's resources serve political ends. Lefebvre's cardinal contribution is to bring the notions of spatiality and territory together, and to show that it is the territorial principle that constituted and was in turn constituted by the state. The inseparability of the territorial articulation of state space and the cultural filling of that space has been highlighted by a whole series of critical philosophers, including Foucault and Agamben. Foucault's ideas of governmentality and biopolitics were developed further by Giorgio Agamben in his idea of 'the state of exception', which the Italian theorist claimed to have assumed canonical position on governance in contemporary politics (Agamben 2005).[10]

We need not pursue these ideas here.[11] The fact is that Lefebvre's work stands in sharp contrast to Agamben's ideas of the state of exception. Agamben collapses the distinction between the public and the private altogether in the state's treatment of the human subject, which he calls 'bare life'. He argues that the modern state rules not only over the public domain of the citizen, but also over the bare and bodily aspects of the human being, thus subsuming subjectivity. Lefebvre, in contrast, has a far more strategic conception of the state, where he says that the state uses its spatial tactics to territorialize the identities of its people. Mathias Albert and Lothar Brock explain the dual constitution of territoriality and citizenship processes. They argue that whether it is that the states created nations or it is the other way round, territoriality was crucial in creating a strong bond of national identity within a given territory.[12]

Conceptualizations in Critical Political Geography

Critical political geographers have compelled IR scholars to give territoriality more centrality, rather than assuming it as unproblematic. While a corpus of writing on the subject has piled up over the years, John Agnew's piece on the 'territorial trap' was the game changer. According to Simon Reid-Henry, who reviewed the impact of this seminal work after fifteen years, Agnew developed the idea of the 'territorial trap' to question some of the assumptions that IR scholars took for granted: 'first, that national spaces are fixed and secure territorial units of sovereign space; second, that domestic and foreign spaces are distinct and separable spheres; and, third, that the territorialized sovereign state is the appropriate container for society' (Reid-Henry 2010: 753). Agnew's work made it possible to question these beliefs, particularly at a time when territoriality seemed to be in retreat in the face of global transformations at the levels of both communications technology and political economy. Agnew's work can be seen in the same tradition of scholars who drew attention to indispensability of social spacing in human lives and the manifold meanings, other than the ones valourized by the modern state, such spaces may have. The discourses on the many meanings of spaces have come together to question the possibility of doing modern IR within the territorial frame of reference.

The important prerogative here for us is to explore how and where the territorial project is lodged. It is particularly poignant to see how margins, borders, and peripheries are critical to territorial projects, which often create identities by territorializing these fluid zones. Critical geographers and anthropologists have shown that this territorializing does not succeed at the edges, and despite surveillance and militarization of borders, different life forms escape the territorial strategies of the state. However, this does not mean that the state refrains from territorial differentiation. Sovereignty has, in other words, a complex relation with people and territory on the one hand, and how people relate to territory on the other. To see only one part of the equation is to inevitably miss the whole dynamic at work, which makes it imperative to relate to national security as a structural face of territoriality, rather than being morally and politically dismissive of it altogether. Therefore, despite the path-breaking contribution it made, Agnew's work is only partial. Agnew asserted, 'Even when political rule is territorial, territoriality does not necessarily entail the practices of total mutual exclusion which dominant understandings of the modern territorial state attribute to it' (Agnew 1994: 53). First, to state that all states would define territoriality fundamentally the same way was cavalier; equally importantly, borders impact not only how the managers of the state think, but also over the imaginations of the population. Territoriality is never an uncontested process. It is not merely a criterion of enclosure, but a form of political rule. It operates not by itself but invariably in cognate terms. Without nationalism and cultural identity, the story of territoriality is hardly a meaningful one. Scaffolding territoriality as a convenient proxy to rubbish the ills of the modern state is thus an unhelpful move.

Perspectives in Mainstream IR Theories

Mainstream IR does not generally ask questions on borders and territoriality; these come packaged with its self-legitimization and are, therefore, taken for granted. Waltzian neo-realism, with its claim that anarchy is immutable, does not find the question about how the world of territorial borders came into being as significant. While in political theory, liberals have opposed the state's claim to legitimate violence on ethical grounds, few liberal IR theorists have problematized boundaries. They had indeed claimed that closed borders were economically redundant and politically hazardous due to their negative consequences for individual rights. However, most liberals stayed away from ethically confronting the puzzle of territorialized borders. Hedley Bull, a leading scholar in the tradition of the English School, was a pioneer in questioning the discipline's silence on borders. As Nick Vaughan-Williams's fascinating survey tells us, 'In the final part of his book Bull explores five possible alternative paths to world order: a system but not a society; states but not a system; a world government; a form of medievalism; or an entirely new arrangement "beyond our own imagination"' (Vaughan-Williams 2009: 46). However, Bull's epistemic bait had virtually no takers within the dominant paradigms of the discipline. Most surprisingly, social constructivist IR scholars like Alexander Wendt and Robert Jackson had their nuanced ontological critique of the neo-realist and neo-liberal approaches. But they stayed away, while recognizing the contingent nature of the inter-state order from investigating the sociology of borders. In

Social Theory of International Politics (1999), Wendt argues that a thorough problematization of the relationship between borders and territory was outside the scope of his analysis: 'an enquiry among states must take territory as in some sense given' (Wendt 1999: 211). Vaughan-Williams regrets that, in effect, 'Wendt's analysis of the formation of identities and interests of states depends upon the prior existence of those states as modern sovereign bordered territorial units in the same way as Waltz's does' (Vaughan-Williams 2009: 47). Robert Jackson's celebrated work on non-intervention questions the normative basis of a state-based order, and yet refrains from digging deeper into the issue. He not only recognizes the historicity of borders, but also their role in exclusivist notions of security, rights, and responsibilities (Jackson 2010).

Scholars like Malcolm Anderson (1996) and J. Williams (2006) are mediators between the mainstream and the critical discourses. They have drawn attention to the nuanced roles that borders play on the one hand, and their connections with complex needs of human identity on the other. The radical schools have branched off in different directions: Ashley and Walker target the conceits of sovereignty and the facileness of the inside/ outside distinction, and the culpability of modernity; ÓTuathail and Agnew point at the different discourses underlying the relations of power, borders, and knowledge; Anderson, Bigo, and Bort attempt to collapse the boundaries of securitization under flows that cannot be disciplined by borders and fences (Ashley 1987; Walker 1993; Ashley and Walker 1990; ÓTuathail and Agnew 1992; Anderson, Bigo, and Bort 2000). These new works have highlighted the complex relations between sovereignty, violence, borders, mobility, and flows (see Vaughan-Williams 2009).

In perhaps one of the most significant works from within the confines of the IR community that looked critically into questions of statehood, territoriality, and sovereignty, Ruggie (1993) advanced three major claims. First, his work highlighted the provisional and contingent nature of all political communities. In essence, Ruggie claimed that the state was neither a materialistic/mechanical framework for the rule of capital nor a universal rational form of organization. The modern state is an entity wrapped up in complex webs of meanings and significations. Second, Ruggie looked into different systems of rule by contrasting the lineage-based, non-territorial, kinship-driven political organizations of pre-modern times with the hierarchical, bounded, and consolidated public authority structure under sovereign command, which came to dominate the political landscape under modernity. The Weberian cast to the trinity of state, territory, and people was, therefore, a modern political form that resulted from the breakdown of the looser feudal structures and the evolution of classical capitalist ones. The modern state system was based on increasing differentiation and individuation of space, centralization of authority within borders, and the regulation of relations with similar entities through the codified rules of statecraft. This cemented a global order based on mutual recognition of sovereign entities. With decolonization, the transition to the modern inter-state system, which is based on sovereign differentiation of territorial space, was complete. Third, Ruggie claimed that the modern state system, though based on territoriality, always contained spaces for non-territorial forms of organizations and practices. In a way, he argued that the state and its attendant institutions (like sovereignty and territoriality) were *fictions*; invented rather than natural, which succeeded in capturing the political imagination of the ruling elites as they could defeat and dismantle other competing or alternative forms of public rule. Ruggie was hopeful that this hard territoriality will not endure for long, and alternative spatial experiments were underway, which would lead to what he called the 'unbundling of territoriality'. While he was essentially making a case for the changes happening in Europe, and emphasized institutions like the EU and epistemic categories like security communities, his work paved the way to investigate the challenges of globalization to a territoriality-based order.

Territory and the Globalization Debate

Ruggie pioneered the transformative thesis within IR, and the globalization debate developed it further, which questioned the meanings of territoriality and sovereignty. Territoriality, the ultimate principle of differentiation that legitimized the international system of nation-states, faced an unprecedented challenge with the developments in information technology and communication sciences, which allowed a time–space compression of the world, which in turn redefined the meaning(s) of temporality and space. Space was fast becoming secondary to the new sovereignty of time. In fact, new technology had created a multiplicity of spacing(s), where different commodities were transacted with little relevance to the settled cartography of borders (Ashley 1987; Harvey 1989). For a host of functions, state boundaries simply did not matter. Like the idea of the state, territoriality was now more a matter of habit, a ritualistic compulsion of unimaginative minds, and a relic of the past, even in symbolic or representational senses. Globalization had breached the artificiality of the inside and the outside, and there was little that territoriality could do to prevent its own transcendence against such massive transformations at all levels of collective existence (see Walker 1993). However, even before the advent of globalization, a whole range of threats had become global, and thus, could not be met by territorialized responses. Humanity had also lived under the looming threat of a (im) probable nuclear holocaust for many decades—a threat that did not respect the differentiating logic of territoriality either. With globalization, borders have become softer, and states have become porous. The increasing significance attached to non-conventional sources of insecurity has further eroded the appeal of territoriality. In fact, it could be shown that territoriality was the cause of many of these global threats. Hence, survival of the human species demanded deterritorialization. Under globalization, control of networks and flows has become more important than the physical or territorial and hierarchical control of space (Biersteker 2002: 165–6).

As territoriality is problematized, it leads to radically different ways of interrogating sovereignty, citizenship rights, and self-determination practices. The dilution of territoriality is often substantiated by taking the actions of the Eastern European states as evidence. These states demonstrated strong eagerness to part with a number of sovereign prerogatives in order to qualify as legitimate claimants of benefits, which were offered by extra-territorial organizations and deterritorialized forms of institutions, the market in particular. The retreat of territoriality is thus a function of the immense expansion of the market forces. To the extent globalization provides the engine to such unprecedented expansion of the market, the former is directly responsible for an eventual unbundling of territory. The logic of territoriality, with its accent on exclusiveness and loyalty, conflicts with the philosophy of the market that emphasizes the virtues of openness, inclusiveness, and functional interdependence.

Globalization debates have indeed pushed IR scholarship to expand its boundaries further.[13] If territoriality is threatened by globalization, the meaning of sovereignty has also changed under its impact. The classical meaning of sovereignty—as undisputed control of physical territory—no longer remains the most significant marker or indicator of sovereignty. Recognition has now become imperative to the life of sovereignty. It is no longer a function of demonstrated physical control over territory, but hinges more on claimants attending a prescribed threshold of democratization and human rights. Transparency and accountability are now more vital to the recognition of sovereignty than raw physical control of territory. Sovereignty and coercive authority are thus delinked. Sovereignty now depends on a broad range of performance criteria, whose ethical foundation is determined by the dominant Western powers—the EU and USA, to be more precise. Once more, the critical evidence to this alleged transformation comes from Europe. The EU and the USA recognized the states of Croatia and Slovenia not on the grounds of demonstrated effectiveness in the physical or hierarchical/military control of their territory, but because of their commitment to endorse liberal democratic practices along with the Western agenda of human rights (Biersteker 2002: 162–3). Writing about the paradoxes of physical boundaries and global flows under a neo-imperial epoch, Wendy Brown states, '...new nation-state walls are iconographic of this predicament of state power. Counterintuitively, perhaps, it is the weakening of state sovereignty, and more precisely, the detachment of sovereignty from the nation-state that is generating much of the frenzy of nation-state wall building today. Rather than resurgent expressions of nation-state sovereignty, the new walls are icons of its erosion' (Brown 2010: 24). As sovereignty has become more fragile, and as the capacity of states to claim absolute control of physical space has significantly waned, the states appear more alarmed and agitated, desperately attempting to cling on to their sovereign powers by erecting physical means.

An excellent rejoinder to this transformation thesis has come from Stephen Krasner (1999), who has described the practice of sovereignty as 'organized hypocrisy'.[14] In brief, Krasner shows that there was never a standard or modular Westphalian straightjacket—the strong Westphalian model was an imagination, a fiction. In practice, the states deviated from the underlying norms and practices of such a system, openly flouting them in their own national interest. Sovereignty in its classical sense, therefore, never connoted uninterrupted control of territorial space. Very few states were sovereign by that criterion, if stringently applied. Intervention has been the norm of the international system rather than an exception. Sovereignty therefore has largely been formal to the majority of states. If, by sovereign, one understands the unconstrained capacity for self-determination and autonomous action, then most states are not sovereign entities (Biersteker 2002: 162).

I take Krasner's analysis to be correct, which makes it an imperative to look at the shifts in the nuances and practices of sovereignty more closely. In brief, there is little evidence to suggest that states mean anything more or less than their traditional understanding of the notion by the term sovereignty. States still need to be in physical control of their territory to formalize any form of government or to create a framework for human rights. The idea of sovereign territoriality has hardly any connection with democracy and human rights, even when one defines sovereignty not as an attribute but as a practice. The more important point, however, is that globalization makes democracy and human rights more crucial to claims of sovereignty (or recognition of sovereignty). At least this is the burden of the argument of those who argue that globalization has altered or mutated the 'meaning' of sovereignty, conceived as a practice.

India's Spatial Imageries: Power, Commerce, and Community

The survey in the previous section has set the tone for this chapter. The bulk of the work on territory, state, sovereignty, and democracy did not originate in the post-colonial world. While the theoretical categories and their justificatory basis may claim a certain ubiquity, the specificity of the post-colonial context does introduce certain unmistakable elements that are missing in the general ideas. I shall not pursue the theoretical agenda of difference here; it is sufficient to recognize that the post-colonial world is not a monolithic construct, and there are wide variations in the manner in which territory, sovereignty, and democracy are triangulated in different parts of this vast geographic expanse. My reading of South Asia says that the subcontinental states have uncritically upheld the public order/security/stability narrative in justifying territorial control and have sought to intervene continuously to articulate a form of 'peoplehood' that would suit this purpose. This is clearly evident in the evolving discourses on citizenship that have sought to travel from the democratic *jus soli* to the more restrictive *jus sanguinis* principle. States seem obsessed over border control and citizenship, both with regards to political/democratic rights and cultural values. The notions of space deployed by South Asian political elites carry these anxieties and fears despite the opposite pulls of globalization, democratization, and human security.

In this study, I attempt to come to terms with the conceptual mapping of India's neighbourhood in South Asia. The territorial configuration of

South Asia involves certain imageries. Regions are configured primarily in terms of space—a particular kind of space, with its distinctive features and possibilities. An area embodies multiple notions, or rival conceptions of space. Accordingly, the meaning of a region not only changes over time but also varies across the concept of space underlying it. India's spatial conception underlying its foreign policy towards its own region is unmistakably driven by geopolitics, conditioned primarily, though not exclusively, by considerations of power and security. A number of recent publications by practitioners like Shyam Saran and Shivshankar Menon, and public intellectuals and foreign policy specialists like Raja Mohan and Aparna Pande, among others, have confirmed this reading. In *How India Sees the World*, Saran has explained a number of discreet episodes of Indian foreign policy with Kautilya's *Arthashastra* as an organizing concept. The book brings out the age-old dilemma of New Delhi's South Asian imagination: a single geopolitical and ecological space with a shared history and economic interdependencies, constantly buffeted by inward looking territorial nationalisms and post-colonial anxiety over border crossings. The ideas of free customs union and walled borders cohabit the space. The desire to integrate and be mistrustful of neighbours unites and divides us all the time. Structural asymmetry only accentuates the unease of India's small neighbours. Aparna Pande also sees continuity of India's foreign policy in the idioms of Kautilya, namely, a strategic culture of independent India, which she breaks down to a self-perception of Indian exceptionalism predicated in its civilizational heritage and the commitment to a culture of strategic autonomy, that keeps it away from the entanglements of international alliances and attracts it to a hub-and-spoke international order made up of many powers that operate through multilateralism rather than hegemony.

In simple terms, I thus argue that a region can be characterized or defined by three conceptions of space, although these definitions are often overlapping and are never exclusive in character or modes of deployment. These concepts are: a region as power; as market; and as a community.

Region as Power

First, a region can be defined in terms of *geo-strategic* references, and looked upon as a zone of conflict arising out of the distribution of power and the patterns of enmity and amity (Bajpai 1995: 31–2). Major powers have often defined regions by the imperatives of national power or of 'space as power'. I use the term 'power' in the sense Joseph Nye defines it. For Nye, 'Power is the ability to achieve one's purposes and goals' (Nye 2008: 94). Power is both material and ideational, including capability and the will to hegemonize the region. When a state defines a region as a space of power, it tends to prioritize national security interests over shared commercial gains or community. Thus, for the Great Britain, Southeast Asia and Asia-Pacific were once referred to as spaces they had to control in their fight against imperial Japan. The Americans have likewise deployed a similar notion of space to define west Asia, that is, in terms of their 'need' for geopolitical control over the oil resources of this region. South Asia has often been understood as an area that arose out of the asymmetric distribution of power between India and her neighbours. While India has sought for a leadership role in the region through the exclusion of other (non-South Asian) powers from it, Pakistan (and also to a certain degree, Bangladesh) has denied its pre-eminence and sought to balance against Indian domination in the subcontinent. The smaller neighbours have at different times resisted India's attempts to hegemonize the subcontinent. India's fear of outsiders, preventing its legitimate domination of its neighbourhood, and its neighbours' unease with a dominant/resurgent India, is the pivot of South Asia's regional politics, and distinguishes it from the other adjacent geopolitical regions.

Region as Space for Commerce

The second reading of a region is to define it as a space of 'commerce and prosperity'. All regions are marked by latent economic interdependence—complementarities in natural resources, primary products, and manufactured goods and services. A region might demonstrate rather weak eco-interdependence by itself. But there are other sources of relationships which are significantly stronger, like the ones emanating from globalization-cum-liberalization that operates on the region from outside. IR in some areas are motivated more by the reasons of market or commerce than by power. The EU and the Association of Southeast Asian Nations (ASEAN) are good examples. Major states in these settings have prioritized economic interests over strategic purposes. The motivation, however, may be explained differently. First, the tragedy of power can induce states to look at commerce. The unprecedented human tragedy of the two World Wars forced major European states to realize the futility of competition over power; they instead focused their collective energies on functional cooperation, based upon free trade across national borders. While this did not make borders, nationalism, and territoriality obsolete, the latter were sufficiently softened to allow cooperation between states at various levels of collective existence. The sovereignty debate did not stall this growing process of collaboration and unification qua regional integration. This suggested that even bitter historical rivals could learn and socialize with new modes of interaction, which offered positive gains to all. Second, shared threats often transform a region. Southeast Asia slowly tugged towards regional integration, as national elites recognized that they could not survive the onslaught of communist threats unless they gave up power for commerce or shared prosperity.

When such changes take place, major states alter the prevalent spatial imaginations. Rather than defining a region as a space of authority and exclusivist control, they start investing in ideas of prosperity and economic cooperation. Moving away from space-as-power to space-as-prosperity is not easy; states need to alter their perceptual lenses in order to make the shift. Liberal institutionalists have demonstrated that co-operation is possible for rational actors (states) despite egoism, provided the institutions take care of free-riding and the enforcement of decisions. Space-as-commerce builds institutions, and argues that interests are malleable. Unlike space-as-power, which emphasizes strategic purposes, the commercial imagination stresses the rational pursuit of common or shared economic gains as the grid which guides policies for states. The idea here is to delink or decouple political and economic interests and allow the latter to craft the spatial imagination of countries.

Region as Community

States, however, can also define a region as 'community'. According to this reading, the shared culture, language group, or social structure represents areas. Yet a region may not, and does not, make a cultural unity; it can equally be an ambit of a distinct pattern of cultural differentiation/contestation and marginalization. The claim to constitute South Asia along cultural lines is always intensely contested. Many believe that South Asia is a space of cultural affinity, its people united by common civilizational values. Others disagree and base their case on the right to cultural difference. After all, the dual partitions (1947, 1971) of South Asia and its multiple ethno-religious conflicts involve questions of cultural difference or contestation, and the fear of severe marginalization.

Of the three modes of spatial imagination, community is perhaps the most contentious. In many post-colonial societies, the boundaries of ethnicity, religion, or language do not overlap with national borders. Substantial kin populations live across boundaries in many such states. It is a little surprising that many states feel they have an obligation to stand by their ethnic kin, particularly if they are persecuted or exploited by their neighbours who come from a different community. States that are created through partition and secessionism are particularly vulnerable in this regard. Multi-ethnic states show a peculiar paradox over community. On the one hand, they categorically refuse rights to national self-determination of communities living within. On the other, they display kin-country syndrome internationally.

As nation-states forge different forms of communities, there is a built-in anxiety in them to relate to other forms of communities both below and above them. Community unites and divides at the same time. The argument is that South Asian states are edgy and excitable over other forms of communities. States have different ranges of resilience, and may be drawn out differently from both within or without. The peculiar history of South Asia has compromised its resilience vis-à-vis other communities. Hence, they both attract and repel the spatial imagination of community, being unsure of what consequences might follow from it. All spatial visions have advantages and risks. With power and commerce, these seem more regular and predictable. Power can mobilize resistance; business can leave security vulnerable. However, with risks come insurance strategies. Power leads to acts of balancing and to coalitions; markets insure against signal disorders and coordination errors. However, the case for community is different. Identity is risky, for it remains agnostic to scale. Borderless communities may empty a state from within. Hence, South Asian states remain suspicious of community, both as an imagery of space and as a lever of policy.

South Asia's Regional Identity

The subcontinent has evolved through the healthy paradox of commonalities-in-difference, which nevertheless provided it with a sense of distinct regional identity.[15] Geography, history, culture, civilization, heritage, and aesthetics came together to mould this complex mosaic of characters that loosely united the inhabitants of the subcontinent, despite their numerous differences. This identity was laid along a community–meta-state continuum, and remained variable for a considerable period of time. The arrival of the Europeans and the dual hypocrisy of territoriality and modernity upset this rhythm fundamentally. Territoriality forged a strong sense of difference as indispensable to the new statist projects in the subcontinent, and, in the process, decimated the community-state character of the subcontinent. As Sunil Khilnani (2003: 20) explains:

> Politics was thus consigned to the realm of spectacle and ceremony. No concept of a state, an impersonal public authority with a continuous identity, emerged: kings represented only themselves, never enduring states. It was this arrangement of power that explains the most peculiar characteristic of India's pre-colonial history: the perpetual instability of political rule, the constant rise and fall of dynasties and empires, combined with the society's unusual fixity and cultural consistency. Its identity lay not in transient political authority but in the social order.

Modernity exaggerated the taxonomical impulses of the modern state and hastened the making of a citizenry who had to be divided and united at the same time. The communalization of the subcontinent under modernity brought modern South Asia into being, pitting religious or communal identities against liberal–secular formations for the first time. Democracy, tragically enough, exacerbated this tendency. As numbers became vital for winning and retaining power, even under the slowly evolving self-governing dispensation under a watchful imperial tutelage, the political attribution of the demography assumed a newfound significance. The politicization of religion was a natural corollary to the process. Caste also began its political career, but its innate complexity, stratification, non-territorial spread, and perhaps most critically, relevance for Hinduism exclusively, prevented it from assuming the trajectory that religion took in the subcontinent.

When the subcontinent was violently divided along the lines of faith in an orgy of bloodshed and unimaginable rapacity, the chasm between community and territoriality was complete. This was the new South Asia, which was wholly anomalous to its past, and destined to remain separated by the very logic of its constitution. There is no way that the model of a community–meta-state can be relived in this context. South Asian states were carriers of these two traits right from the start—they justified their exclusivity by contrasting narratives of victimhood and made territorial nationalism existential to them. South Asia, in other words, became a fearful pathology of securitized nationalism, which required a strong politics of difference and exclusion, no matter what the domestic attributes of social or collective identity the member states had. In other words, the character of the state—be it democratic or authoritarian—and the nature of its nationalism—whether civic or ethnic—did not impact the project of 'other-ization' within the subcontinent. A secular India would have as much penchant for conflict as a non-secular Pakistan. In fact, over the years, the elite discourses in South Asia tended to veer towards a sanitized version of regular realist discourse. In other words, states would fiercely compete in an anarchical setting, unsure of their own security, and regardless of the character and motivations of other countries. As the community/state linkages were abrogated in South Asia, a realist imagination of the subcontinent took hold across the states. This study does not extend to the analysis of other South Asian states in detail, but the central argument of the predominance of a power/security-centric understanding of the subcontinent would apply across the discourses of state elites. However, this study argues that there is a sociological subtext to this power-imagination. This generic realism would not have emerged but for the effacing of the narratives of civilizational commonalities by those of nationalistic differences.[16]

India's 'Power' Imagination

India has a complex power-imagination of its neighbourhood. The reason for it is that India's preferences in South Asia are paradoxical. India seeks to lead the subcontinent, owing to is natural material preponderance over all other South Asian states. However, while it achieves limited domination on occasions, it cannot lead the subcontinent. Its advantages over its neighbours are purely material and not cultural or ideological. It achieves, therefore, intermittent and rudimentary power, but fails to hegemonize the subcontinent. It offers little by way of ideas that others can comfortably share. India's narratives of democracy, pluralism, and economic growth are strong, but they remain unattractive to its neighbours. India has not believed in the promotion of democracy as a norm (either internationally or regionally) and its record of dealing with democratic regimes in South Asia (virtually across board) remains awkward and hesitant. India's pluralism is again suspect not only for some of its domestic contestations which have border-jumping consequences, but primarily for the fact that this model problematizes the relations between communities and the state. India's economic growth spawns a neo-liberal imagery that is undocumented by facts and figures. Although intuitively appealing, it requires porosity of borders and prioritizing economic well-being over state security interests, which fundamentally contradicts the prevailing dynamics of the subcontinent.

India betrays an agony over its perceived role in South Asia. The frustration of a perennial arriving converges with its inability to keep the subcontinent free of external interferences. The more India's bilateral problems with its neighbours continue, the more China gets drawn into South Asia; China's ties with Pakistan, Nepal, Sri Lanka, and Bangladesh balance India, and pull it to the subcontinent more closely. India's security concerns are serious in the subcontinent. It has unresolved territorial conflicts with Pakistan (over the state of Jammu and Kashmir) and China (both along the eastern and the western sectors of their long border)— two nuclear-powered states that are hostile to India on different counts. It suffers from terrorism and insurgency, with external links and support from a number of South Asian states, from disputes over water and illegal migration, and kin-group treatments across South Asia.

There is also the growing realization amongst Indian elites that the success of India's economic growth demands more imaginative articulations of space, one that will liberate it from the claustrophobic clutches of South Asia. The formal inclusion of Afghanistan in South Asia and the dilation of Myanmar's significance as a gateway to Southeast Asia are pointers to this effect. In the northwest, India seeks a stake in Afghanistan's future, as the state is vital to its security interests. India has made considerable investments in Afghanistan's economy and infrastructure. The gradual drawdown of the US-led North Atlantic Treaty Organization (NATO) forces in Afghanistan in the near future weighs heavily on India's security-planning. This reinforces the traditional realist imperative of its foreign policy, for there is a gradual realization that India needs to be an active player in Afghanistan if Pakistan's designs of reclaiming its strategic depth are to be thwarted. In Southeast Asia, on the other hand, we have a more complex overlaying of economic and geo-strategic imperatives, which is in line with India's steady rise in naval capabilities and the deepening of its political ties with the ASEAN and Asia-Pacific states. India's 'Look East' policy and its conceptualization of South Asian regionalism reflect these complementary and opposed preferences in full.

Identity and Selfhood

The making of India as a modern territorial state has produced rich literature, perhaps most iconic of which is Manu Goswami's magisterial *Producing India: From Colonial Economy to National Space* (2004). Goswami uses Lefebvre's work on space to explore the production of a national space in India through the intricacies of colonial economy, and geopolitical ideas and culture. In her words, 'It suggests that social spaces—colonial and national, political and economic, material and imagined—do not emerge from self-evident geographies, nor do they exist in mutual isolation. Rather, they are co-constituted through the complex "superimposition and interpenetration" of socioeconomic structures, state practices, cultural forms, and collective agency on multiple spatiotemporal scales' (Goswami 2004: 6). Her text draws attention to the role of the global processes that were critical in manufacturing a territorial and national India. She finds the standard accounts of colonialism and nationalism deficient, as 'these works have paid less attention to the ways in which broader social processes and institutions—such as the dynamics of the interstate system, the expansive logic of capital, the institutionalized tie between nationhood and statehood—shape the political-economic and discursive structure of nationalism' (2004: 15). Goswami's path-breaking work describes the global socio-economic processes through which a national space was imagined in India under the aegis of imperial capital, which produced a fragmented spatial imagery within which the cultural imagination of India was possible. Her work leads us to important questions in post-colonial times, over the technologies of state required to perpetuate the cartography of differentiation, the contestations over the meanings of citizenship, and the role political economy (global capitalism) plays in shaping major political debates in South Asia. Niraja Jayal, Joya Chatterjee, Ayesha Jalal, Vazira Zamindar, and Anupama Roy, among others, have examined the nuances and transmutations in the meanings of citizenship in India and South Asia, and have shown how territorial considerations played a critical and important role in the process.

Changing Connotations of Identity

India's identity can be gleaned from several sources, and there are different registers to this identity. However, we need to clarify in what sense the term identity is deployed here, given the mass of complex and often contradictory definitions of the concept that already exist.[17] In the older sense, identity 'refers to the (often legal) association of a particular name to a particular person—the quality of being a particular person, or the same person as before' (Fearon 1999: 8). Eric Erikson's concept of the 'identity crisis' further advanced the idea, by implying that identity refers to one's feelings about one's self, character, goals, and origins (1999: 10). But identity is not merely a matter of feelings; it is a definition of the self. Personal identity is a set of those attributes of a person that are considered essential by the individual for his selfhood—the properties that are necessary but not contingent. But a person is not a prisoner of a given identity. In his personal life, the matter is simpler, for in most liberal societies, at least people are granted a space where they become what they are. Personal identity is a predicate, and anything can provide its content if the individual approves of it. However, identity is not just a matter of innocent personal choices. Identities are social and political. Social status also asks the question about who we are, but narrows the scope of definition by enjoining stricter rules of membership and certain attributes attached to the chosen group/s and expectations of accepted modes of behaviour of the members. As used in IR literature, the definition of Alexander Wendt (Wendt 1994: 395) comes closer to capturing the meaning: 'Social identities are sets of definitions that an actor attributes to itself while taking the perspective of others, that is, as a social object.... [Social identities are] at once cognitive schemas that enable an actor to determine "who I am/we are" in a situation and positions in a social role structure of shared understandings and expectations.' This means that it is often forgotten that people take certain social categories as natural, inevitable, and unchanging facts about the social world, while these are in actuality, consciously created for them.

For India, the meta-contestation over its selfhood remains the one between liberal, secular nationalism on the one hand, and the Hindu communitarian vision on the other. Given that the Congress party has ruled India for most of the period since Independence, and the brief interludes of non-Congress rule have seen complex coalitions of both regional and national parties—barring the Bharatiya Janata Party (BJP) government that has come to power in 2014 with an absolute majority— the secular, liberal nationalism has dominated India's image of itself. In the words of Judith Brown:

> That most articulate and influential founding father, Jawaharlal Nehru, Prime Minister from 1947 to 1964, had envisaged India as a composite

nation that included a great diversity of peoples and reflected a many-layered sense of 'being Indian' that grew out of the subcontinent's long history of dealing with outsiders who lived there, some as rulers. Despite the partition of the country in 1947 and the creation of Pakistan as a Muslim homeland, he retained this vision of a national identity born of diversity and sustained by tolerance and secularism. (Brown 1998)

What is done in the following sections is to pay attention to this identity and see how this is related to some of India's foreign policy preferences in the subcontinent.

India's identity can be addressed at two levels. The first is the historical processes through which the idea of India took shape in modern times, though it borrowed freely from the past, both real and imagined. Indian political and social thinkers, like Gandhi, Nehru, Tagore, Savarkar, and Ambedkar, among several others, have contributed to this process, with each defining the Indian differently. The philosophical differences among these constructs have been pivotal in providing the registers in which Indians would anchor their chosen definitions of their political identity. The term 'political' is crucial here because some of the stable social categories that had provided a sense of continuity and meaning to collective life were already there—the immense intricacies of the brahminical caste order in particular, which seemed to have been instrumental in configuring a sense of social identity by providing a set of expected roles, and modes of behaviour that varied across regions, spaces, and over time. But the idea of political India was quintessentially modern; it arose primarily out of a contest between a broadly liberal and secular model of nationhood on the one hand, and a faith-based determination of selfhood on the other. While Gandhi had, for the first time, politically connected the modern subcontinent, and had emerged as the uncontested national leader, a venerable father figure of the nation, his vision of India as a state-less society—put out most ambitiously in his *Hind Swaraj*, which rejected modernity and embraced the traditional community—never caught the popular imagination of the masses. While India could trust Gandhi as a political liberator, they remained fundamentally alienated from his social ontology of being (Khilnani 2003).

Nehru's Articulation of 'Identity'

That imagination was provided instead by Nehru, who vigorously put across the idea of a modern and industrial India, embracing secularism and a broadly liberal orientation to life—which was opposed to colonialism and imperialism in all its political manifestations—and invested in the ideas of fraternity and a silent self-confidence that came from its civilizational and ethical lineage, and its commitment to a functional democratic political order. According to Varshney (1993: 247), Nehru feared invoking India's past as the basis of its post-colonial identity, as all past interpretations were likely to be controversial. Instead, 'he tried to make modernization and economic development the basis for national identity, something on which presumably everyone could agree. National identity, by this reading, could dissociate itself from a common past or from common origins, and gravitate towards a common future or a common purpose' (1993: 247). As is well-known, the Muslim League and the Hindu nationalists had both challenged this paradigm of liberal, secular nationalism as being fundamentally alien to the subcontinent, which defined a sense of community by religious affiliation. After the vivisection of the subcontinent along the lines of faith, through unprecedented bloodshed and displacement of population, which partially vindicated Muslim League's claim that Hindus and Muslims were two different communities whose peaceful and dignified political coexistence was an impossibility, the Nehruvian perspective of the idea of India, with suitable adjustments and accommodations now and then, remained the dominant vision of and for India that regulated both domestic life and structured India's ties to the outside world.

Nehru's conception of India's identity is more crucial in IR, as he virtually singlehandedly defined the contours of India's foreign policy. Most importantly, Nehru had an internationalist perspective, and conceived of India's role in foreign affairs in global terms. He remained an ardent enthusiast of pan-Asianism for the better part of his life (see Jain 2011), and his imagination of India's role in South Asia was largely conditioned by this. He believed that India and China were heirs to ancient civilizations, and having suffered colonial or semi-colonial exploitation, they would work together towards a new order in Asia that would bring back to the continent its lost glory and restore peace, prosperity, and progress, based on cooperation and modernity. In this idealistic grand vision, South Asia as a distinctive geopolitical space had no place.[18] Nehru's attitude towards India's neighbours remained pedagogic and aloof, and he primarily thought of India's role in South Asia as a part of its larger role in Asian affairs. India's war with Pakistan in 1948, and the subsequent acrimony over Jammu and Kashmir, had already indicated the weakness of this grand design; the border dispute with China that led to the disastrous 1962 Indo-China war demolished this discourse of being a moral power of global standing without sufficient material capabilities.

However, the weakness on Nehru's part to imagine South Asia as vital to India's geopolitical interests, and also for its image as a state claiming post-colonial difference must be read into the nature of the nation-state and its relation to territoriality in the post-colonial world. Identifying the contested process of decolonization as the primary cause of contemporary inter-state territorial conflicts in Asia, Itty Abraham analyses the political implications of establishing a fixed territorial homeland as a necessary starting point for both international recognition and national identity. Colonial nationalists sought to redefine the prime criterion for independent statehood as unified political control over a defined piece of land, or territorial sovereignty. Once territorial sovereignty was established as the way out of the impossible one land-people-state trinity, the loss of state territory could become nothing less than the loss of state power. His conclusion is that states cannot compensate for land, as it is vital to the legitimacy of the post-colonial nation-state, which has little to do with their potential for economic gains or imagined narratives of historical memory. In his words, 'The core problem with territorial loss is that it opens the door to an excavation of the relationship of state and nation. It exposes the nation as a historically contingent formation and being, and brings into question the state's claim to represent this nation, now and in the past' (Abraham 2014: 12–14).

Post-Colonial Notions of Identity

The post-colonial articulation of sovereignty has created the ultimate paradox for the national elites. They realized immediately the artificiality of their constructs and the historical anomaly involved in this model of nation-state, and hence, invested completely in the idea of territoriality, which was much more than the mere physical land: it was a terrain of political legitimacy for the new state. In an essay on India's competing national identities, Varshney (1993: 238) contrasts the territory—plural–secular and cultural—and argues:

> Since the territorial principle is drawn from a belief in ancient heritage, encapsulated in the notion of 'sacred geography', and figures in both imaginations, it has acquired political hegemony over time ... India's

most explosive moments concern its 'sacred geography', the 1947 partition being the most obvious example. Whenever the threat of another breakup, another partition, looms, it unleashes remarkable passions in politics. In India, however, they become desecrations of the sacred geography.

Borders thus became exclusionary and non-negotiable, and if the space outside was disorderly and dangerous, this was also the raison d'être for disciplining the inside, lest weakness is exploited by others in challenging the legitimacy of the state-led nation-building project, which sought to bring about the trinity of one land–state–people. The conflict between India and Pakistan over Kashmir is a good example of this. As Khilnani puts it, 'Kashmir remained contested by India and Pakistan throughout the 1970s and 1980s, remaining as "a test of Indian state sovereignty, its capacity to protect its citizens, keep order and justify its territorial ownership"' (Khilnani 2003: 31). Abraham argues that in the Indian context, 'With sovereignty in 1947, fluid imperial boundaries became fixed borders of the nation-state. These borders now incorporated territories and peoples that could not easily be identified as culturally "Indian" and, who, moreover, soon came to define themselves in opposition to a predatory Indian nation-state' (Abraham 2014:14). Whether the state has been predatory or not remains debatable, but the general argument, that the state's foreign policy was not merely a matter of realizing international or global purposes but was also a forging of the national project in peripheral regions, remains healthy.

'Identity' of the Hindu Right

The other model of India's selfhood comes from the Hindu right wing, building on the writings of a pantheon of brahminical and nationalist writings dating back to Bankim Chandra Chattopadhyay and Swami Vivekananda through Veer Savarkar and Golwalkar. But there is a significant difference in these different lineages that the modern Hindu right-wing parties draw from. The early brahminical writings, mostly penned by Bengali writers, wanted a revival of a mythical, resplendent and glorious Hindu past that has been lost through the Muslim invasions and the British colonial subjugation of the subcontinent. But Savarkar's ideas were not a throwback to the past. It was a model of Westernized nationalism that uses Hindu cultural symbols to make a wholly new body of citizens that is homogenous and ruthlessly efficient in building a modern Hindu state. It is this idea of India that the BJP, which came up as a successor to the old Jan Sangh, came up with in the early 1980s. In the words of Sunil Khilnani:

> But the BJP's definition of Indian nationalism was precisely the contrary of Nehru's. It explicitly declared allegiance to the Savarkarite idea of *Hindutva*, 'Hinduness', and celebrated a glorious Hindu past.... But Hindu nationalism also embraced the armoury of the modern state. Its ambition was to complete the project of achieving an Indian nation state by piloting it towards what it saw as its logical terminus: a culturally and ethnically cleaned-up homogenous community with a singular Indian citizenship, defended by a state that had both God and nuclear warheads on its side. (Khilnani 2003: 188)

According to Thomas Blom Hansen, the ideology of Hindutva and 'positive' or 'true' secularism amounts to the principle of rule by Hindu majoritarianism. He notes that it is a 'peculiar co-articulation of Brahminical ideologies of purity, romanticist notions of fullness and authenticity, and quasi-fascist organicism and celebration of strength and masculinity which characterizes the Rashtriya Swayamesvak Sangh (RSS) and its affiliated organizations' (Hansen 1996: 608). This idea is fundamentally opposed to the secular model, inasmuch as while the latter had followed a hands-off policy vis-à-vis the cultural practices of society, the proponents of Hindutva 'hope to bring the array of Indian religious and cultural activities under [the] command of the state, to tidy up the compromises and accommodations that litter Indian life and bring them into a regimented design, presided over by a single legal system' (Khilnani 2003: 190). Its ambition is much more austere: to build a model of state-society relations that is opposed to any legal or political recognition of cultural and religious differences.

Debates on Indian Secularism

The onslaught of the Hindu right has led to a significant debate on what will ensure the toleration of religious, ethnic, and cultural differences in a state like India. The liberal, secular nationalist model had proposed the idea of secularism. The Indian model of secularism, however, is different from the classical European one, for it connotes equal tolerance of all religions, rather than a strict separation of state and religion. The model had come under criticism not only from the Hindu right, who castigate it as being 'pseudo-secular', but also from a number of noted Indian social scientists, who consider it deficient. The Hindu right argues that while Indian secularism is tolerant of the many religious practices of the minority communities, it is harsh and derogatory towards those of the majority Hindu community. They therefore want a non-discriminatory secularism that would be equally just to all communities. According to Partha Chatterjee, 'positive secularism' is meant not only to deflect accusations of its being anti-secular, but also to rationalize in a sophisticated manner its campaign for intolerant interventions by a modern, positively secular state against the religious, cultural, or ethnic minorities in the name of 'national culture' and a homogenized notion of citizenship. The argument is that the modern state is the principal ingredient of this concoction, as it is predicated on the fusion of modernity, science, rationality, sovereignty, and the massive facilities of statist coercion (Chatterjee 1994).[19] The modern Indian state put the powers of the state into secularism; the same skills, more streamlined, and turned more predatory at the auspices of the political right, can now be used to articulate the notion of 'positive' or 'real' secularism.

India's understanding of South Asia must begin here. However, it is curious to dig into the concept of land and territory in the Indian context. In his *Discovery of India* ([1946] 1987), Nehru repeatedly mentions how, in his dialogues with people across the subcontinent, he was at pains to understand their 'idea of India', and after repeated probing, they would identify India with the *dharti* (sacred land), which gave them life and vitality, and was sacred in an existential sense. This notion of identifying land with 'Mother' or with something sacred that demands reverence and conviviality meant that people had a sense of land as something more than a mere political economy of possession. Land was a vital aspect of their sense of being, which located them and provided them with an ontology, no matter how obscure and beguiling it may have been. However, this ontology was not one of settled non-negotiable borders. It was a distinctive cartography of little communities living local lives but feeling a fraternal bond in this imaginary space of India. As Khilnani (2003: 154) writes:

> After all, before the 19th century, no residents of the subcontinent would have identified themselves as Indian. There existed intricate, ramified vocabularies of common understanding, which classified people by commonalities of lineage, locality and sect; but 'Indian' would not have figured among its terms. Subcontinental society was hardly static, yet most people never ventured beyond their own or neighbouring loyalties.

With Partition, however, territory became a site of political legitimacy, a vital criterion of state power and capacity. This demanded doctrines of insulation against capricious forces, and projection of power in 'South Asia'—a new entity that altogether lacked precedent in the history of the subcontinent. South Asia was thus a complex space, overladen with a series of binaries—danger and fraternity, insecurity and hegemony, power and progress. Hence, I argue that India's imagination of South Asia is never seamless and unitary; it has always encapsulated different and complementary images, with the picture of power overshadowing others.

Imagining Space as Power

Why has this image of power dominated the rest? The reason for this must be sought in the mismatch between the community and the state in South Asia, which has been in the past an Indo-centric space, modelled not on territoriality but on a meta-polity of diverse communities that competed and coexisted over time. The making of modern South Asia was thus the very onset of a new logic of geo-strategic understanding of space, which is predicated upon sovereign territoriality. It is only far from home that one could be what his national identity demands. This has been the archetypal colonial experience, and the same is also demanded of post-colonial subjects. This explains the anxieties of the state in South Asia—the citizens could not separate themselves from the neighbours, and even if they did, this differentiation would not have made any anthropological or social sense. The political impossibility of the image of the community under the new sovereign dispensation guaranteed the domination of the imagination of power in the subcontinent, which made India's post-colonial geopolitics 'wholly consistent with imperial strategies of defending and extending colonial Indian territorial boundaries' (Abraham 2014: 16).

The Impossible 'Other': India's Rivalry with Pakistan

The conflict between India and Pakistan lies at the heart of the geopolitics of South Asia. In fact, the reason why India's spatial imagination of its neighbourhood has been so distinctly realist is because of this fundamental and intractable conflict.[20] The conflict originated in the history of colonialism and the subsequent violent denouement of the partition which gave birth to the two states in 1947.[21] Very broadly, there are two rival explanations for it: one based on territory and the other on identity (Paul 2010). T.V. Paul marshals several arguments against both territory-based and identity-centric accounts of the enduring rivalry. He extends his own explanation based on the concept of truncated power asymmetry, observing India and Pakistan's relative capabilities, their conventional military and nuclear strategies, and the role of alliance politics. That may well be the case.

On the other hand, I argue that post-colonial sovereign territoriality and rival national identities are the key drivers that cause enmity and bitter rivalry between India and Pakistan.[22] What makes territorial concessions virtually impossible in this case is the peculiar imprint of the nationalist identity on them. Had the dispute not been on Kashmir but on some other issue unrelated to the divergent national discourses, a resolution would have been much easier to achieve. But a cursory glance into the elite discourses shows that a zero-sum mindset prevails on Kashmir, as both India and Pakistan consider it as a crucible of their nation-building projects. Truncated power asymmetry builds on this fundamental divide. As years went by, new complications emerged. The increasing Islamization of Pakistan has exaggerated the value of the 'faith as people' model of nationalism. The importance of Muslim Kashmir for Pakistan has therefore increased over time. The Hindu right wing in India, on the other hand, has also a tight integration model of the nation that demands the withdrawal of separate status to Jammu and Kashmir.[23]

The traditional Indian statist discourse has been to view separatism as a wrong position on the national narrative. Kashmir has thus been looked upon as a security issue. Moreover, dialogue with the Hurriyat or with forces demanding independence of Kashmir has been resisted on grounds of being opposed to the national integration of India. India's sensitivity to Pakistan's influence with the separatists is easily understandable; it sees it as a nefarious ploy that challenges India's national integrity and invites third parties to resolve the conflict. In fact, the Indian narrative is that there isn't any conflict over identity at all, and that the discourse of identity dispute has been smuggled in from Pakistan to polarize the argument. Similarly, from the perspective of Pakistan, there is no contradiction over identity, for to recognize the dispute is to challenge the very narrative of the seamless nationalist identity. In this paradoxical game of mutual denial, they understand the blind spots of their national narratives.

Dilemmas of reputation and status aggravate the negative dialectics of identity and sovereign territoriality between India and Pakistan. Hence, I propose that explanations based on either reputation or status 'are not opposed to but are complementary' to the one based on identity and post-colonial sovereign territoriality.

India has fought four wars with Pakistan and faced many severe crises under the shadow of nuclear armament. Pakistan has persisted with a strategy of sub-conventional warfare and supported insurgency and terrorism in India since the 1980s. The Indian state, despite its manifest superiority on many indicators of capability, has apparently had variable success against this strategy of a thousand cuts against it. India was able to actually cut off Pakistani support to pro-Khalistan Sikh militants in the 1990s and thereby terminate this domestic conflict. However, India has had limited success against terrorist violence in Kashmir. What is most significant is the role Pakistan's army and the Inter-Services Intelligence (ISI) have played in supporting the war of terror against India. There is corroborative evidence linking Pakistan's state agencies with the daring terrorist strike against the Indian parliament in 2001 and the Mumbai terrorist attacks of 2008. However, such evidence has not been accepted by Pakistan, and some of the masterminds of these attacks have found a safe haven in that state. India has had little success against Pakistan's militarism and New Delhi has not been able to formulate any definite security strategy or doctrine against its rival (Paul 2010). Nuclear weapons have brought in an asymmetric deterrence in the subcontinent and have virtually ruled out the potential of long wars, although the possibilities of small-scale military exchanges are not entirely ruled out (Basrur 2008; Ganguly and Hagerty 2006; Paul 2005). One of the reasons that makes India seriously wary about its role in South Asia and strengthens the transcendentalist discourse in its neighbourhood policy is its limited success against Pakistan. There is an increasing realization that a policy of dialogue and friendship does not work with a Pakistan bent upon inveterate enmity against India.

(Re-)Imagining the Neighbourhood: Extension or Transcendence?

India has thus found itself constrained in South Asia by both, a strong revisionist state and a number of relatively smaller countries, which have neither agreed to bandwagon with India consistently nor accepted its claims of leadership. There underlies India's abortive regionalism in South Asia.

Structural Asymmetries

Why could the South Asian Association of Regional Cooperation (SAARC) not transform South Asia? The problems with SAARC as a regional organization are multifarious. But the point that the structural asymmetry that India has vis-à-vis its South Asian neighbours remains moot. India's aspired power projection goes beyond South Asia, and it apparently wants liberation from the South Asian quagmire, so that it can play a more assertive role in Asian, if not global, affairs. Indian security thinking takes it that the prospect of a status quo and strategically united South Asian subcontinent is dismal; hence, it is perhaps legitimate for her to seek to expand its influence elsewhere, by transcending the troubled neighbourhood.

Transcendence in Economic Imagination

When it comes to commercial policies and the economic imagination underlying it, the logic of transcendence assumes even more clarity. South Asia as an economic space is too claustrophobic for a growing Indian economy. The logic of scale—more than anything else—demands rapid integration of India with Southeast Asia and Asia-Pacific, with or without the existing South Asian states. The structural difference between the economy of India and those of its neighbouring states impedes the establishment of a free trade regime in South Asia, which would be truly remunerative and economically attractive. India clearly prefers bilateral economic deals with its South Asian neighbours over genuine economic multilateralism for obvious reasons. The relatively weak and smaller neighbours want just the opposite. The pull of globalization has further compromised the chances of success for a liberal regional economic arrangement. The logic of the market (to which the liberal imagination is inextricably wedded) and the present direction of India's foreign and domestic economic policies militate against the idea of suboptimal gains in the interest of altruistic considerations. The meta-assumption of self-interest or egoism as the driver of the liberalization policies preclude any counter-economic reasoning that makes regionalism at the level of the SAARC—as it is presently constituted—an attractive option for India.

Finally, the SAARC is structurally committed to being a collective of sovereign nation-states, the only form of community that has a claim to being a legitimate political arrangement. The fixity and exclusionary nature of South Asian borders rule out its transmogrification into a looser form of political community which would radically question the inside/outside or citizen/others distinctions. India suffers from grave difficulties in its capacity for identity transformation within the subcontinent, because territoriality as a container of national specificity trumps attempts at redefinition over and above the state. The neighbours have problems of community vis-à-vis India, and these cannot be ignored in fashioning a vision for regional cooperation along communitarian lines. In simple words, South Asia remains too state centric to allow itself to be redefined as a community of people. India arguably has little incentive in such a move, since its existing conflicts over community remain intense and often violent; any attempt by New Delhi to espouse a vision of a society is liable to be translated as socially hegemonic by the neighbours. The dilation of the state and the contested nature of community-state ties trump the community imagination of South Asia. Given the centrality of India in the subcontinent and the unsettled claims of nationhood in virtually all South Asian states, there is little possibility, realistically, of carving out a new South Asian identity at the level of a community that might provide fresh conceptual basis for building a strong regional organization here. At the least, India's unsettled historical residues of conflicts over community vis-à-vis its neighbours rule out such a vision as a serious paradigm for regionalism in South Asia.

Logic of Extension

The failings of conventional political geography of South Asia have encouraged India to re-imagine the boundaries of its neighbourhood by extending it in both eastern and western directions. India has therefore tried to problematize the nature of geo-strategic interactions of South Asia. In the west, India was pivotal in getting Afghanistan into SAARC.[24] It is pertinent to note here that the British, whose geopolitical framework India inherited and remained broadly committed to, never fully mastered Afghanistan, and treated the state as a buffer. It still retains its character of being a classical buffer state. It theoretically provides India a much-needed corridor to connect with Central Asia and Iran for reasons pertaining to energy and oil, and affords an opportunity to counter Pakistan's policy of strategic depth in that state. Afghanistan's geo-strategic location at the crossroads of the Silk Route made it the meeting point of great philosophical and cultural traits, with influences of the Indian and Zoroastrian traditions, and the Greco-Persian and Roman empires. Talibanization had thwarted this syncretism, but it could not destroy the heritage and historical links. India has primarily sought to invest in infrastructure and industrial development in order to promote economic growth and reduce poverty in Afghanistan, to lay the new road and railway connectivity and thereby enhance Kabul's cross-border and transit trade with neighbouring countries. However, Afghanistan poses a huge challenge for India. India has no little geopolitical purchase in the state. The drawdown of the US-led NATO troops might put the security of the civilian government in jeopardy, unless the much vaunted Bilateral Security Agreement (BSA)—which would allow a force of 8,000–10,000 troops to remain in Afghanistan beyond 2014—materializes, and international financial assistance continues to pour in. India, with its panoply of economic, political, and strategic investments in Afghanistan, therefore, has a profound interest in ensuring that the NATO forces stay. However, India has done precious little in diplomatic terms to facilitate that agreement. While India wants Western powers to arm the Afghan security forces more heavily, it has continuously vacillated over its own role, preferring to remain content with training 1,000 Afghan internal security force personnel annually (Joshi 2013). The limited role India plays in Afghanistan, despite the state's crucial importance to its national security, follows from the perceived threat of the Taliban and extremist or terrorist elements that have harried India in the past. While the sagacity or appropriateness of this approach is debatable, it indicates a conservative approach to an extended spatial imagination of South Asia to the western front.

Spatial Metaphors and India's 'Look East'

India's attempt to redefine its neighbourhood in the East is not merely an exercise in broadening the subcontinent, but in transcending it in several important ways. In keeping with India's self-identity and the spatial metaphors underlying its imagination of neighbourhood, one finds that there are three visions of India's 'Look East' initiative, each underpinned by a particular conceptual orientation (see Chapter 5 in this volume). These conceptual maps are framed through the deployment of the notions of power, commerce, and community, and would be developed in Chapter 5. Like India's conceptions of a regional order in South Asia, the power imagination undergirds the official discourses of the 'Look East' or 'Act East' policy.

India has in fact started to move beyond Southeast Asia. It has flagged off a policy of looking Far East in 2012, which seeks to take her to the South Pacific. India's economic aid to the small islands in this region has grown steadily. While the figure is low when compared to the USA, China, or even Australia, given India's distance and India's economic capacity at the time, the investment is commendable.

There are reasons as to why India is expanding its reach. But perhaps more importantly, given the potential for liquefied natural gas extraction through deep sea mining, particularly off the coast of Papua New Guinea (PNG), and with India's improving deep sea mining capabilities, engaging with these islands contributes to a further widening of its energy import basket. With the advent of the idea of the 'Indo-Pacific', which sees the region stretching from Madagascar to the Marshall Islands as one unit, deepening partnerships with the Pacific Islands might help India gain a more overarching presence in this 'two ocean' region. In the words of Kailash K. Prasad (2014), 'With new opportunities for trade and with resource based interests stretching further into the Pacific ocean, New Delhi could also make a stronger case for playing a greater role in ensuring freedom of navigation through the maritime highways of global commerce in South and East Asia—a role India's rapidly modernizing navy might not find entirely unwelcome.' However, as I shall argue in Chapter 5, geopolitical concerns and strategic considerations have gradually come to overlay the trappings of prosperity. Business is good if it contributes to national security. The fact that a more ambitious and riskier open doors/borders policy could result in far more economic gains for all stakeholders and forge new bonds among kin groups is understood, but not entertained. Space-as-power trumps the other imageries in India's foreign policy, even when it comes to new experiments to transcend the limitations of geography.

***

The national imagination in India has naturally favoured a power reading of its immediate neighbourhood, which is fundamentally a defensive and security-centric vision based on its claims of difference. The heritage of being an old civilization, its democratic culture and institutions, its preference for strategic autonomy, and a sense of defiant affirmation of its role in world politics have contributed to the articulation of this feeling of difference. India has not only sought hard to become a modern state but has also tried to imagine South Asia as such. Modernity and territoriality have fused in this geopolitical imagination of space as power. It is interesting to note that India's imagination beyond South Asia has changed more smoothly when compared to its vision near home. India has increasingly stood by a neo-liberal international order, though retaining a moral critique of its discriminations and excesses. While it occasionally bandwagons with the less developed countries against the developed West, its role in the global political economy is now far more confident than in the past. In the words of Rahul Mukherjee (2014: 461), 'Embedded liberalism has driven the country to make decisions to spur growth and welfare within a secure international environment.' However, no sustained politics of liberalism is visible in South Asia, and though India's official position has often been to urge South Asian states to make good of India's economic growth, the discursive framing has chosen the language of power over commerce. South Asia's regionalism is thus stillborn.

India's imagination of South Asia can be thought of as a two-level process. First, it has its sources in India's own identity, and thus contains the fragility of its models of selfhood. The secular, liberal model of civic nationalism which came to dominate India's self-imagination has become contested over the years. The contestation is manifold: on the one hand, it is about the silences—the politics of dignity and recognition questioning the innocence of India's civic nationalism, thereby strengthening the social cleavages of caste and ethnicity; on the other, more drastically, the liberal model is now under threat from the Hindu right wing, which blends culture, faith and nationalism to create a new ideology of honour and unity. However, in terms of foreign policy, the new political forces led by BJP are yet to make any radical departure in India's South Asia policy on the basis of its Hindu politico-cultural agenda. A discourse of power based on sovereign territoriality continues to be the guiding mantra of India's policy towards its neighbourhood. The increasing militarization of India's ties with Pakistan may be explained along the axis of Hindu cultural nationalism, though there is clinching empirical evidence against it. The claim that India's bold surgical strikes across the international border are the manifestation of an increasing Hindu revivalist masculinity may seem attractive, but will not stand close scrutiny.[25] In other words,

India's domestic identity contestations have little impact on its spatial imageries of its neighbourhood. No matter what kind of power rules India, the range of policy remains, by and large, constant. In case of South Asia, however, territory, more than any other marker, serves as the defining element of national identity of states, and accounts for the remarkable consistency in the way the subcontinental elites define their political relations with neighbours.

This means that India's imagination of South Asia 'cannot be' entirely reduced to domestic politics. This would neutralize the very foundation of the inside/outside distinction that the politics of post-colonial sovereign territoriality entails. Hence, India imagines its neighbourhood as a space different from itself. This difference is not easy to make. Culturally, anthropologically, and socially, South Asians were always a meta-community. The only way this difference works is through the discursive practices of citizenship, which increasingly invoke the principle of territorial separation as the sole basis for relating to its neighbours. This inevitably makes realist power politics the most appropriate basis for imagining South Asia, and perhaps the only inexorable one under the circumstances. South Asia's liberal imagination is inherently weak, given liberalism's problematic relation with territoriality, and the tendency of the market to transcend fixed or bordered spaces. India, like other South Asian states, fears the meta-community of its past. This delegitimizes the politics of community, which perhaps would have been the most appropriate spatial imagination for the neighbourhood.

South Asia, after all, is a very geopolitical, Curzonian construct; it is entirely opposed to South Asians as a people, as they had historically been, notwithstanding their political identities and nature of the rule. But modern South Asia is a territorialized space, valourizing sovereignty and control. Hence, India's engagement with the region has been through strategies of national security. While Nehru was not keen enough to factor in the neighbourhood as a vital element of India's regional security, his successors have had to respond to security challenges in a far more direct way. India gradually developed a more assertive and interventionist discourse over the 1970s and 1980s (which caused significant problems with its neighbours), and moved to a more fraternal discourse based on non-reciprocal concessions vis-à-vis the smaller states of the region. However, its rivalry with Pakistan did not transform; it assumed a balance-of-terror character, with both becoming recognized nuclear powers after 1998. This intractable conflict prevented the possible redefinition of the region. India's difficulties over Sri Lanka and Bangladesh, which exposed the superficiality of the inside–outside distinction as demanded by the states, limited returns to its new politics of friendship or fraternal power. Frustrations over its incapacity to lead the subcontinent, and the constraints imposed successfully by its neighbours, have compelled India to gradually start redefining the geography of South Asia. It has done this by incorporating Afghanistan in the west and linking up with Southeast Asia, and then the remote Southern Pacific islands in the east. But this re-articulation is also based on India's perceived geopolitical needs. In Afghanistan, India needs security guarantees against Pakistan and a corridor to the energy economies of Central Asia. In the east, it needs to exploit economic opportunities and balance against an increasingly assertive China that threatens India's rise. Hence, its new regionalism is also predicated upon 'the geography of power' and fear. The confidence required for imagining alternative spatial imaginations is lacking in India; India uses foreign policy to streamline, discipline, and crush the challenges to its territorial nationalism, and in the process, reinforces the imagination of South Asia as a space of power.

Notes

1. This means that other forms of collective imagination of India and the region are available. Civil society groups, for example, are not constrained by the statist conception of a region. They have often deployed the categories of class and gender to define India and South Asia. Artists and radical scholars also engage in different forms of spatial imagination, which are very different from the existing political narratives. However, these imaginations do not engender concrete decisions and policies that decide domestic and foreign policies of states. That does not mean that the alternative constructions are irrelevant. They have enormous normative salience, and indicate the different horizons of possibilities. However, unless any of these imaginations become politically dominant, they cannot rival the dominant elite discourses of the state.

2. Newman defines borders as '...the process of bounding, drawing lines around spaces and groups, is a dynamic phenomenon, of which the boundary line is, more often than not, simply the tangible and visible feature which represents the course and intensity of the bounding process at any particular point in time and space. A deeper understanding of the bounding process requires an integration of the different types and scales of boundaries into a hierarchical system in

which the relative impact of these lines on the people, groups and nations can be conceptualized as a single process' (Newman 2003: 134).

3. A similar view comes from Nimmi Kurian. In her words,

> A geopolitics of knowledge has closely accompanied the geopolitics of borders, often mimicking reasons of the state. For from offering alternative imaginaries, mainstream IR has largely tended to faithfully mirror the 'cartographic anxiety' of the state. The mimetic nature of formal research has meant that many of these questions have been studied in fractured frames, with scholarship often taking the cue from statist frames. It has been disinterested in the everyday struggles and contestations of the borderlanders, preferring instead the esoteric diversions of systemic battles that structuralism wages. A politicomilitary reading of border landscapes is conspicuous by what it leaves out of its research remit; that there is alongside an anthropology, a history and a sociology of borders to negotiate. (Kurian 2014: 145)

4. On European borders, see Balibar (1998, 1999), Bauder (2011), Carens (1987), Kearney (1991), and Eder (2006).

5. On the US–Mexican border, see Nevins (2000). Also useful are Andreas (1998–9) and Andreas and Biersteker (2003).

6. Raffestin says that the construction of territory is the outcome of territoriality. He defines territoriality as 'the ensemble of relations that a society maintains with exteriority and alterity for the satisfaction of its needs, towards the end of attaining the greatest possible autonomy compatible with resources of the system' (Raffestin 2012: 121).

7. Critical geopolitics and border studies have spawned an astonishingly large literature. The works of Agnew, David Newman, Dalby, Toal, Spark, Sassen, Rumford, Ansi Paasi, and Sanjay Chaturvedi, among several others stand out.

8. See the debate between Abidzade and Miller for contrasting views on this issue.

9. Stuart Elden has contributed significantly to bring sociological substance into geopolitical constructs. Also useful is Brenner and Elden (2009).

10. The novelty in Foucault's idea lies in the concern about how individuals understand the places in which they live. The spaces do not exist in a vacuum, but are rather defined by a preconceived set of relations. In 'Of Other Places', Foucault is mostly concerned about the historical development of Western space perception, beginning from what he identifies as 'espace de localization' in the Middle Ages, through the 'etendue' [extending] from the time of Galileo to the modern 'emplacement'. Foucault deduces that contrary to time, space is still in the process of reaching the synthesis: secularization and sanctity are the guiding principles that cleave space. Foucault argued that our spatial understanding is better sorted in temporal terms. However, sanctity still divides space by separating the inner form the outer, the internal from the external, and signifying spaces

by the prevailing standards of the normal and he deviant. In Foucault's words, 'And perhaps our life is still governed by a certain number of oppositions that remain inviolable, that our institutions and practices have not yet dared to break down. These are oppositions that we regard as simple givens: for example between private space and public space, between family space and social space, between cultural space and useful space, between the space of leisure and that of work. All these are still nurtured by the hidden presence of the sacred' (Foucault 1984: 2). Spaces are always relations distinguishing the familiar and the curious. Foucault calls the latter 'heterotopia', which, like a mirror, is a space that is real and yet unknown.

11. For an excellent account of how the political history of territoriality is to be read in general, and the contributions of Foucault in particular, see Elden (2013).

12. Albert and Brock argue, 'Both historical processes converged, however, in the understanding that nation refers to a uniting of the people living on a state's territory as a community of citizens with certain rights and duties but also with feelings of solidarity, vis-à-vis the state and fellow citizens. This way, territorial rule was reconstituted, through nation building, as a three-dimensional spatial arrangement of social practice' (Albert and Brock 2001: 35).

13. Globalization and critical geopolitics are issues that have pushed IR scholars in different ways to look at territoriality, statehood, and sovereignty more closely than ever before. Opinion regarding the nature and extent of the impact of sovereignty on territoriality, globalization, and statehood is extremely varied. Most commentators believe that globalization has profoundly affected the meanings of territoriality, globalization, and statehood, with some going on to argue that it has fundamentally altered the conventional meaning of these concepts in terms of their empirical referents, while others have been somewhat less radical in their perception of the change. Against these analysts is staked the views of the no-changers, who are equally variegated in their response, with some arguing that the fundamental understanding of these concepts has survived the onslaught of globalization, while others claiming that the empirical transformations brought about by the forces of global dispersion are a fact, but these can be cognitively accommodated within the regular meaning of these concepts. For a survey of these positions, see Chatterjee, 'Globalization'.

14. For a different interpretation than mine, see, Albert and Brock (2001). Also see the discussion in Biersteker (2002).

15. On the various facets of this fascinating discourse, see Kohn (1996), Dirk (2001), Bandyopadhyay (2004), Chatterjee (1986, 1993), Metcalf (1997), Guha (1997), and Guha (2011).

16. In terms of theoretical positioning, the arguments developed here are close to constructivism. Theoretically, constructivists are more comfortable dealing with community as a social category, compared to realists and neo-liberals.

17. Identity is a messy concept. For excellent analyses of conceptual difficulties surrounding it, see Brubaker and Cooper (2000). For a methodologically informed analysis, see Fearon (1999).

18. On the gradual evolution of India's conception of region, see Michael (2013). On the role of Nehru in shaping India's post-colonial identity in international affairs, see Chacko (2011).

19. For a very useful discussion, see Pantham (1997).

20. On the various dimensions of the India–Pakistan conflict, see Ganguly (1986) and Paul (2005). For the origins of the Kashmir dispute, see Dasgupta (1968).

21. On the various perspectives, history and historiographical debates on the partition of the Indian subcontinent, see Philips and Wainwright (1970), Khan (2007), Chakrabarty (2004), Chatterji (2007), Kumar (1999), and Samaddar (2003).

22. For a discussion of identity and ideological differences between the two states, see Jalal (1995).

23. I draw a distinction here between what causes the rivalry and what keeps it going.

24. India's Ministry of External Affairs noted in a statement issued on August 2012: 'In regional cooperation, Afghanistan joined SAARC at the 14th SAARC Summit held in Delhi in April 2007, opening possibilities of Afghanistan becoming a trade, transportation and energy hub linking together the countries of the region from Central to South Asia. India has also encouraged Afghanistan's efforts at capitalizing on its unique geographical location at the heart of the Asian continent by supporting regional initiatives like the Istanbul process and RECCA [Regional Economic Cooperation Conference on Afghanistan] that seek to assist in Afghanistan's development through cooperation in a various sectors of the economy' (Ministry of External Affairs 2012).

25. Take the recent example of surgical strikes allegedly made by the Indian armed forces across the Line of Control in Kashmir in retaliation to terrorist strikes in a place called Uri, which killed eighteen Indian soldiers (18 September 2016). BJP claimed this as a display of virility and strength, something which was lacking in the past. Apparently, military strikes against terror camps were undertaken by the Congress-led United Progressive Alliance (UPA) regimes as well, though were not advertised. In contrast, the BJP-led government invokes a language of homogenous nationalism and militant sacrifice, not only in matters of national security, but in domestic politics as well.

2 Globalization, Democratization, Liberal Peace, and Human Security in South Asia

T HIS CHAPTER CONSIDERS three alternative arguments for possible transformations and changes in South Asia, which have remained empirically and ideationally relevant to the subcontinent for the last two decades. These are arguments based on globalization, democracy and liberal peace, and human security, respectively. Globalization entails transformation qua softening of territoriality, questioning of sovereignty, economic interdependence, and the onset of conditions that require going beyond nation-state-based solutions and policies. The liberal peace argument is about the growth of liberal democracy as the most efficacious antidote to violent conflicts between states, particularly the more powerful ones. Finally, human security entails freedom from want and fear; it means having the most robust solutions to the endemic problems of human insecurity, involving democratic institutions, participatory development, and civil society initiatives.

These arguments are not necessarily opposed to each other. While their specific analytics are distinct and cannot be collapsed into a common thesis, in the final analysis, all three arguments are about creating positive security interdependencies in South Asia. They also entail commitments to democracy, human rights, development, and legitimacy. Above all, they possess significant positive heuristics. Hence, their normative case is hardly a matter of contestation. Serious differences remain over the role of the market forces, the relation between the community and the individual, the most desirable models of development, the preferred agencies of change, and the meaning of democratic empowerment. But there is a broad consensus on the need to discipline states, legitimize sovereignty, strengthen the discourse of rights, cultivate civility, and move away from the logic of national security to that of democratic development. However, none of these projects have so far succeeded in transforming the face of South Asia. South Asia remains a space of power, despite embracing globalization, achieving sustained democratization, and investing consistently on virtually all the indicators of human development. The realist spatial imagination constitutes the subcontinent, and has proven to be remarkably resilient in the face of all the transformative projects. My argument here is that South Asia's strong territoriality proves remarkably resistant to any qualitative change. Intense geopolitical rivalry casts its shadow across the subcontinent. Deep internal conflicts, based on various bases of identity, prevent any change in the underlying spatial imagination held by the elites, virtually irrespective of ruling ideologies.

Globalization and Change in South Asia

We have discussed IR literature at length in Chapter 1, focusing on various dimensions of state, sovereignty, and territoriality under globalization. The principal arguments propounded by scholars who feel globalization has changed the meanings and practices of statehood, sovereign entitlements, and territoriality can be summarized as follows. First, it is argued that globalization transforms the idea of the state from a regulative entity to a general human collectivity, or an organization bereft of any particular claim to hierarchy or legitimacy. To the extent these states have become dysfunctional owing to the forces of globalization, there is a corresponding deflation of the state by a new politics of global cosmopolitanism from above, and fragmentation by the politics of identity from below. Globalization has thus turned the state largely inconsequential to the life of its people. Second, it is widely believed that globalization trumps territoriality by time–space compression of the globe. Networks have become more important than direct control of borders/territories. Territoriality is softened by globalization, as the critical threats have become extra-territorial, and moved beyond the capacity of the states to resolve them. The geopolitics of territorial or border security thus has little value in times of global transformation. Third, critics urge that sovereignty as a practice is transformed by the forces of globalization, which amounts to greater transparency and accountability in domestic affairs that no longer hinges on the capacity for authoritative and hierarchical control of the territory. Democratization and human rights mean more to sovereign practices than the traditional idea of physical or territorial control.

A recent perspective on globalization[1] is fashioned by Matt Sparke, who has sought to bring the imperatives of fluid geography, social commodities, labour, and geopolitics in an integrated narrative. He highlighted two important aspects concerning globalization; first, some of its contemporary conceptualizations; and second, the material transformations resulting from political, social, and economic reorientation and its impact on geography. Through this exercise Sparke challenges the given notion about globalization being an inevitable and levelling process. He cautions that the unevenness is getting worse. Spark departs from the neo-liberal fixation on capital to emphasize the role of labour in the global economy. He argues through the later part of the book that despite spatial differences, globalization has created an interconnected global working class. He also provides a detailed discussion on how social life is being increasingly designed on the imagination of an interconnected world, as opposed to traditional geopolitical focus on nation-states. The book also explores matters of space, territoriality, locality, spatial fixity and mobility, and issues of geopolitics and geo-economics and their changing conceptions in the twenty-first century. Furthermore, like Castells (1996, 1997, 1998) and other theorists of social communication, Sparke sees more value in the idea of a networked world in contrast to the differentiated statist imagery of the traditional geopolitical thinking (with its focus on territorially defined nation-states) as the dynamic shaping fresh ways of organizing social life, and opines that even new military models of warfare tend to reflect it (Sparke 2005).[2] Sparke's thesis is nicely complemented by the connectivity argument by Parag Khanna, who argues, 'Competing over connectivity plays out as tug-of-war over global supply chains, energy markets, industrial production, and the valuable flows of finance, technology, knowledge and talent... Another way this competitive connectivity takes place is through infrastructures alliances; connecting physically through across borders and oceans through tight supply chain partnerships' (Khanna 2016: xvii).

The rise of geo-economics has, in contrast, brought to the fore the centrality of economic tools in service of geopolitical goals. In a gripping narrative, Blackwill and Harris have shown how the game of geo-economics is changing the American game as well as the contours of world politics. They defined geo-economics as 'the use of economic instruments to promote and defend national interests, and to produce beneficial geopolitical results; and the effects of other nation's economic actions on a country's geopolitical goals' (Blackwill and Harris 2016). Geo-economics is accounted for by three factors. First, the contemporary rising powers use far more of their economic instruments as part of their repertoire to gain geo-strategic influence and wage geopolitical conflicts across diverse theatres of the world. The contrast between calculations of Soviet and Chinese national power estimates to policymakers in the USA is a clear example. However, modern geo-economics is not simply about what great powers do; every conceivable state seems to prefer its economic means to get to whatever goals it may have. In a twist to the democratic peace argument, it seems plausible that the coalition of democratic states may use geo-economics against states that refuse to cooperate and trade fairly on level terms. Russia and China, as authoritarian states, might prefer bribes and other strategies to increase their influence among weaker neighbouring states. Geo-economics in today's world has become related to other aspects of statecraft; hence, its newfound attractions and effectiveness. Second, great powers have far more resources at their disposal than they did in the past, which is partly due to the return of sate capitalism after the financial crisis of 2007–9. As state enterprises have gained steadily, the marriage of coercive and economic capacities appear more potent and lethal than it did in the period of strong globalization. The third factor behind the resurgence of geo-economics is the changing nature of the markets and their growing impact on foreign policy of states. This, however, is not an argument against geopolitics; it only draws attention to the care that powers need to take to adjust to markets, lest their geopolitical leverage is undercut by better performers.

In this section, I articulate a contrarian perspective in the context of the prevailing contentious politics of South Asia. Virtually every South Asian state has responded to globalization by way of liberalization policies, which saw variable degrees of opening up of their economies and the withdrawal of the state from a range of economic activities. Therefore, globalization has indeed impacted South Asia in various ways.[3] But has South Asia undergone any identity transportation as a result of globalization? Do South Asian states relate to each other any differently than in the past?

Is there a veritable threat to the notions of territoriality, sovereignty, and statehood in South Asia that is a consequence of globalization? The study does not find this to be true. In this section, I develop a set of arguments in support of my claim that globalization has been largely inconsequential to the political configuration of the subcontinent.

Geopolitics Shaping Identity in South Asia

The central argument of this chapter is that the prevailing geopolitical dynamics of South Asia still continue to be the chief component of the region's make-up. The continuity of that dynamic is primarily responsible for trumping the macro-transformational consequences of globalization in the subcontinent. Unlike most other regions of the world, military expenditure, in both absolute terms and as a percentage of Gross Domestic Product (GDP), increased in South Asia between 1990 and 2000. India and Pakistan in particular maintained high expenditures in the period between 2006 and 2015. In more specific terms, I offer three reasons as to why South Asia is unable to transcend its self-identity, or rather fails to evolve an identity at the regional level which is commensurate with the needs of contemporary globalism, particularly in terms of evolving novel regional institutions and practices.[4]

First, nationalism remains rather widespread and strong in South Asia, with a large number of unsettled cultural, ethnic, and historical issues stoking the fires of nationalist passion. Second, South Asians continue to assign high value to sovereignty and independence, which can be attributed to their memory of birth through partitions, and having lived under long colonial occupation by an alien power. It is no mere coincidence that some of the strongest resistance to the dilution of the principle of non-intervention in the domestic affairs of the state—as inscribed in the Charter of the United Nations—came from the South Asian states. South Asian states continue to betray extraordinary sensitivity to the idea of border control or physical occupation of territory as top prerogatives of sovereign states. The unresolved issues of ethnic subnationalism have only reinforced the resolve of the states (in South Asia) to reconfirm their territorial dominance. The same fear undergirds South Asian concerns for 'illegal' migration and/or clandestine border crossings. In fact, South Asian states seldom recognize the existence of migrants and refugees, and betray a strong hostility towards the immigrant population. Third, the identity of South Asia still continues to be drawn along strategic lines. South Asia emerged as a critical regional security complex during the Cold War, and continues to be so after the demise of that systemic bipolarity (Buzan and Waever 2003: 94). The nuclearization of the subcontinent has further reinforced this strategic configuration.

Conflicting Strategic Configurations

In strategic terms, South Asia remains divided by the status quoist integration of the subcontinent by India and the revisionist account held by Pakistan. While India has always emphasized on the geo-strategic unity of the subcontinent, Pakistan has worked for extra-regional engagement to offset the strategic advantage held by India. These contradictory efforts have generated complex interactional problems in the subcontinent. While the two other larger South Asian states— Bangladesh and Sri Lanka—have stayed neutral to this fundamental divide, they have also, by and large, refrained from joining hands with India, being mistrustful of its hegemonic intentions. For both Sri Lanka and Bangladesh, subnational issues have prevented normalization of bilateral relations with India, exposing the enormous salience of internal security considerations within the subcontinent. The binaries of inside/ outside, citizen/people, hierarchy/anarchy, and friend/foe, along with being progressive within and necessitous without, continue to mark South Asia's existential reality. The borders do not show any signs of retreat; identities do not appear to be broadening or becoming inclusive. This does not mean that people-to-people contract or civil society initiatives are absent in South Asia. It also does not also indicate absence of trade, commerce, and other modes of communication amongst the South Asian states. What it shows is the overwhelming dominance of strategic configuration as the constitutive norm of the subcontinent, which automatically results in the valourization of the principle of differentiation, and the concomitant strong legitimization of the territorialized practices of sovereignty.

Globalization, Nationalism, and Subnationalism

Against these, the proponents of globalization may argue that nationalism has weakened in the last ten years in subnationalist or ethnic mobilization in different parts of South Asia. However, in what way has globalization triggered this? By most accounts, the cultural narrative of globalization is essentially homogenized—it is the culture of Western cosmopolitanism that finds an unprecedented opportunity for global dissemination qua modern technological means. If the global cultural narrative is singular, then it is a threat not merely to the culture of nationalist particularity, but also to the cultural forms below the nation, which the nation subsumes through representation. My argument here is that globalization produces an unintended effect—homogenization deforms into fragmentation. Ethnic communities, or subnational groups, find new opportunities for accentuating their difference from others and for articulating the same. Even the changed character of nationalism, far more contested now than it was in the past, is not an obvious threat to the framework of the nation-state. The specificity of the nation in terms of its value articulation is not necessarily a threat unto itself, unless the value (on which the nation is based) rails against the framework itself (Das 2003: 107). In fact, even communitarian writers concede that ethnic subnationalism in South Asia is unable to transcend the imagination of the nation-state as a spatial category. They replicate or mirror the nation-state in their secessionist discourses, demanding their own nation-states by exercising their right to self-determination on ethnic grounds (Das 2004). There is little evidence of any imagination of network communities, or a politics of deterritorialized peoplehood, where the exercise of political authority would not be coterminous with a given territory, but would extend to people or communities identified by a given criteria. There is no sign of any movement towards 're-medievalism' in South Asia, towards the creation of political communities unattached to discreet territories. The argument of subnationalism, or ethnic mobilization, as triggered by globalization, is a non sequitur: it can make sense only if the transformation attests to the spatial imagination inherent in the framework of the nation-state. Anti-state activities and secessionist tendencies are therefore logically unrelated to the relevance of the sovereign state as a political framework.

There is a second line of argument, which relates globalization and territory but again without any implication for the legitimization or delegitimization of the frame of the nation-state. According to this argument, globalization can engender secessionist tendencies within large heterogeneous federal states, which are unable to grow a unified sense of national identity by decisively overriding particularistic or local attachments. As a federal polity globalizes, the benefits accrued out of the process get unevenly distributed amongst the units, since units have come to enjoy greater autonomy than they did in the past in articulating relations with sovereign state and non-state actors. Productive or developed units succeed in reaping greater benefits in this process than their underdeveloped counterparts, and hence, beyond a certain threshold, might begin to harbour secessionist proclivities, as the cost or burden of subsidizing the inefficient units (that are insufficiently globalized and weak) threaten to lower the level of prosperity that could have been achieved otherwise (Patnaik 1995: 247).

Two observations attest to this line of argument. First, this is a perspective on secessionism, and 'not' on the unbundling of territoriality. The prosperous provinces merely want to be wealthy states. Second, the empirical correspondence of 'this argument to the South Asian reality is missing. None of the most-developed units or parts of the larger South Asian states have demanded secession from their present bodies. The correlation between relative deprivation and the politics of secessionism on the other hand, is quite high in the subcontinent. This is true for India's northeastern states, the Tamil-dominated provinces of Sri Lanka, and to a lesser intensity, Baluch and Pathan mobilizations in Pakistan. The one rich province in India that experienced a violent secessionist movement, Punjab, witnessed collapse of the demand before globalization began in India. Hence, the variable prosperity induced by globalization is no threat to the durability of the nation-state framework in the subcontinent.

Globalization and Domestic Trends within South Asia

The fact about South Asia is that its domestic and regional patterns have remained unchanged despite or notwithstanding globalization. The general pattern of violent internal politics in virtually all states has remained unchanged, along with the pattern of spillover to the regional level (Buzan and Waever 2003: 106–7). Neo-liberal policies and progress towards democratization have done little to reverse this trend. As Frances Stewart and Taimur Hyat argue, 'Over fifteen conflicts have occurred in a span of five decades. Indian has witnessed eight, followed by three in Pakistan, and one each in Sri Lanka, Bangladesh, and Bhutan ... A dozen ethnic conflicts have become big enough to be described as internal wars. Most have lingered on, and led to large scale economic and human losses' (Stewart and Hyat 2002: 112).

In Sri Lanka, the conflict between the LTTE and the Sri Lankan state, an intense ethnic conflict between the Tamils and the Sinhalese populations, continued throughout the 1990s. Although the mediation effected by Norway promised to translate the occasional and intermittent truces into a durable political settlement and trends in international politics went against the extremist activities of the LTTE after 2002, the promised political agreement did not materialize. Each party seemed to have entrenched its gains further in this period, thereby making a military solution to the conflict look rather impossible. Bangladesh, on the other, has undergone a disastrous political polarization in its democratization process, threatening to plunge the nation into large-scale political violence. The growing Islamization of the polity has complicated and accentuated the crisis further, causing adverse repercussions for Indo-Bangladesh relations (Buzan and Waever 2003: 106–7). Nepal's domestic turmoil is at its peak, with the monarchy usurping all authority by nipping the country's incipient democratization process at the bud on one hand, and the Maoist insurgents capturing several parts of the state on the other. Bhutan witnessed massive infiltration of various anti-Indian insurgent outfits throughout the 1990s, but a spectacular military counter-offensive by the monarch against these elements in 2003, aided by the Indian army, seemed to have reversed this trend. There is, however, no evidence of democratization in Bhutan, and the ethnic relations between the Bhutanese of Nepalese origin and the ethnic Bhutanese continue to remain tense.

The evolution of domestic trends in Pakistan has been very convulsive. On the one hand, its state apparatus continues to be distorted by its frenzied zeal to strike military parity with India, which has made the political system parasitic on the politically active military establishment. The active involvement of Pakistan in the Afghan crisis (1979–90) began to cast an ominous shadow on the body politic of the former, with democratization becoming the scapegoat for the country's persistent ills and growing sectarian violence. The distinction between state and regime security was evidently collapsing in Pakistan, with the elites becoming more self-aggrandizing than anything else. The impact of the Afghan civil war on Pakistan was direct—it led to vast immigration of Afghan refugees, some of whom became the conduits for a billion-dollar trade in arms and narcotics, and propagated a culture of violence amidst a network of corrupt warlords and mafias (2003: 107). It was responsible for the new-found salience of Islamic fundamentalism in Pakistan, since Pakistan's support for the Taliban regime was open. The rise of General Pervez Musharraf—the new military dictator of Pakistan, saw the collapse of parliamentary democracy and the disbanding of democratic forces in the state.

The situation in Pakistan assumed a new twist after 9/11, since Pakistan regained its lost geopolitical significance in the strategic calculations of the USA. As a leading state in the American war against terrorism, Pakistan began to get valuable military hardware from the USA once more. The Musharraf regime obtained a de facto legitimization, which derived out of its security-/military-dispensing role rather than out of any commitment to democratization. The triumph of geopolitics over the alternative politics of democratization underscores the irrelevance of globalization in the subcontinent. It also renders the assumption redundant that transformation in the meanings of sovereignty is more contingent upon democratic norms than territorial/physical control. Even with the democratic regimes coming to power after the military went back to the barracks, there is no empirical evidence of any let-up in the geopolitical logic of the state. Pakistan remains a warrior state, obsessed with its need to obtain strategic parity with its 'other'—India. National security decides the broad contours of the state, and with the renewed conflict with Indian security forces across the Line of Control in Kashmir and the international border with India across Punjab since the summer of 2016, militarization of the major state apparatus has steadily increased.

India since the 1990s

The proponents of globalization might draw inspiration from trends unfolding in India 1990 onwards, but upon closer scrutiny, there is no evident correspondence between the dynamic of globalization on the one hand and the nature and prevalence of the pattern of domestic violence on the other. The period under review has seen continued violence over territoriality (Kashmir), separatism (Kashmir and the northeastern states), governance and social justice-related issues (the ultra-left insurgency in more than ten states and caste atrocities/violence in north India), communal divide (Hindu/Muslim riots), and demands for autonomy (leading to the creation of a number of states by breaking up larger ones).

The nature of the Indian state has undergone a change. It has distinctively laid aside its intrusive welfare role and taken the direction of neo-liberalism. Globalization has multiplied the intensity and extensity of urbanization, and has engendered complex social dislocations in response. The liberal, Western, consumerist, and cosmopolitan culture of globalization can be found in India's leading cities, reflected in the modes of popular representation in media and entertainments of all forms. Globalization has also unleashed a great developmental debate, with the country's intelligentsia being divided on its relative merits and demerits.[5]

The Indian state has become more xenophobic about its frontiers in the east, despite the promise of the 'Look East' magic. There is little domestic support for a new politics of regionalism, which might redefine South Asia more consistently with the demands of globalization. There is little evidence of any concrete problematization of territoriality, or sovereignty, other than in the critical narratives of a group of social scientists. The state has undoubtedly become more contested and fragmented, but notwithstanding the claims to the contrary, there are no visible signs of a politics of deterritorialization, or any imagination of a form of political community, which may transcend the framework of the nation-state (Samaddar 1998a, 1998b, 2001a, 2002; also Das 2003). More people and communities have become sensitive about their claims to political specificity or particularity; they now actively demand that their homeland be either autonomous or independent of the existing state. But they all continue to imagine within the territorial metaphor. They demand complete universalization of the state, as against the existing framework in which there are muted possibilities for the satisfaction of the political aspirations (territorially conceived) of multiple communities, which forcefully cohabit within the bounded space of existing structures.

Globalization as State Empowerment in India

It appears that globalization is embraced more in the interest of national vitality or national power than anything else. Neo-liberal policies are often explained along geopolitical axes. The argument here is that if

India needs to realize its potential of becoming a genuine great power (an ambition that no longer remains utopian, owing to India's successful economic policies of greater free trade and more extensive marketization), it has to pursue neo-liberal economic policies of greater free trade and more extensive privatization. According to this view, strategic depth and economic non-interventionism coincide. Successful globalization is then a means for state empowerment, the best path for the country's inevitable graduation to the pantheon of great powers (Nayar 2005; Nayar and Paul 2003). One need not ascribe to this (neo-)realist cum liberal mix to stand against the radical claims of globalization in the South Asian/Indian context. However, the argument is useful, inasmuch as it shows that there is no inevitable contradiction between the pulls of geo-economics and the pressures of geopolitics; coexistence is at least as conceivable as mutual opposition.

Continuity vs. Change

The regional dynamics of South Asia, as an extension of the domestic trends of the constituent states, emphasizes the element of continuity rather than change. The primary reasons behind India's wars with Pakistan, or the fundamental issues under dispute, remain unresolved. India is still to sort out its territorial disputes with China, and the Kashmir issue is yet to be addressed (Chellaney 1999a, 1999b). On top of India's territorial dispute (over Kashmir) with Pakistan, other aspects of their conflict include societal/identity issues (communal *vs.* secular) and a general or broad dynamic of arms competition, particularly over nuclear warheads and missiles. The last decade has witnessed continued rivalry on defence-related matters, despite a big increase in the quantum of trade and business, notwithstanding the sustained process of dialogue and normalization. Till the territorial issue over Kashmir is not settled through the mutual consent of both the states, the use of low-key violence or support to terrorist groups (in Kashmir) would continue to remain a viable policy option for Pakistan, to which India would need to respond in 'statist' terms.

The contemporary political discourses in South Asia seem obsessed with illegal migration, fundamentalist Islam, and cross-border terrorism. This is 'not' to suggest that an alternative regionalism cannot grow in South Asia. Nor is this argument an investment in geopolitical determinism. Unfortunately however, going by available evidence, no such alternative vision seems to be gaining political traction over the prevailing politics of alienation and fear in South Asia.

Explaining South Asia's Puzzle

I find that the effects of globalization come in the form of complex mediations rather than direct effects. Globalization facilitates the construction of certain discourses of power, 'given the prior existence of a form of politics'—a form that is neither ubiquitous nor universal. Globalization is creative on the cartography of liberal politics, and its power of issuing a politics of liberalism is always contested. The persistence of the imperatives of geopolitics, or the prevalence of continuity over change in South Asia, is explained ultimately by the absence of an organic liberalism in most South Asian states. This also partly explains the weak democratization of the subcontinent. The idea that if states started the globalization game, things would suddenly move out of control and floodgates would open is wrong. It does not imply either that this would inevitably remove the artificial territorial divisions by unleashing an inexorable logic of commercial prosperity fuelled by an ever-growing market. Globalization does make the state powerless in certain things, but it would not necessarily threaten the politics of territoriality or vertical sovereignty by implication. For globalization to be that creative, there has to be a certain political foundation, an ideational edifice. South Asia lacks that political foundation on which globalization can transform state identity, territoriality, and sovereignty.

Democratization and Liberal Peace in South Asia

A second set of arguments claims that as democratization gains ground in South Asia, along with economic interdependence fostered by changes in the global economy, the constitutive principles of the subcontinent are bound to transform over the long run. In this section, we will first discuss the opportunities and challenges of the democratic project in South Asia. This will be followed by a brief excursion into the applicability of democratic peace to the fraught relations between India and Pakistan.

Although the South Asian states began their journey with distinctive national projects, their unity lay in their commitment to become strong states with consummate national identities. This commitment, however, had to be worked out through complex social structures, which inevitably got intertwined with the political dynamic. All South Asian states had three goals in common: to achieve rapid economic development; to create a strong national identity; and to preserve territorial integration in the face of a myriad challenges to state authority, including the threats of secession. The nature of social elites who came to dominate these South Asian states decided the character of political rule. As Ayesha Jalal's comparative analysis of three South Asian states, namely, India, Pakistan, and Bangladesh, has shown, democracy and authoritarianism were never clearly differentiated ideas in the subcontinent, and therefore, their pairing (rather than exclusive treatments) allows a more incisive historical analysis of the structures of dominance and resistance in this part of the world (Jalal 1995: 1–9).

Roots of Democratization in South Asia

History is important here for two reasons. First, it explains the opportunities and betrayals of democratic projects across South Asian states, in terms of both ideology and class. Second, history is significant for indicating the malleability and flux of South Asian societies, their transformation(s) and challenges, and the inevitability of continuity and change. Trends suggest that democratization has strengthened in South Asia as a whole, although problem(s) of democratization have multiplied. Three factors are crucial here. First, states of South Asia face a remarkably similar political challenge: how to respond to the growing pressure of the demand of the underprivileged, the marginal and the weaker sections, to enter the political arena and be heard. In brief, all South Asian political systems face a challenge of representation, and need to respond to the accusation of serious representation(al) deficit. This provides a great opportunity for democratization, since no other political system exists that can accommodate the marginalized, the dissidents, and the hungry yet politicized masses.

Second, the South Asian states also face a crisis of centralized authority and tight federal models. Centralization no longer seems to work. Coalitions of regional formations are increasingly becoming vocal, and in some cases dominant, and authoritarian devices of displacing their demands show decreasing efficiency. The aspirations of the outlying regions have acquired greater strength due to globalization and the weakening of the direct economic capacity of the state. As regions can now directly articulate networks of capital by escaping central vigilance and control in various degrees, their bargaining capacity vis-à-vis the centre has increased substantially. Although regionalism by itself can be no guarantee to democratization, as the example of Pakistan shows, it increases the mobilizational content of the political system. High mobilization within a polity tends to give rise to a democratic framework. As regions become more and more important, the impetus for democratization is likely to steadily increase.

Third, with globalization, information revolution, a new consciousness for human rights (however repressed it might be for such South Asian states), the expansion of the middle class, and the rapid spread of consumerism, the profile of the civil society is bound to change in the South Asian subcontinent. An autonomous civil society might not develop in the short or medium run in South Asia; the civil society might also not escape its domestication by the territorial nation-state qua a deadly and recursive logic of national security. Yet, it forces renegotiation of identities by the state, or impels their politicization. As identities acquire strength and are politicized, they cannot be left outside the political power game. In this sense, identity politics, despite its many hazards and shortcomings, trumps authoritarian practices and accentuates the tendency towards democratization.

Discerning Threats to Democratization

Despite these opportunities, there is no guarantee that democratization would become an uncontested norm in South Asia's political culture. There are problems threatening the democratic experiment at two levels. The first relates to the issue of how the 'logic of territoriality', or the authority pyramid of the modern state, along with its culture of citizenship, relates to the various subnational/transnational identities, which are based on a plethora of primordial markers. For India, there are two contrasting theses.[6] The first argues that despite many problems and serious misgivings, 'the federal reconciliation of regional identity with autonomy' has been democratically achieved.[7] The second interpretation argues that the state was forced to define communities as relations of power vis-à-vis the nation, and it devolved a strategy to negotiate with them, which sought to harmonize, universalize, and totalize, rather than liberate, particularize, and empower the communities as subjects of rights.[8] The need to reproduce the reason of the nation in the life-worlds of the diverse communities turned the former into a perverse other of the latter. This, by default, consigned Indian democracy to a complex competition for spoils among shifting coalitions of groups, defined along communal lines. No South Asian state is free from this danger, although the manifestation of the same has tended to vary considerably among them. This is a theme that requires a more detailed exposition.

Religious Threats to Democracy

All South Asian states face a crisis in the relations between state institutions and religious identities in one way or the other, with Pakistan increasingly being engulfed by *jihadi* violence, and a distinct hardening of religious identity in all the provinces of the state. Sectarian violence has wrecked Pakistan in the last decade; the state is convulsed by the violence unleashed by a host of fundamentalist groups with different political projects. Bangladesh is struggling to reconcile its Islamic heritage with its secular commitments, which are predicated upon Bengali linguistic nationalism. Islamist organizations and political outfits have remained on the country's landscape, despite occasional harsh measures adopted by the Awami League government to curb religious extremism and terrorism. India is also gripped by a politics of cultural nationalism under the active patronage of the BJP, a Hindu nationalist political force, which now governs the state with a clear legislative majority. Inter-communal relations blow hot and cold across the nation, particularly during elections in states where the BJP has a strong organizational base. The controversies over the ban on cow slaughter, a Hindu turn to the educational curricula, the worshipping of a new politics of masculinity that celebrates Hindu dominance over the national imagination, the martial virtues of a Hindu past, and the need for cultural homogeneity as an essential condition to graduate into a great power—all these unmistakably point towards a right-wing turn in Indian mass politics, though its longevity and ultimate destination remain to be seen. Sri Lanka still struggles to recreate a new social contract between the dominant Sinhala community on the one hand, and the minority Tamil and Muslim groups on the other. The religious extremism of organized Buddhist organizations had been the bedrock of the majoritarian Sinhala ethnic nationalism, which ultimately ended the civil war by force. Even in Myanmar, Buddhists have taken on minority Muslim migrant communities like the Rohingyas, who are constantly on the run, being hounded by the state-backed forces.

Democracy and the Liberal Logic

Liberals believe that democratization, when combined with market forces, or liberal economic policies, works strongly towards peace. The liberal case for economic cooperation builds on the prosperity-induced or welfare-induced effects of the market, which is claimed as a long-term solvent of ultra-nationalistic conflicts. If the progress of market forces results in greater wealth and higher welfare (wealth causing welfare), then it can be reasonably expected that the constituencies benefiting from such wealth/welfare would contribute to the cause of peace. If liberalization via market forces, however, merely increases relative deprivation and diminishes welfare, there will be little domestic public resistance to oppressive, overtly nationalistic policies, particularly if such policies are shown to have beneficial economic effects for the development of the state.

The impact of market liberalization, free-trade policies, and privatization on South Asian economies is an extremely contested issue. Going by the prevalent opinions, it may be safe to assume that there are powerful arguments both for and against liberalization policies, and a comparative analysis of South Asian economies show that despite the free market doctrine becoming the new orthodoxy in South Asian economic thinking, the role of the state still continues to be pivotal. The so-called compulsive compressions of globalization seem to have made little progress in the subcontinent.

Enduring Rivalry between India–Pakistan

That liberal peace argument is hardly relevant to India–Pakistan relations is clear from the turn of events in the past as well as in contemporary times.[9] While Pakistan experienced a peaceful democratic transition, with Nawaz Sharif becoming the prime minister in 2012, the relation with India has gone from tense to worse, with the possibilities of war looming dangerously large between two nuclear-armed adversaries. Relations improved after the Agra peace talks between Vajpayee and Musharraf, which continued with Manmohan Singh on one hand, and the partnership of Yousaf Raza Gillani and Asif Ali Zardari on the other, till the dreaded Mumbai terror of 26 September 2008, which destroyed the gains of the past few years. However, a similar pattern erupted during Vajpayee's premiership when the Indian prime minister's unilateral offer of peace through the Lahore bus diplomacy was followed by the Pakistani military mobilizations that led to the Kargil War of 1999. While the conflict was largely the result of the refusal by Pakistan's armed forces and security services to hand over authority to the civilian government in matters of defence and foreign policy, it nevertheless exposed the limits of democratic political forces across borders in fostering a relation of peace and cordiality. With Musharraf staging a coup in Pakistan in 2001, democracy existed till 2008. No sooner had the democratic forces made a spectacular comeback in Pakistan, the Mumbai attacks occurred and the relations between the two adversaries plummeted.

The Kargil conflict apparently presents an enormously difficult case for the democratic peace theory, both in its dyadic and monadic versions.[10] As far as the monadic version is concerned, it presents a grave anomaly, as a democratic state hatched a military plot against another democratic state without any serious provocation. It gives evidence to the view that democratic states are capable of violence against their adversaries, which is independent of the nature of the political system of the latter. The Nawaz Sharif government, which was in power when the Kargil crisis erupted, apparently spared no thought for the nature of the political system in India. This puts the dyadic version of the theory under severe stress. Why did Pakistan, a democratic state in 1999, use a military strategy against the democratic Indian state, particularly after the conclusion of the Lahore Peace Drive? There is no answer to this to be gleaned from the democratic peace theory.

The nature of India's political system hardly mattered in this context. Having offered an olive branch to a democratic Pakistan under Nawaz Sharif, India found the Kargil imbroglio virtually thrust upon it from nowhere. Although intelligence reports had hinted at irregular troop movements and gathering of insurgents/mercenaries, the government was caught completely off-guard when Pakistani troops had moved in. It is rather far-fetched to argue that the Indian reticence and moderation to begin with can be accounted for by the nature of the political system in Pakistan. India's forbearance and patience might have been influenced by its understanding that Nawaz Sharif's government was committed to peace towards India, and that this regime could be trusted since it was democratic in nature. The institutional variant of the theory would thus appear to explain the anomaly. While shared democratic norms created a general expectation of peaceful relations between India and Pakistan, the actual course of action was decided by the institutional factors, which frustrated the peace effect also stem from the shared norm. The broad argument is that the Kargil War took place despite democratization of Pakistan. This is also not an historical aberration. Even in the early 1990s, when Benazir Bhutto was in power in Pakistan, despite an agreement between Rajiv Gandhi and Benazir Bhutto that ruled out attacks on each other's nuclear facilities, relations continued to remain strained, primarily over Kashmir. In fact, throughout the 1990s, the relationship between India and Pakistan remained highly charged, particularly since the insurgency in Kashmir peaked 1989 onwards. Pakistani governments, whether ruled by Benazir Bhutto or Nawaz Sharif, despite their democratic credentials, did not budge from adopting a strategy of low-key violence against India, which has been described as a war by proxy. A democratic Pakistan has shown as much of an appetite for conflict with India, as a non-democratic Pakistan had in the past.

Pakistan's Internal Politics and Democracy

A quick look into Nawaz Sharif's policies since he returned to power in February 1997 reveals the fragility of democratic norms, and the tenacity of extended social interests within institutions. Nawaz wanted to rid the political system of the fateful dualism, and the domination of the non-elected executive in the figure of the president, which he believed to be the root cause for the weakness of the parliamentary system. He introduced the Thirteenth Amendment, which made the president powerless and entrusted the office of the prime minister with the power to appoint and dismiss the chiefs of all the three armed services. However, like his predecessors, he made no investment in democratic norms and practices, and began dismantling the putative checks and balances that were expected to constrain as well as restrain concentrated power. Rather than encouraging political debate and a culture of dissent, he began to silence his critics at all levels of governance, including the civilian administration, the judiciary, and even the army. This was a critical moment in Pakistan's political history. The most immediate danger, recognized both within the army and in the political system at large, was Sharif's intention to destroy the authority of the army and turn it into a partisan tool, as he had done to the bureaucracy and the judiciary. This was surely the climax of his powers, for the establishment of the armed forces, the real bastion of strength within Pakistan, was destined to resist any bid to tame it into submission.

In the post-2008 period, the essential parameters of the Pakistani state have not changed, and the exceptional salience of the national security state, securitizing both Kashmir and Afghanistan, despite a non-performing economy and a looming energy crisis, continued to determine civilian–military relations. The USA's 'War on Terror' in Afghanistan against the Al-Qaida terrorists and the Taliban forces after 9/11 had revived the geo-strategic worth of Pakistan as a frontline state; military and economic assistance had flown freely till the Bush regime was in power. Even afterwards, with Obama deciding on a steady drawdown of US forces in Afghanistan, aid to Pakistan did not cease. Added to this was the constant military, economic, and infrastructural support of China, whose motivations include balancing/constraining India and keeping potential energy links open through Pakistan. The unceasing eruption of jihadi and sectarian violence in Pakistan further contributed to the militarization of the state. Democracy, and the desiccation of the vestiges of the liberal project, happened simultaneously, which guaranteed the centrality and the continued dominance of the national security state.

Moreover, India–Pakistan rivalry is not limited to the two states. China and the USA have played critically important roles in conditioning the nature of this rivalry through their strategic alliances with Islamabad at various times. In fact, the Chinese role in arming Pakistan is central to the geopolitical competition in the subcontinent. The role of the USA has waxed and waned, depending upon Washington's perceived strategic needs. At the least, democratic credentials have played no independent causal role in shaping its policy towards South Asia. To sum it up, democracy and globalization have not contributed to peace in any way in India–Pakistan relations; their intense geopolitical conflict, overlaid by the larger strategic competition of China and the USA, is largely responsible for the peculiar resilience of an intensely power-centric imagination that underlies the subcontinent. The theory of liberal peace has no manifest empirical purchase in South Asia, and given the poverty of a strong liberal political culture, it is hardly expected to change elite mind sets in the region.

Perils of Human Security: Ethnic Violence in South Asia

The nature and strategy of the South Asian states have played a crucial role in designing the 'freedom from fear' campaign. All South Asian states feel they are safe when their core values can be preserved without recourse to war, and even when under attack, these values can still be maintained. Thus, communalism is widely accepted as a threat to human security because it violates the logic of secularism, which is understood as a core value of any multicultural society. This makes it evident that the nature of the threat posed by communalism cannot be fathomed without reference to the two other interrelated 'issues': nationalism and secularism. Communalism is usually viewed negatively across South Asia, though the politics of the subcontinent remains deeply enmeshed in communal sentiments. Communal affiliation is thus a critical aspect of South Asian politics, despite the negative connotations of the term.[11] Secularism also assumes a new meaning specific to South Asia, where it does not require an exclusionary insulation of state and religion from each other; rather, it demands an equal respect of the state for all faiths. However, religious communalism is not the only form of group violence dominant in South Asia. Ethnic violence is also a major threat to the human security of groups in various parts of the subcontinent. In fact, all the states in South Asia are witness to ethnic competition and occasional violence between estranged groups. Both primordial and instrumentalist explanations have been offered, and have often been corroborated by evidence. Moreover, incidents of ethnic violence have not been limited to states, but have had transnational ramifications. Kin-country syndrome is a common phenomenon in the region, with caste and tribal identities often relaying group conflicts from one state to another.

Minorities in Bangladesh

The relevance of faith as one of the two bases of national identity in Bangladesh creates serious difficulties for religious minorities in the state. Saleem Samad writes:

> Fifty years ago in 1941, 28.3 per cent of the total population was minorities. The population of Hindu was 11.88 millions, while 588 thousand was other religious and ethnic minorities (Buddhist, Christian and animist). Evaluation of government statistics of 50 years,

from 1941 to 1991, indicates a large drop in the figure for minorities. A comparative picture shows that the number of the Muslim majority increased 219.5 per cent while the Hindu community increased by 4.5 per cent. (Samad 1998)

There is a considerable body of work that documents the deprivation of the hill tribes in Bangladesh, owing to forceful evictions and land-grabbing by the state. Despite the presence of a vibrant and essentially secular civil society in Bangladesh, the state's overwhelming preoccupation with issues of religion and language has relegated the question of tribal rights to the backburner. The relative deprivation, both material and symbolic, of these groups remains high, and their human security low in Bangladesh.

Minorities in Pakistan

The plight of the minorities in Pakistan remains grave. A report on the state of the minorities in Pakistan argues:

> Demands for greater autonomy by the major ethnic groups have, over the years, provoked severe government repression. At the same time, non-Muslim minorities have continued to be the victims of particularly harsh religious laws. The system of separate electorates, which was in place until recently, confined non-Muslims and some Muslim groups to second-class citizenship, and undermined their claim for equal rights. (Lattimer 2002: 3)

The clashes between extremist Sunni and Shia groups have continued in Pakistan, with the Shia minorities suffering more in terms of life and property. The violence and the denial of constitutional rights of worship and culture against the Ahmadias have proliferated since the 1980s, as Pakistan slipped into religious fundamentalism under the patronage and encouragement of the state during the military rule of General Zia ul Haq, and has only exacerbated in recent times (Jalal 2014; Nasr 2009). Religious minorities are insecure in all the South Asian states, at all levels of collective existence. While the secular democratic framework of the Indian political system provides for stronger constitutional rights to the minorities than most other states in the subcontinent, the political salience of communal cleavages continues to remain active. For as long as minorities are deprived of their cultural rights, the social security of the subcontinent remains fragile.

Statist Strategies to Cope with Ethnic Violence

Ethnic violence causes grave insecurity and fear in many parts of South Asia. Nation-states in South Asia, in fact, have responded to this by often setting communities against each other, and used other divisive techniques available to them to weaken militant ethnic groups that were challenging the authority or legitimacy of the state. The techniques range from co-opting ethnic elites into the mainstream political process, splintering of mono-political ethnic movements both from within and without, controlling the timing and quantity of developmental or aid funds, and disbursing other privileges to the members of the mobilized ethnic community. The state would also set up and improve, to the extent feasible, the surveillance and intelligence activities amidst conflicting groups, identifying intra- and inter-group differences, and usually building on the predicament of the weaker side. The state also confronts insurgent groups by using counter-insurgency methods, including the deployment of armed forces (often in the form of massive military operations) to crush the military organization and the support systems (including external linkages) of the anti-state militant outfits. India has practised such policies extensively in the northeastern states, with varying degrees of success. Pakistan, Sri Lanka, and Bangladesh have also largely followed similar trajectories when dealing with ethnic problems.

The designs of the state and human insecurity have set in motion changing patterns of conflict and cooperation. In cases where the civil society sympathizes broadly with the anti-state ethnic group, the success of the state in diluting the intensity of conflict remains tenuous and marginal. This gives rise to long stalemates, punctuated by occasional armed clashes, with both the state and the ethnic group suffering sizeable casualties. In this situation, even when the militant organization is the one on the run, hounded by the massive fire power of the national armed forces, they succeed in inflicting heavy losses on the latter, usually by hit-and-run tactics and sabotage. The Naga insurgents, the LTTE till the recent past, and the Kashmiri militants have tended to prevail even in the face of disproportionate opposition, since they received broad social or community support, although not 'approval', of everything they did. Extortion and torture of local communities, and kidnapping and killing of innocent people, on the other hand, have distanced the militants in Punjab and the United Liberation Front of Assam (ULFA) from the people, making it relatively easier for the state and its armed forces to tackle these groups. The South Asian experience reveals, as much in other cases throughout the world, that state armed forces can restrain insurgency, prevent the occurrence of violence, or weed out terrorism; but it cannot make for greater security.

Human Casualties in Internal Violence

As the domestic conflict/civil war data in South Asia shows, ethnic violence is a major cause of fear for people caught in crossfires, be it that of the irredentist ethnic outfits, or of a revanchist state. Ethnic and communal conflicts claim hundreds of lives in South Asia. The sectarian violence in Karachi and parts of Sindh, Balochistan, and Khyber Pakhtunkhwa in Pakistan, terrorism and insurgency based on ethnic/communal affiliation in Manipur, Kashmir, and Assam in India, the bloody war between the Sinhalese and the Tamils in Sri Lanka, have claimed innumerable lives, and have made thousands of refugees. Though ethnic violence in Sri Lanka began twenty-eight years ago, the numbers of Tamils who died during the war's final phase (2008–10; during the Sri Lankan Army's final offensive against the LTTE), according to a United Nations panel set up by the Secretary General Ban Ki-Moon, go up as high as 40,000. And since 1983, Sri Lankan Tamil refugees have come to India in waves (Giri 2015). Sri Lankan authorities steadfastly refuse to accept these figures. What is significant is that for nearly three decades, most Tamils besieged by the state—LTTE violence had lived under constant fear of being targeted by either of the actors. The LTTE's destruction has not opened up genuine reconciliation, either political or social, and for Tamils living in refugee camps, the talk of human security is a rude mockery of their fate. The status of Bangladeshis living in India also remains unsatisfactory, for they are not recognized as refugees by the Indian state, and are denied recognition by their state of origin. In essence, these migrant workers are virtually stateless people, with no state taking any responsibility for their basic rights.

The Sri Lankan state defeated the LTTE militarily, which resulted in massive displacement of Tamils, and exceptionally high figures for refugee flows were recorded in Tamil Nadu in India. While the Tigers were crushed in 2009, the Sri Lankan government refused to respond to global demands from the international community for an investigation into alleged war crimes committed during the final stages of the conflict. Like most South Asian conflicts, internal ethnic conflicts cross international borders. The ethnic Tamil problem has always been a transnational one. As Tamils were displaced in huge numbers, their properties looted without compensation, women raped, and basic rights violated, India could not remain neutral to the situation. Though New Delhi had acted with utmost caution and self-control, Tamil parties in India began to put enormous pressure on the centre to act. While India did not put any overt pressure on Sri Lanka, when twenty-five countries passed a US-sponsored UN Human Rights Council resolution calling for a probe into increasing accusations of ongoing human rights abuses, including extra-judicial killings, disappearances, and torture, India supported the resolution. Colombo called the measure a threat to Sri Lanka's domestic reconciliation efforts; the Sri Lankan government has vehemently denied the allegations and has accused the USA of undermining efforts at national integration and reconciliation. The same culture of recalcitrance and domination of the dominant ethnic community prevails in Colombo, as is found in most comparable cases in South Asia. Without political integration and meaningful empowerment of the Tamils, there cannot be any solution to this crisis, but Sinhala recalcitrance—paired with the distrust of the Tamil community—has prevented a more meaningful peace from taking hold.

The Maoist Crisis in India

Perhaps the most dramatic site of the contrast between the national security discourse and its other, a radical version of human security, is the Maoist or Naxalite movement in parts of India. The Indian state sees it as India's gravest internal security threat, and describes it as a war between the government of India and the Maoists. The latter call Indian elections a sham, deny the sanctity of the parliament and the judiciary, and have taken up arms to overthrow the Indian state. While the state discourse does mention the absence of development as a possible cause for the rebellion, its narrative is squarely lodged in the conventional doctrines of state security, which sees salvation in their military defeat.[12]

The Maoist insurgency is both a violent renunciation of the state, and the culmination of decades of ruthless and systematic exploitation of the most vulnerable sections of the population. It combines the insecurity of want and fear, of losing livelihood, land, culture, and dignity in a paroxysm of violent outburst against a democratic state. Here comes the other paradox: if democracy enfranchises with impunity the basic rights of a vulnerable minority, can it deliver human security to them? It is this double dilemma of modernity/democracy that informs the struggle of the refugees of India's progress, and the Indian state's response against it.

Terrorist Violence in Pakistan

Terrorism and sectarian violence have claimed innumerable lives in South Asia. But in the new millennium, no state in South Asia has suffered more than Pakistan. According to the data compiled by the South Asia Terrorism Portal (SATP), Pakistan continued to face the brunt of the Islamist extremism and terrorism that it has long produced and exported. In 2012, Pakistan suffered a total of at least 6,211 terrorism-related fatalities, including 3,007 civilians, 2,472 militants, and 732 Security Forces (SF) personnel, as opposed to the 6,303 fatalities, including 2,738 civilians, 2,800 militants, and 765 SF personnel, in 2011 (Singh 2013). Terrorism has flourished in Pakistan due to the easy and abundant availability of weapons, the control of the state apparatus largely by the Punjabi elite, which alienated other ethnic groups, the generic weakness of the democratic institutions and practices, the use of Islam as a binding force for society and polity, and the poor economic performance that multiplied rentier interests and corroded the economic base of the state. While East Pakistan openly revolted against the framework and seceded in 1971, the movements in Baluchistan and rural Sindh were the result of unfulfilled provincial demands. As the state became increasingly delegitimized, the reliance on the army and Islam increased steadily. General Zia took this policy further, and openly patronized Islamists in the Pakistani Army, which ultimately took its toll upon this relatively secular institution. The war and the post-9/11 War on Terror were turning points in triggering the recent wave of unprecedented sectarian violence and terrorism within Pakistan, which further radicalized the role of Islamic orthodoxy in the arc between Kabul and Islamabad. The Afghan Wars have fundamentally altered the dynamics of Pakistan. It has led to a deadly combination of arms, extremely orthodox brands of Islam, Talibanization of parts of the society, drugs, and considerable weakness of the state institutions. As the role of the USA in Pakistan has divided its people as never before, the appeal of orthodox faith has once again come to dominate politics and society. Pakistan is thus waging a bitter internal war, and terror and sectarian violence have come to convulse the contours of the state.

State Security as the Referent

South Asia's elite, consisting of politicians, military personnel, and civil servants, monopolize the official prerogatives of security. Although security encompasses non-military dimensions, the historical pre-eminence of military power has not changed fundamentally. The referent of security is therefore the state. Thus, most policymakers consider South Asian security in statist terms, although some of them recognize the significance of non-state actors and forces in shaping the security agendas of the subcontinent. The centrality of the state is variously attributed to a host of factors; the immaturity of the youth (the states being relatively new in comparison to their Western counterparts), the propensity for forceful reassertion of sovereignty, the centrality of territoriality, and even the rural background of the South Asian elite (which makes them particularly sensitive to the issue of land and boundaries), and the nature of the political boundaries that constitute these states. The idea seems to be that one cannot have security without dominant statehood. In the light of the analysis presented earlier, it becomes apparent that the discourse of human security has not dominated South Asia in the post–Cold War era, and the predominance of realism and national security thinking explains this.

Explaining the Lack of Regional Self-Identity

Why are the South Asian states unable to transcend their sectarian, geopolitical self-identities and evolve a regional identity commensurate with the needs of globalism in terms of evolving novel institutions and practices? Sovereign territoriality is the constitutive principle of post-colonial South Asia, and all the South Asian elites who have so far come to rule these states are dealers in unsettled cultural, ethnic, and historical conflicts, stoking the fires of nationalist passion to cement their rule. A subcontinent premised on exclusivist sovereignty runs counter to the innate history of its people, who have dwelled in fluid geographies of frontier zones, rather than fixed linearity drawn arbitrarily on political maps. This inevitably creates tugs to defy the logic of territoriality, which must be buried if the nationalist projects are to achieve fruition. The fact is that having lived under settled borders that are not necessarily good at stopping people from crossing over, the South Asians have come to fear alternatives that may throw their nationalist and territorial projects haywire. No common project of human security has emerged in this region because of bitter memories of long colonial occupations and a history of violent partition as a midwife to at least three major states on the subcontinent (Buzan and Waever 2003: 93–4). Ethnic and religious conflicts that cannot be contained within territorialized states and a political culture that consciously socializes the fiction of territoriality against spatial imaginations of shared living are also responsible. These states remain extraordinarily concerned with border control, and claim territoriality as an absolute right of sovereign states.

There are radical alternatives to this politics of power. However, these have no policy purchase and give no peace dividend to the subcontinent. India has been singularly unable to provide an alternative to a securitized solution to the Kashmir dispute, and its spatial imaginations of South Asia and beyond remain anchored in a strategic logic of power and control. Commerce and community are thus ultimately subordinated to the needs of territory effect. In Sri Lanka, an intense ethnic conflict between the Tamils and the Sinhalese populations continued throughout the 1990s and came to an end with the military defeat of the LTTE in a full-scale war. The wanton human rights violations accompanying this have remained completely unaddressed. Ousted Tamils still suffer in ramshackle refugee camps without basic minimum needs. The solution, if any, is not premised on reconciliation, democracy, participation, or justice; it was brought about by brute force and successful state action. Bangladesh remains divided on its national identity role, and this division gets externalized in its ties with India. Nepalese politics continues to remain volatile, and the geopolitical importance of Nepal as a buffer between India and China continues to frame its foreign policy in the subcontinent. Even the peaceful state of Bhutan does not welcome Nepalese refugees, lest its cultural capital necessary to build the seamless nation-state within fixed borders is compromised by such influx of 'outsiders'. The success of the territorial project has guaranteed that a frenzied discourse of foreigners and outsiders define the politics of South Asia.

Can a discourse of human security, premised in an alternative spatial imagination, come to being in South Asia? Not unless the elites switch from the discourse of realism to that of human security. In a piece that brought together realist concerns, globalization and human security in South Asia, Rajesh Basrur concluded:

> The region's sole military confrontation—between India and Pakistan— is likely to diminish for two reasons: because the military option is no longer feasible, and because the economic imperative of globalization is pressing nations in general to cooperate rather than fight. Yet, short of the emergence of high-intensity interaction—whether in the economic or the military realm—the possibility of military conflict cannot entirely be ruled out. (Basrur 2001: 6)

My argument reinforces the same cautious optimism.

* * *

Globalization has indeed impacted all states of South Asia strongly, some more, some less. Democracy has become confident and stronger since 2008. The need to fashion a bolder human security regime has also gained ground. However, liberal attitudes and values have decidedly declined in the last thirty years. None of these trends have transformed the generic character of the subcontinent. The existing politics of South Asia 'cannot' and 'will not' redefine South Asia or unmake it. It is indeed a politics of survival, continuity, and difference. It is essentially realist, but also market oriented. Being exposed to global market forces is not a mortal threat to the existential reality of territorial statehood. Memory and geopolitics combine to rehabilitate nationalism and the politics of territoriality in South Asia.

Are there theoretical alternatives to this? By way of a clarification, I may add that such a resolution cannot bypass territoriality. The potential for change critically hinges upon the normative defence of the ethics of nationhood and its rival communitarian formulations. Without getting into such a comparative exercise, it seems clear that there is evidently no politics of unbundling of territoriality following globalization, which is in site in South Asia. In any case, none of the hypotheses concerning the transformative promise of globalization, democratization, and human security seem to hold true for South Asia.

Notes

1. For recent perspectives on globalization, see Sparke (2005), Khanna (2016), and Blackwill and Harris (2016).

2. For details, see Sparke (2005).

3. A look into the export–import figures, both intra-regional and international, reveals the increasing significance of international trade for South Asia. Yet, in a comparative sense, the opening-up of South Asia still remains insignificant vis-à-vis many other developing regions. There is little economic impact of the process thus far at the sub-regional level.

4. Viewed in this way, I agree with the perspective that strong regionalism and strong globalization are not incongruent or contradictory; the imperatives of the latter in fact generate tendencies towards the former. The areas that are in the forefront of the globalization process are areas where regionalism has become increasingly powerful. This holds true for Europe, the Asia-Pacific states, Southeast Asia, and North American states. The fact that South Asian states have responded positively to the demands of globalization do not extend, however, to any evidence of rigorous regionalism. Despite some positive trends around the beginning of the new millennium, the SAARC has remained hostage to the politics of apathy and mutual suspicion, which is a good indicator of the continuity of the past, rather than a bold promise to transcend the prevailing tragic collective amnesia by new imaginations of space and identity.

5. With BJP's ascension since 2014, a new politics of cultural nationalism has gained ground in India, which threatens to weaken the liberal-secular project of nationhood even further.

6. There is extensive literature on India's democracy. For details see, Vanaik (1990), Varshney (1995), Mehta (2012), Ruparelia (2008), and Samaddar (2002).

7. For a comprehensive discussion, see Harihar Bhattacharya (2004: 74–100).

8. For details, see Chatterjee and Sen (2004: 184–99).

9. For T.V. Paul, in his provocative title, *The Warrior State: Pakistan in the Contemporary World* (2014), the primary reason for Pakistan's intransigence is the state's Hobbesian view of the world. Its consistently high spending on the military stems from an obsession to achieve strategic parity with India. The Pakistani military magnifies threatening perceptions of India to corner a disproportionate share of the state's resources, and deliberately expands its military assets. As a result of such arming, India feels worried, and a vicious cycle of arms race gets locked in, often destabilizing the subcontinent. Paul's thesis is that Pakistan suffers its own 'resource curse' in the form of a geostrategic curse. Sumit Ganguly (2016), in contrast, proposes that Pakistan is a 'greedy state', whose security establishment has not yet reconciled with the territorial status

quo in South Asia. The author has effectively shown that India's concessions have not changed Pakistan's aggressiveness. This surely goes against the expectations of conventional security dilemmas. Despite being a product of the territorial partition of British India, Pakistan remains hostile to a subcontinental security order in South Asia bequeathed by the British, and unilateral Indian concessions would hardly transform such Pakistani military attitudes and behaviour.

10. Democratic peace has spawned extensive literature. For classic statements, see Doyle (1983a, 1983b), Russett (1993a, 1993b, 2009), Russett and Oneal (2001), and Gelpi and Griesdorf (2001). For a very useful discussion, see Levy (1988) and Elman (1997).

11. For an interesting discussion, see Bose and Jalal ([1997] 2011) and the various essays in Jaffrelot (2007).

12. The Maoist insurgency, which picked up significantly after the unification of the erstwhile People's War Group and the Maoist Communist Centre in September 2004, was described by Manmohan Singh, the then prime minister of India, as the country's 'gravest internal security threat'. But Maoist violence witnessed a dramatic decline in fatalities. From a high of 1,080 fatalities recorded in 2010, the figure came down to 602 in 2011 and a further and substantial drop to 367 in 2012 (SATP 2016).

phenomenon, some preferring systemic compulsion, while others going for state preferences. In a nutshell, India and Pakistan are impelled by the 'logic of the system' to join the war against terrorism. Given the gross asymmetry between the cost of their remaining outside the coalition and the 'benefits' of association, the choice is indeed simple. However, this does not explain the whole story, as India and Pakistan perceived the 'system effect' rather differently, which is explained by their vastly dissimilar domestic structures that mediate such effects.

Security Interdependence in Post–Cold War South Asia

Two other issues deserve independent treatment here. First, the relationship between security interdependencies and the international system needs some clarification in light of the post–Cold War changes to the latter. Buzan defined security interdependence as a hostile or friendly pairing of two states, and the regular interaction between them (quoted in Kapur and Wilson 1996: 28). Scholars disagree on the number of security interdependencies in South Asia, and the relative significance of each pair. Buzan and Rizvi (1986: 14) found Indo-Pakistan rivalry to be the only strong security interdependence in South Asia. However, employing Buzan's own definition of the concept as 'a pattern of amity, enmity and indifference', Kapur and Wilson (1996: 28) identified 'multiple security interdependencies—within South Asia, as between South Asian states and external powers'. Buzan again referred to higher- and lower-level security complexes, the former consisting of how great powers impact regional security subsystems, and the latter being a formation of local actors alone. For Buzan, the higher-level security complex had a unilateral impact on the lower level. But Kapur and Wilson differ here. They argue that 'no security interdependency can enjoy a dominant position in South Asia, and the "impact" of the "higher" on the "lower" has decreased over time' (1996: 29). This position indicates further relaxation of the global structural determination of regional security dynamics in South Asia. Kapur and Wilson postulate somewhat controversially that the Indo-Pakistan conflict, described as the 'hitherto dominant security interdependency', has 'lost its importance in both the South Asian regional subsystem, and the international system' (1996). Needless to say, the bulk of the work done on South Asian security, and/or the Indo-Pakistan conflict contradicts this finding of Kapur and Wilson. Following this argument, one can advance the proposition that the higher the number of security interdependencies in a regional subsystem, the lower the impact of the higher security complexes on the lower.

Alliance Behaviour and Polarity

The second set of issues that directly links the constituent states of a regional subsystem with the international system are alliance behaviour and polarity. Most scholars of the subject deal with the nature of polarity and alliances within the regional subsystem, agreeing that bipolarity has been the dominant pattern, which forced Pakistan, the weaker state, to compensate for its material weaknesses vis-à-vis the dominant player, India, through alliances with the USA and China. Did transformation in the international structure, from bipolarity to unipolarity, have any impact on the polarity and alliance behaviour in Asia? The answer is in the negative. The nature of Pakistan's alliances shows no change: both the USA and China are still central to Pakistan's security paradigm. Relations between the USA and China, although assuming increasing complexity and new difficulties, show no fundamental or qualitative change either. Similarly, India's linkage(s) with external powers have not markedly changed. Although India still espouses a non-aligned foreign policy and refrains from direct entanglement with existing military alliances, the difference between India's security needs and American strategic compulsions in southern Asia has diminished quite dramatically. Despite this, however, Russia still remains India's closest security partner, and India's defence requirements continue to come primarily from that state. Therefore, one scarcely finds any decisive impact of international structural changes on India's and Pakistan's alliance behaviours.

This analysis agrees with Rasul B. Rais's (1993: 29–39) view that the impact of post–Cold War global détente and a change in the essential elements of the triangular system operating in South Asia have had marginal consequences for the regional subsystem, because the local actors have not altered their understanding of the central issues of the conflict. Regional subsystemic frame(s) of analysis, such as that of Barry Buzan, therefore, remain incomparably more efficient analytical tools for explaining South Asia's conflicts, than deterministic structural ones. Scholars like Buzan, however, claim that they are modified neo-realists. To that extent, then, a modified structural mode of neo-realist analysis is not completely irrelevant to the security concerns of South Asia. This is also in line with Buzan's analysis that ruled out any fundamental change in the South Asian regional security complex until 2011.[2]

Structural Analysis and India's Power

Most Indian officials regard their country as a middle-level power with the potential to become a major one, and seek greater international recognition of this status. India, as a middle-level power, interacts constantly with great powers and lesser states. One can offer a structural explanation to these relations, and argue that it is the structure that determines the schedule of interests for states, and no state can, therefore, pursue policies vis-à-vis another state that goes against the logic of the given structure. As Rajagopalan and Sahni (2008: 13) put it:

> Thus, our focus should be on the state of global balance of power, and the nature of the international system that it gives rise to. The nature of their systems exerts a certain amount of influence on the strategic policy choices of the states in that particular system. Examining such [international systemic] pressures on national policies and on the outcomes of inter-state relations is different from examining the foreign policies of great powers or the policies of regional actors.

However, the fact cannot be glossed over that pure structural theories cannot efficiently explain foreign policy approaches of states and the changes over the time. Structural theories employ the concept of polarity to define a system; poles are defined by concentrations of power at the unit level. They change when the number of states (units) inhabiting a system that have the power to inflict unacceptable damage on their adversaries, vary. But how does power accumulate in a state? A pure structural theory of world politics is unable to account for this.[3]

In other words, deviations do happen and irregularities do occur in foreign affairs, and unless one were to concede more ground to non-systemic factors, no proper explanation of such behaviour is possible. Two fundamental points beg consideration in the light of this tension. First, the systemic or structural effects are not free-standing; there is hardly a pure structural effect. The distribution of power is never automatic, and no structural realist has ever provided a convincing explanation to why it should be treated as a system-level variable at all. A large number of intervening factors are involved here. To dump them on to the unit level is most unhelpful as a theoretical move. The nature of the global structure is vital, but this global entity has multiple modes of working, which leverage the units diversely. Second, the constraints and opportunities of the system structure are invariably filtered and mediated through domestic-level variables. The fact that states often do not behave the way structural realists predict is because of the role played by the domestic variables. What is distinctive about the contemporary global system is brilliantly brought out by Ashley J. Tellis. He says that in the last one millennium, the motives of the states have not changed at all (Tellis 2007: 118–30).

Survival remains the unique leitmotif for all states. Again, the modes of survival have also not undergone any radical transformation; states either produce the deterrence capacity themselves through internal mobilization of resources, or join with other states in alliance for that purpose. The nature of the global system decides the choice of strategies. In the Cold War's bipolar system, the warring camps were close-unit universes; they were not required to communicate with their rivals or adversaries for economic growth and prosperity. In the present system, globalization has altered the logic of the relations between adversaries. The adversaries now compete in connection with each other for mutual economic development and prosperity. Unlike the past, they do not have the luxury to cut off themselves into autocratic camps. The resulting gains from such economic exchanges are, however, fed into the rivalry itself. This complex dynamics of the present global order is the structure within which major powers strategize vis-à-vis each other. Just as the USA faces competition from China in a condition of extremely high mutual economic interdependence, so must India and China manage their competitions in the days ahead. Even if relations were to deteriorate for political/power-related reasons, the states would continue to condition the overall dynamics of their ties in each other's economy (2007: 127–9).

Decoding Levels of Security in South Asia

South Asian security must be understood at several levels. First, the security of each state which constitutes the region called South Asia; second, subcontinental or regional security vis-à-vis that of other regions and the international system; and third, (although security encompasses non-military dimensions) the historical and unchanged pre-eminence of military power as security. The referent of security is, therefore, the state.

I have interviewed several ex-policymakers and retired army officers on various dimensions of the security of South Asia in general, and India in particular. Needless to say, the responses were too varied to be standardized into any distinctive pattern. Nevertheless, a few observations regarding the perceptions held by the dignitaries reinforce the prominent attributes of the mainstream discourse(s) discussed thus far. Most policymakers and army officials consider South Asian security in statist terms, although some of them did grant the significance of non-state actors and forces in shaping the security agenda of the subcontinent. The centrality of the state is variously attributed to the immaturity of youth (the states being relatively new when compared to their Western counterparts), the propensity for forceful reassertion of sovereignty, the centrality of territoriality, the rural background of the South Asian elite, which make them peculiarly sensitive to the issue of land and boundaries, and the nature of political boundaries that constitute these states. The idea seems to be that one cannot have security without dominant statehood.

The states of South Asia struggle for security within an anarchical system. In their search for security, these states must individually assess the political and security environment in which they are located, and also must examine the nature of ties with their neighbours in a strategic or interactive mode. They concentrate mostly on developing appropriate military doctrines, acquiring the weapons needed for the safety of their borders against possible external intrusion/threats, and articulate appropriate force deployment postures. States guard both against capability and threats, but the latter is more relevant to its security. States must assess continuously the threats coming from other sources, never let down its vigil against potential and/or real enemies, balance threat(s) by either internal mobilization or external alliances, and invest sufficiently in technological upgradation to preserve security in a fast-changing, high-tech information age.

India's South Asia policy bears testimony to such an understanding of security. That is not to argue that India gets the policy right every time, in terms of achieving its goals. Concrete decisions are guided by ever-changing exigencies in foreign relations. However, states make policies within a given structure of possibilities. They invariably subscribe to certain mental maps. India's cognitive map stems from its subscription to a territorialized ontology of space-as-power that has ruled out alternative ways of engaging with the subcontinent.

India's Regional Security Doctrine during the Cold War: From Indifference to Arrogance of Power

This section discusses India's security discourses vis-à-vis the smaller neighbours in South Asia. While India did not develop conscious regional security doctrines, elites since Indira Gandhi have contributed significantly towards developing India's approach to South Asia. In the remaining part of this chapter, I survey these discourses closely, and argue that there is an unmistakable rendition of the subcontinent through the image of power in them. Power here does mean military domination. What India has sought in the subcontinent are two closely related objectives:

1. South Asia remains immune to external or outside interferences, and disputes are bilaterally negotiated and resolved.
2. A manifest recognition of India's post-colonial difference that, more than its disproportionate material capabilities, legitimizes its pedagogic discourses in South Asia.

While neither of these objectives has ever been fulfilled, this has not led the Indian elites to redefine the subcontinent in a different manner. The tragedy of South Asia's regionalism, and India's relative success in transcending South Asia physically through its 'Look East' policy, by effectively linking up with Southeast and East Asian states, both commercially and strategically, reinforce this diagnosis.

India's Approach to South Asian Security

If South Asia is viewed geopolitically, it shows some attributes of a loose regional subsystem (Paul 2010: 8–9). While the traditional literature on regional subsystems has emphasized the role of states, Paul extended the concept further to include 'societal level insecurities'. Paul also recognized that many clusters of relationships could not be accommodated within the concept of a regional subsystem. His general argument has been that South Asia's insecurity is explained by '... two critical factors: the presence of weak states, and weak cooperative interstate norms' (2010: 4). The character of the South Asian subsystem that he develops emphasizes the region's India-centric nature, its multiple cleavages of religious, ethnic, and other identities, and its inability to qualify as a hegemonic order. The absence of hegemony is explained as follows, 'Part of the reason for this lack of hegemony is the unwillingness of key states to accept Indian leadership, let alone dominance on many issues. The region is not economically interdependent, and as a result a potential source of power that India could exert is missing' (2010: 9–10). It is this contested geopolitical neighbourhood that India negotiates. It is therefore logical enough that the space is imagined primarily as one of power, requiring appropriate security insurance against untrustworthy neighbours.[4]

India's deep pessimism regarding South Asia stems primarily from a realist conceptualization of space, which puts territorial control and cartographic anxiety in the forefront.[5] Such cartography of fear is largely a result of colonial heritage. Olaf Caroe, in particular, left a legacy upon India's strategic thinking, by anticipating the centrality of South Asia and some of the later great power involvements in the subcontinent. Caroe served as foreign secretary (1939–45) and as governor of the North West Frontier Province (NWFP) from March 1946 to June 1947. Throughout his career, he pleaded British decision makers to factor in geopolitics in their imperial strategy. Brobst's work on Caroe has been instrumental in tracing the Indian post-colonial geopolitics based on the old imperial notions of inner and outer boundaries, buffers and strategic borders. Caroe, for Brobst, was the chief architect of the notion of 'the subcontinent's geospatial centrality', particularly as an antidote to Russian expansion. In this, however, Caroe was only echoing a whole line of British officials whose geopolitical ideas were marked by intense Russophobia. Caroe, nevertheless, was systematic in his approach and believed that a unified South Asia was integral to a robust defence of Asia in general, and the Middle East in particular. In fact, Caroe's unerring concerns about the Asian Great Game influenced much of post-colonial geopolitical thinking as well. He insisted in his correspondence with various British officials that British geo-strategic interests even at the time of withdrawal required facing up to 'the new political forces ... at work in Eastern and Central Asia' (Chester 2007: 676). In a major paper titled 'Whither India's Foreign Policy', dated 26 April 1942, he wrote that 'a realisation is needed in the highest places that India cannot build a constitution unless the frontiers are held and the ring fence in some manner kept standing' (Noorani 2006). Caroe referred to the 'outer ring'—including Persia, Afghanistan, Tibet, and Southeast Asia—that constituted 'a secure shield under which India could progress free from care' (Brobst 2005: 36). This was a bulwark against Soviet adventurism and possible

Chinese incursions as well. Caroe also reflected on the notion of India's 'inner ring'—comprising frontier zones of Baluchistan, Nepal, and the Naga Hills of northeastern India, that afforded much needed security cover for the British army. Caroe, however, was neither popular with the British officials nor with Nehru, who was instrumental in rubbishing his thoughts. While Caroe's impact was modest by all means, he, along with Lord Curzon, was responsible for articulating the idea of South Asia as a geopolitical construct, and emphasizing the importance of India as a lynchpin of an Asian security order. Caroe had, therefore, linked the 'concept of India and [the] centre of [an] Asiatic System', thereby anticipating Nehru's great power imagination of India and its legitimate centrality to Asian affairs (Noorani 2006).

From Jawaharlal Nehru to Rajiv Gandhi, there was no fundamental shift in this orientation. The Indian approach to security in the subcontinent remained essentially wedded to its colonial heritage, wherein protecting the subcontinent and the Indian Ocean from external interferences assumed cardinal significance. However, unlike the British, India had limited success in achieving its goals. While Pakistan frustrated India's efforts for a strategic unity of the subcontinent through its formal and informal alliances with the USA, the smaller states refused to buckle under Indian pressure. Afghanistan and Burma had remained key states in the colonial defence architecture, as they soaked in pressures from the west and north, and from the east, respectively. Independent India had no comparable strategic depth on either state. While the Himalayan states retained their value as buffers, China's ascension and hostility towards India after 1959 meant a considerable decline in New Delhi's leverage vis-à-vis Nepal in particular. While Nehru was opposed to balance-of-power and alliance politics, his variant of liberal nationalism was predicated solidly upon territoriality and fixed borders that valourized post-colonial sovereignty above other normative goals. India's crusades for a just world order was a firmly Westphalian project, one that rejected ideas like soft borders and shared jurisdictions in its neighbourhood. Given the history of its constitution, it was impossible for a post-colonial state like India to experiment with territoriality in an area where borders and nationhood never coincided. Every state in South Asia had to valourize territoriality, despite its historical irrelevance, as settled borders were the primary ingredient of their contested projects of nation-building.

Nehru's India

Nehru was indeed in many ways an exceptional figure, as he not only dominated Indian foreign policymaking like a colossus, but also laid the philosophical foundations of non-alignment, which will dominate India's approach to international affairs for many decades to come. More pertinently, Nehru was obsessed with considerations of competition among the great powers and the Cold War alliances, and paid little attention to the immediate neighbourhood. In the words of K. Subrahmanyam, the doyen of India's strategic thinkers,

> In the thirties, he was of the view that after India became free its security problem would not be a major one. In this he was influenced by his perception that India was too valuable a stake to be allowed to be dominated by any one power and hence the international balance of forces with some minimum efforts on India's part should be able to ensure her security... But within two or three years after that event it should have been obvious to him how Pakistan constituted one core of our security problem. His continuous efforts throughout the fifties to maintain an arm's lead over Pakistan would tend to support such a view. He had clearly realised that the greatest security threat to India came through interventionism of the big powers. (Subrahmanyam 2008: 1186)

Regarding Pakistan, despite the war in Kashmir in 1947–8, Nehru remained an optimist. He argued:

> We are convinced that India and Pakistan must, as quickly as possible, revert to normality in their relations. The two countries are so situated that it is imperative that the relations between the two should be the most cordial. Being neighbours, they have a certain identity of economic interests. It is only when they promote their trade relations arising from their economic interdependence that their relations can return to normality. In the meanwhile, we cannot escape from the problems that detract from improved relations between Pakistan and us. We try to overcome them, not to lose hope and give them up as insoluble. Struggling in our search for agreement, we proceed slowly and patiently. (Nehru [1950] 2013)

It was only after the disastrous war with China in 1962 that Nehru began to think seriously on security issues, though there is little evidence of any systematic discourse on the subject. However, the fact that India was the natural heir to the legacy of British policy towards the subcontinent seems clear from the controversial policies Nehru pursued vis-à-vis Nepal. Nehru seemingly uncritically sold himself to British India's policy of Nepal as an indispensable buffer between India and China, and sought to keep the Himalayan kingdom under tight Indian supervision. The fact that India was unnaturally sensitive to political developments in its immediate neighbourhood can be easily read in New Delhi's machinations in Nepal during Nehru's tenure. This anxiety only increased with India's ignominious capitulation before the Chinese troops in the 1962 war.

Regional Security Environment Post-Nehru

India's regional security environment assumed increasing complexity during the second half of the 1970s, though this seems rather paradoxical, as India defeated Pakistan and dismembered its eastern part, which emerged as the sovereign country of Bangladesh in 1971. What is even more crucial is that the victory came in the wake of an exceedingly difficult geopolitical situation that saw Pakistan, China, and the USA align against India. India signed the Indo-Soviet Treaty of Friendship and Cooperation in August 1971, which was a cleverly concealed defence agreement to balance this unfriendly coalition. Its decisive military victory meant that the fear of Pakistan opening a second front in the east and cutting off the 'Chicken's Neck', a thin corridor along northern West Bengal's *terai* region that joins India's mainland with the volatile northeastern states, was exorcised once and for all. While relations with China remained strained, the prospect of a Chinese incursion, given the security of the Indo-Soviet treaty, was negligible.

And yet, India's prime minister found the country endangered both within and in the neighbourhood, and justified her fear by theories of foreign (read American) conspiracies. Relations with Sri Lanka and Nepal deteriorated, and Bangladesh, whose independence was impossible without India's war, took little time to turn against New Delhi. The exceptionally demanding strategic environment, combined with the fears—both real and imagined—of an increasingly insecure supreme leader, produced the 'Indira Doctrine' that clearly articulated India's unabashed articulation of the power imagination. While Raja Mohan described Indira Gandhi's policy to tie up with the Soviet Union to prevent the USA and Chinese meddling in South Asia as 'paranoid' (Raja Mohan 2001), it was primarily an attempt to reconstruct the South Asian theatre in line with India's newfound strength after the decisive defeat of Pakistan in the 1971 war.[6]

India's Security Involvement in Sri Lanka

India got involved in Sri Lanka's civil conflict over the rights of the ethnic Tamil population against an increasingly centralizing and authoritarian state (Raja Mohan 2001). Several factors motivated India's decision. First, there was domestic consideration, and the fear that, if India did nothing to help the Tamil community in the island, not only would there be an increasing exodus of refugees to Tamil Nadu, but this might also rejuvenate the secessionist constituencies of that state. Second, there were fears of external (American) involvement in the Indian Ocean, as Sri Lanka was increasingly looking up to the West for support in its domestic conflict. Third, India thought that as the problem involved the Tamil community, the resolution of the conflict demanded an active Indian role. What motivated such thinking? Scholars differ in their interpretations. In the words of Barbara Crossette (2008: 37):

> In virtually every country on India's borders, Indira Gandhi and her Congress Party, using Indian intelligence agencies—the domestic Intelligence Bureau and, after the late 1960s, the new Research and Analysis Wing (RAW), developed for international operations— left a legacy of meddling, subversion, and mistrust. Not infrequently, smaller countries were effectively tipped off balance or crippled, which is apparently what she intended.

Sankaran Krishna (1999) argues that it was India's penchant for hegemony or domination in the subcontinent that pushed it on the proactive path. Priya Chacko (2011: 138–43), in contrast, says that it was India's defensive mentality—the fear psychosis that Indira Gandhi suffered from—that made India get involved in Sri Lanka. If fear had provoked Indira Gandhi, her son, Rajiv Gandhi, who succeeded his mother with an unprecedented majority, was motivated by a new sense of confidence and quick modernity as panacea to all troubles in life, whether domestic or regional. It was his restlessness and confidence in India's ability that he thought needed to be showcased to the world that made him intervene militarily into Sri Lanka's domestic conflict, in wanton disregard of the post-colonial rules of territorial sovereignty.

India's Involvement in Nepal

The period also witnessed high-handed tactics from India in its dealings with Nepal. India, on the one hand, flaunted its special relations with this Himalayan kingdom as something that underscored their deeply shared cultural, ethnic, and religious ties. On the other hand, Nepal had consistently expressed dissent against what it considered to be the unjust Indo-Nepal Treaty of Peace and Friendship, and had been sceptical of India's intentions, particularly after Sikkim was turned into a part of India on 15 May 1975. The intricacies of the crisis between Nepal and India in the 1980s were complex, and rooted in a controversy over the expiration of two trade and transit treaties. It was a classic confrontation between an emerging regional superpower and a strategic yet landlocked nation that was not only geopolitically vital to India—being a buffer to China—but one that survived economically through the years, largely through Indian generosity.

Nepal enjoyed favourable treatment from India, but became increasingly concerned about its own security and sovereignty in the recent years, particularly after Indian Prime Minister Rajiv Gandhi ordered his troops into two other small South Asian neighbours, Sri Lanka and the Maldives. In what many diplomatic observers viewed as a symbolic gesture, Nepal decided in 1988 to purchase military equipment from China. The Nepalese government also announced that it was imposing restrictions on Indian residents and business people in Kathmandu, who in the past had enjoyed the same freedom that tens of thousands of Nepali migrants had enjoyed in India. India took this as an act of betrayal. When the two treaties expired on 23 March 1989, the Indians closed fifteen of the seventeen land entry routes to Nepal, which relied on India for all of its petroleum and 35 per cent of its other imports. India has been the lifeline for imports from Third World countries. The blockade led to Nepal to compromising, and restored the traditional benefits enjoyed by Indians working there. However, the event left a bitter memory in the minds of the Nepalese political elite, and relations between the two states, despite India's prime minister, V.P. Singh's success in getting assurances against Chinese involvement in Nepal, did not regain the warmth and mutual trust of the past.[7]

Intervention in Maldives

India's desire to play an active security role in South Asia was further manifested in the military operations it undertook in Maldives in 1988, when India intervened to prevent an attempted coup by mercenaries.[8] In November 1988, a force of some 80–200 mercenaries, largely drawn from a Sri Lankan Tamil insurgent group, the People's Liberation Organization of Tamil Eelam (PLOTE), infiltrated the Maldivian capital of Malé and took control of key points in the city. However, the rebels failed to capture the then Maldivian president, Abdul Gayoom, who took refuge in the Maldives National Security Services headquarters. It is clear that President Gayoom requested military assistance from several countries, including India, the USA, Britain, Pakistan, Sri Lanka, Malaysia, and so on, for help. New Delhi responded to the crisis with uncharacteristic speed and decisiveness, seeing it as India's prerogative and responsibility. The Indian troops took control of Malé within several hours, and rescued President Gayoom. India recalled the bulk of its troops after the mission had been achieved, with around 150 troops staying back for a year as a security cover. While India saw its intervention in the Maldives as a model for the benign security role that India could play in the Indian Ocean, many analysts saw this as a part of the new regional doctrine that India has espoused in the 1980s. It is noteworthy that India undertook the intervention alone, demonstrating its ability to airlift troops over long distances, and to successfully intercept the miscreants at sea, thereby signalling a growing confidence in its maritime power.

India's Insecurities with Bangladesh

India's ties with Bangladesh, whose political freedom came through the joint military operations by the *Mukti Bahini* (Freedom Army) and the Indian armed forces against Pakistan, became complex after the initial period of warmth. Several factors contributed to this: the tragic assassination of Mujib, the chief architect and the first prime minister of Bangladesh; the coming into power of a military government under Ziaur Rahaman; the problematic basis of Bangladesh's dual identity; the unresolved land and maritime boundaries; and the sharing of water. Sharing of river waters became contentious for the first time during Mujib's rule. India decided in 1951 to construct a barrage at Farakka, a village in Murshidabad near Bengal–Bihar border, about eleven miles from Bangladesh's border. Pakistan had objected to it, as it would have affected the flow of the Ganges waters into East Pakistan. The barrage and the feeder canal were finally commissioned in 1975, following an interim agreement signed between India and Bangladesh on 18 April 1975. But differences arose over augmentation of the fair-weather flow of the Ganges. An agreement on 5 November 1977 for a five-year period provided for the withdrawal of 20,500 cusecs and 34,500 cusecs water from the Ganges by India and Bangladesh, respectively, during the leanest period (21–30 April). But this did not receive favourable response from many quarters in India.[9]

After the coming of the first non-Congress Janata Government in 1977, Morarji Desai began talks with Zia, that paved the way for a five-year agreement on river usage. The return of Indira Gandhi in 1980 and the assassination of General Zia, leading to the military takeover of Bangladesh under General Ershad, prevented any finalization of the treaty. Bangladesh urged for a dam construction upfront in Nepal, which India saw as a ploy to regionalize the issue. The stalemate ultimately gave way to the two-year agreement between Rajiv Gandhi and General Ershad in 1985, but Ershad was forced to resign in 1990. Under the rule of the Bangladesh National Party that followed, despite a number of protracted and acrimonious meetings, no agreement on water sharing could be inked. Looking at the period under review, Devin T. Hagerty's (1991: 362) analysis seems to hold good. In his words, 'Based on the available evidence, it is impossible to support the notion that New Delhi's regional security policy from 1983 to 1990 was characterized by flexibility or ambivalence. The denial of external influence in South Asia was a consistent and overriding current running through India's South Asian policy under the governments of Rajiv Gandhi and V.P. Singh.'

South Asian Security in the Post–Cold War Order: Power as Fraternity

India's approach to regional security changed considerably as tumultuous changes began to affect the international order. The end of the Cold War and the disintegration of the Soviet Union posed enormous security burdens on India. More crucially, India met with an unprecedented economic crisis in 1991, which led to a qualitative structural shift in its economic policy, paving the way for economic liberalization. As these changes unfolded, new priorities emerged. International trade and development of close economic ties with the West became essential prerequisites for growth. Hence, it was perhaps necessary that India's perception of South Asia as a space would also need to adjust to these new priorities. Unfortunately, the immense increase in terrorism that engulfed India since the late 1980s—much of which was sponsored by Pakistan, as it took full advantage of India's domestic troubles in Kashmir and Punjab—and the increasing violence in the northeast, particularly in Assam, which also had close international linkages, did not allow India to fundamentally alter its spatial conception of South Asia. The realist understanding of space as power and security continued to shape its understanding of the immediate neighbourhood, though the policies required to meet the challenges began to change.

The Gujral Doctrine

The framework of a new policy was articulated by Inder Kumar Gujral, India's prime minister between April 1997 and March 1998. As the minister of external affairs under the governments led by V.P. Singh and Deve Gowda, Gujral had shown inclination to improve India's ties with its neighbours in South Asia to regain the trust lost due to the more interventionist policies pursued during the 1980s. Gujral formulated the 'Gujral doctrine', which articulated the concept of 'non-reciprocity'. In his words:

> The 'Gujral Doctrine', if I may call it so, states that, first, with its neighbours like Bangladesh, Bhutan, Maldives, Nepal and Sri Lanka, India does not ask for reciprocity, but gives and accommodates what it can in good faith and trust. Second, we believe that no South Asian country should allow its territory to be used against the interests of another country of the region. Third, that none should interfere in the internal affairs of another. Fourth, all South Asian countries must respect each other's territorial integrity and sovereignty. And finally, they should settle all their disputes through peaceful bilateral negotiations. (Gujral 1997)

During his tenure as the prime minister, India signed crucial water-sharing treaties with Bangladesh and Nepal, agreed in principle to allow Nepal physical connectivity with Bangladesh, signed an investment promotion with Sri Lanka that changed the trajectory and quantum of New Delhi–Colombo trade significantly, and offered unilateral tariff concessions on many commodities to facilitate the realization of the South Asian Preferential Trade Area (SAPTA) (Chako 2011: 163). Gujral's doctrine was, however, more of a continuity of than a fundamental break from India's understanding of its neighbourhood. Its conciliatory note was further legitimized by India's traditional commitment to fraternity and autonomy, which built on India's identity as a democratic civilizational state. However, near home, apart from underlying the need to offer more to weaker neighbours who may not be able to reciprocate in kind, no fundamental re-reading of the South Asian space happened. As in the past, the territorial order premised upon sovereignty was vindicated, and non-interventionism and bilateralism were reemphasized as the drivers of policy. As Gujral's own statements on Sri Lanka suggest, India's legitimate concerns over the fate of Sri Lankan Tamils could not be brushed aside (2011: 163). The Gujral doctrine, in brief, was not a fundamental alteration of India's spatial imagination of South Asia. It was a change in the drivers of policy, brought about by the pragmatic realization of the limited efficacy of the earlier and stronger interventionist doctrine of the 1980s.

Vajpayee and India since 1998

Atal Bihari Vajpayee's tenure as a prime minister saw paradoxical developments unfolding in India's dealings with its neighbours in general, and in its ties with Pakistan in particular. The period was overshadowed by the overt nuclearization of India and Pakistan, the momentous developments following the Al Qaeda strikes against the USA, leading to the destruction of the Twin Towers in New York, the Lahore Bus diplomacy and the Agra Peace Summit, the war on Kargil heights, and the terror strikes in Kashmir and on the Indian Parliament. These led to dangerous military mobilizations across the India–Pakistan border, and complications over deteriorating ties with Bangladesh, Sri Lanka, and Nepal.[10] With regard to these three lesser states, the complications primarily stemmed from domestic developments, which were detrimental to Indian interests. The security scenario was further complicated by growing internal challenges to India's security, which had external backing in a fraught neighbourhood. The Indian position towards the region remained by and large unchanged. Vajpayee complained of the region's inability 'to forge an integrated economic understanding, circumventing political differences', while at the same time praising Bhutan for its 'outstanding example of sensitivity to the security concerns of a neighbour' (Vajpayee 2004).

The complex and troubled colonial legacy continued to decide the politics of South Asia, which failed to make any fundamental breakthrough in connectivity, shared economic development, collective efforts to fight underdevelopment and poverty, and to forge closer economic ties to remake the subcontinent as a zone of prosperity. As Vajpayee, in his prime minister's speech at the SAARC Summit in Kathmandu on 5 January 2002, put it in a pithy manner, 'Mutual suspicions and petty rivalries have continued to haunt us. As a result, the peace dividend has bypassed our region' (Vajpayee 2002).

UPA Regimes and India's South Asia Policy

The UPA-I and II regimes, led by Manmohan Singh, did not show any radical departure in India's understanding of its neighbourhood. The policy continued to vacillate between the two points of reference, which had long remained constant in Indian spatial imagination of its surroundings. On the one hand, it summons the narrative of regional peace based on the transformational potential of market-based co-operation, and on the other, it deploys the realist logic of insuperable political difficulties that belies this transmutation in the absence of political goodwill.[11] In Manmohan Singh's (2005b) words:

> It is also interesting to note that the response of other countries to our national security concerns is being shaped by perceptions of business and economic opportunities.... Regrettably, however, South Asia has been slow to recognize the win-win aspect of economic cooperation.... We can jointly create reciprocal dependencies for mutual benefit. So far, this potentially benign process has been hobbled by narrow political calculations.

The logic of self-help in shaping security policies, the primary attribute of realism, is clear from Singh's submissions (Insight IAS 2009) before the Indian Parliament: 'In the final analysis, the reality is that ... when it comes to matters relating to our national security and defence, we will have to depend on ourselves. Self-help is the best help. There is no substitute to strengthening our defence capabilities, our internal security structures and our emergency response mechanisms.'

End of Sri Lanka's War

India's conceptualization of South Asia had followed the lines of the Gujral doctrine on most occasions since the new millennium. Relations with Sri Lanka took an interesting turn. Sri Lanka decided to militarily liquidate the LTTE, taking full advantage of the post-9/11 international mood against terrorist and militant groups. The USA named the LTTE a terrorist organization and froze its overseas assets. The Rajapakshe Government of Sri Lanka approached the issue with a great deal of planning and resolve.[12] It purchased both offensive and defensive weapons from China, knowing that owing to domestic sensitivities, India would not give Colombo arms. The story of the violent decimation of the LTTE need not detain us. The fact is that in January 2008, the Sri Lankan government pulled out of the 2002 ceasefire agreement and launched a massive offensive. In May 2009, it declared the Tamil Tigers defeated, after army forces had successfully overrun the last patch of rebel-held territory in the northeast, killing the supreme Tiger commander and the dreaded rebel leader, Velupillai Prabhakaran. During this time, the Sri Lankan army launched a massive and superbly orchestrated military offensive to wipe out the armed rebellion for good.

What explains the Indian approach to the terminal phase of the Sri Lankan civil war? One needs to recall that from 2003 to 2009, India had supported the goal of a 'negotiated political settlement' for Sri Lanka through forms of power devolution, which would satisfy 'the aspirations of all communities'. In keeping with my central argument that post-colonial territoriality and sovereignty were the critical ingredients of India's imagination of its neighbourhood, India held on to its unambiguous preference for the 'unity, sovereignty and integrity' of Sri Lanka. During the final phase of the conflict, known as the Eelam War IV of the period 2007–9, the escalation of violence in Sri Lanka, and the growing pressure from Tamil Nadu influenced New Delhi to put some degree of pressure on the Sri Lankan government with regards to the wanton violation of human rights of many innocent Tamils. However, this did not detract from the real policy, which actually supported Sri Lanka, both militarily and diplomatically, to help eliminate the scourge of the LTTE through what New Delhi had come to believe as a massive and just counter-terrorism operation. According to Sandra Destradi, in 2007, India began to abandon its rigorous non-involvement approach and started to take an indirect but highly significant role in the military conflict through the crackdown on LTTE networks in Tamil Nadu on the one hand, and on the other, in the provision of military hardware, mainly in the form of 'defensive' equipment, and in other forms of military cooperation with the Sri Lankan government (Destradi 2010: 13).

Tackling Nepal and Bangladesh

India's relations with Nepal and Bangladesh had also been difficult till 2008. While the Bangladesh Nationalist Party, led by Begum Khaleda Zia, was in power, India had significant security concerns regarding Bangladesh. In addition to long-term problems over river-water sharing, demarcation of boundaries, and alleged illegal migration of Bangladeshis into India, the Bangladesh Nationalist Party (BNP)–Jamaat coalition pursued a rabidly anti-India policy and became a safe haven for religious extremists and terrorists operating freely across the international border, in addition to patronizing camps that trained anti-Indian insurgents active in the volatile northeastern states. Both the National Democratic Alliance (NDA) and initially the UPA-I governments had great difficulty dealing with Bangladesh during this time. With the return of the secular Awami League to power with a massive mandate, relations with Bangladesh improved significantly. India and Bangladesh signed a historic agreement to settle the land boundary, and made considerable progress towards drafting a water-sharing treaty on river Teesta (a river that flows through Nepal and northern West Bengal and drains into the river Padma in Bangladesh). But due to the intransigence of the West Bengal government, the treaty could not be ratified in the Indian Parliament, and no agreement was signed on the sharing of Teesta river water (see Chatterjee [2016]).

These setbacks notwithstanding, Bangladesh was quick to operate against the terror groups; it dismantled the anti-India insurgent camps within its territory. India's ties with Bangladesh hinges critically on the nature of Bangladesh's domestic politics, or rather upon the dual basis of Bangladesh's national identity, which had led to the double partition of the state. The complex socio-cultural relations between Bengalis across the border point to the difficulties of the community–territoriality disjuncture in the subcontinent. For many Bangladeshis, crossing over into the other side is habitual; this has been the normal pattern since the remote past. The same migratory pattern, however, has altered the demographics of at least one province in India: Tripura, where the original inhabitants gradually lost out to the migrating Bengalis in numbers, and also over the languages of power, and is deemed existential in a number of other provinces in the northeast. The increasingly violent riots and killings in the Indian province of Assam in the last five years, particularly between the Bodos and the Muslim migrants across Bangladesh, also point to the intractable nature of the problem. Bangladesh and India are intertwined in a serious human security imbroglio, which cannot be solved through the sovereignty–territoriality model that pervades the imaginations of both the states. However, the inability to open up the issue of community, and fearing unknown consequences for territorial sovereignty, ties the hands of both.

Since India's coercive attempts to bring Nepal to line in 1989, relations between India and Nepal have remained frosty. Before Prime Minister Narendra Modi's visit to Nepal in 2014, no Indian prime minister had visited the country in the past seventeen years that have seen major political instability due to the Maoist insurgency, changes in governments, removal of the monarchy by the people's movement, and elections to the Constituent Assembly to write a new constitution. India distanced itself from the pro-democratic struggles in Nepal, and was deeply concerned over the Maoist movement. To the manifest disappointment of the pro-democratic forces, India, during this period of political instability, did not wish to get embroiled in Nepal's domestic politics or in government formation. The situation had been more complex, given the role of China in Nepal's political system. However, India followed the course of events in Nepal closely. In 1990, the popular participation by the masses overthrew the Panchayat government and replaced it with a democracy, consisting of constitutional monarchy and multi-party democracy. In 2006, democratic political forces, through yet another movement, got rid of the constitutional monarchy and declared Nepal as a federal democratic republic. As the people were instrumental in making these remarkable changes, India found it imperative to adapt to the situation.

However, the Indian government had grave difficulty in dealing with the Maoists, as they declined the special privileges that India had always enjoyed in Nepal, showed eagerness in moving closer to China, and indulged in strong anti-India propaganda. Moreover, intelligence reports in India pointed to certain linkages between the Maoist guerrillas in India and their Nepalese counterparts. In fact, India was more comfortable in this period with the conservative elements in Nepal, who had been the traditional bastion of strength for New Delhi. However, India's careful but consistent narrative of sovereign territoriality held its ground. In fact, Prime Minister Modi maintained that India wanted Nepal to develop its own political course, and would develop relations with governments irrespective of ideology. While addressing the Constituent Assembly, Modi stated that 'India would always support Nepal's sovereign right to choose its own destiny' (PM India 2014). He also assured, 'Nepal is a truly sovereign nation; we have always believed that it is not our job to interfere in what you do, but to support you in the path you decide to take.'[13] Domestic politics in the two countries have immense impact in shaping their relations. India's policy towards Nepal has made a dramatic shift from the 'twin pillars' approach to a 'people's choice' approach. Both the choices in foreign policy sprang from the changes in the domestic politics of Nepal. India's policy towards Nepal, as a result, came to support the 'people's choice'.

These domestic changes had a strong impact on the bilateral relations between India and Nepal. There seems to be stability in Nepal after the second Constituent Assembly-cum-Parliament elections in 2014. All the major parties are in agreement of writing the Constitution by January 2015. This fits with India's approach to the subcontinent, which is premised upon post-colonial territoriality and sovereignty. As Sangeeta Thapliyal (2014) puts it, 'These historical bonds are unseen between any two countries in the world. The cultural ties have worked well between the people and leaders of the two countries but it cannot be synchronised with similar foreign policy interests or goals and security interests. Every sovereign country works to the best of its national interests defined by time and context'. There is a critical threshold, beyond which community cannot be invoked in South Asia. India's relations with Nepal, despite the attractions of the popular narratives of being another theatre for rivalry between India and China, are better approached through the prism of India's post-colonial difference based on the community–territory disjunction.

Theorising India's Understanding of South Asia

Taking all factors into account, India's understanding of South Asia has largely followed the trajectory suggested by the Gujral Doctrine. There is a complex intertwining of realist and neo-liberal metaphors to it. Shivshankar Menon, India's foreign secretary, noted in one of his speeches:

> The challenge for us in our neighbourhood is to build inter-dependencies, which not only integrate economies, but also create vested

interests in each other's stability and prosperity in the subcontinent. Interestingly, today India is not the issue in any of our neighbours' political transitions; rather, the countries of the neighbourhood look to the Indian market and economy as positive factors for their own economic growth... We will continue to work with each of our neighbours, through the innovative use of development partnerships, our economic and technological capabilities, the development of cross border infrastructure projects, as well as our civilisational linkages, to achieve the goal of a peaceful periphery. In this process we are ready to provide benefits to our neighbours without necessarily insisting on reciprocity. (Menon 2007)

Similarly, his predecessor Shyam Saran maintained, 'It is true that as the largest country in the region and its strongest economy, India has a greater responsibility to encourage the SAARC process. In the free markets that India has already established with Sri Lanka, Nepal and Bhutan, it has already accepted the principle of non-reciprocity' (Saran 2005). And yet, simultaneously, he also brought back the subtext, one that harps on India's post-colonial difference, the claims of sovereign territoriality, and privileges security over everything else:

The sub-continent is now home to several independent and sovereign states and this is a compelling political reality ... As a flourishing democracy, India would certainly welcome more democracy in our neighbourhood, but that too is something that we may encourage and promote; it is not something that we can impose upon others. We must also recognize, regrettable though this may be, that the countries of South Asia, while occupying the same geographical space, do not have a shared security perception and hence, a common security doctrine. This is different from EU or ASEAN. In South Asia, at least some of the States perceive security threats as arising from within the region. (Saran 2005)

Modi's Engagement of South Asian Neighbours

Prime Minister Narendra Modi's style of foreign engagement has been noteworthy in this respect. As Brahma Chellaney (2014) shrewdly points out, with the invitation extended to all South Asian regional leaders at his swearing-in ceremony in May 2014, Modi rendered clear his priority to regain India's 'lost ground in the backyard'. An impromptu and 'friendly' visit to meet Prime Minister Nawaz Sharif in Pakistan in December 2015 was preceded by extensive, scheduled, high-profile trips to Bhutan,

Nepal, Bangladesh, Mongolia, South Korea, Afghanistan, Singapore, Malaysia, the United Arab Emirates, and various countries of Central Asia throughout the year. But at the same time, in an overt endorsement of diplomatic symbolism, he remained non-committal to Pakistan in November 2014 during the SAARC Summit, when the latter refused to prosecute the masterminds of the Mumbai terror attacks. Modi shook hands with Nawaz Sharif only the following day at the Dhulikhel retreat. He has also tried to institutionalize the idea of 'Asian solidarity', defined through three key markers: the Regional Comprehensive Economic Partnership (RCEP); cybersecurity architecture for the ASEAN Regional Forum; and the settlement of disputes through multilateral rules. On maritime concerns in Asia, Modi has calibrated the Indian position, without straying too far from the traditional line. The India–Japan Joint Statement of 2015 referred to the 'Indo-Pacific', officially bringing this strategic phrase into India's foreign policy lexicon. However, the prime minister's speeches on the subject themselves allude to the Asia-Pacific and Indian Ocean as distinct regions connected by history and destinies, 'however we choose to define them' (Sukumar 2015). Thus, as India struggles to settle on national narrative(s) of foreign policy moves, its search for external legitimacy in the neighbourhood continues to remain increasingly complex and challenging.

Two major developments require special attention under the new dispensation in India. First, there are claims to an increasing muscularity in India's approach to its adversaries, coupled with a newfound bravado, which takes pride in ostentatious demonstrations of power. Nowhere is this clearer than in India's offensive against Pakistan in response to stepped-up incidents of terror strikes in Kashmir. The massacre of eighteen Indian army men at Uri in Kashmir led to the much advertised 'surgical strikes' by India against terror camps across the Line of Control. The fact that such operations had apparently taken place under the UPA regime as well is beside the point. Modi's strategy has been to relentlessly orchestrate against the export of terror by Pakistan and mobilize public support by widely publicizing India's military strikes. The fact that India and Pakistan are involved in regular gun battles across the border, leading to deaths and loss of property on both sides, has not resulted in any policy reversal so far. Referring to Pakistan, Modi complained:

> There is one nation in Asia whose aim is to ensure that the 21st century does not become Asia's century, and that it remains associated with

terrorism.... That country wants South Asia's history to be splattered with blood, killings and terror.... Whenever a terror attack takes place, only one country is blamed. Whenever we hear about terror strikes, news follows that either the terrorist went from there or, like Osama bin Laden, they settled there afterward. (Quoted in Mathew 2016)

Addressing the people of Pakistan, he said:

Your rulers are misleading you by singing songs on Kashmir and reading out scripts written by terrorists on Kashmir. You should ask your leaders why India, which was created along with Pakistan, exports software and Pakistan exports terror.... You should ask them why they were not able to handle East Pakistan, and why they cannot handle PoK, Gilgit, Sindh, Balochistan and Pakhunistan...? (Quoted in Mathew 2016)

The evidence thus far suggests that the conflict with Pakistan has worsened in the last one year in particular. In the words of one of the most astute analysts of Indian foreign policy, 'In his dealings with India's other adversary, Pakistan, given his ideological proclivities and Islamabad's seeming inability or unwillingness to eschew its ties to terror, it is highly unlikely that he will evince much interest in or expend much political capital in seeking a rapprochement' (Ganguly 2015: 11).

To claim that this line constitutes a clear qualitative change in India's approach will not be appropriate. The subcontinent remains fixated on a narrative of terror and confrontation. However, as India's military and economic capacities have grown, a new power-speak has come to dominate the discourses. There is not only allusion to superiority over its rival, but also a clear indication to 'pay back in its own coin'. The lines between the internal and the external have gotten blurred officially. Territoriality once again proves incapable of solving the vexed issues of nation-building. The unabashed admission of blind spots within the territorial borders of two nuclear-powered states is a manifestation of the 'territory effect' and also the failing to bring together the impossible triad of land, people, and citizenship.

Second, Modi's approach to the immediate neighbourhood evolves within the given frame of reference, frequent claims to boldness, pragmatism, and sincerity of purpose notwithstanding. Therefore, Modi's South Asia policy shows the traditional Indian concern for security of borders vis-à-vis difficult neighbours, perhaps a more pronounced sensitivity to the growing presence of China in its backyard, the need to counterbalance a growing Chinese naval presence in the Indian Ocean, and the paradoxical invocation of the language of connectivity and the discourse of surveillance and discipline at the same time. The vicissitudes of these relations are ultimately tied to domestic developments in all the states. To this is added the unmistakable trends of fashioning a brand of cultural nationalism that is opposed to the idea of a secular and pluralist order. This vision offers the alternative of an austere and homogenous nation, culturally united along Hindu values, committed to redeem a mythologized, glorious, martial past, extolling the virtues of order, hierarchy, and supreme sacrifice for the 'motherland'. While this policy relentlessly crusades in favour of augmenting India's material capabilities, it self-consciously deploys the language of what Rahul Sagar has termed as an 'assertive and exclusionary nationalism' (Sagar 2014, quoted in Ganguly 2015: 6). As we discussed in Chapter 1, the turn towards a policy of cultural nationalism is both new and old in India. It builds on a lineage that has politically reinvented itself since the early 1990s, and is inextricably intertwined with the inter-community relations in the subcontinent. The ruling political elites in India have a clear Hindu world view. Now unencumbered by difficult coalition partners, as was the case before (NDA-1), they have conjured up a powerful narrative of pride, humiliation, shame, and indignation, which may lead to unforeseen consequences in the neighbourhood.

India's Strategic Community

This section looks into the discourses of the strategic experts, who are either directly or indirectly related to foreign policy decision making. Most Indian analysts consider the security environment of India to be grave. Thus, J.N. Dixit (2003: 380), one of India's most respected security and foreign policy analysts and former foreign secretary, remarks:

> India's immediate neighbours remain apprehensive of its intention and regional potentialities. The only way to overcome this situation is for India itself to structure equations with the major centres of powers on the basis of intermeshed and interdependent interests and, within India, to cross the threshold of economic and military strengths which would persuade neighbours as well as the international community that adjusting to India rather than controlling its potentialities would be a more realistic option.

Similar caution has been expressed by defence analysts like Brahma Chellaney and L.P. Singh. According to Chellaney (1999b: xviii):

Like the real elephant that has teeth for show but separate teeth for biting; 'elephant' India needs to understand that a state should put its desire for friendship with neighbours and major powers on public display while continuing to sharpen its capacity to deter aggression. India's main failing has been that it has always wanted to be a state that is liked, not a state that is respected. Respect can come only if a state knows the ways and means to secure well-depicted interests and acts determinedly.... India has been so comfortable in the role of a victim before international audiences that it has overlooked some basic principles of international relations, including that national strength brings international respects....

Again, L.P. Singh (1999: 1) says:

Through the centuries, India has attracted invaders (as distinguished from those who made India their home). They came out of greed, to plunder its famed reaches and its cultural treasures.... The Chinese attack in 1962 and Pakistan's aggression in 1947–48 and 1965 stand apart in their motivation and objections. They were partly territorial in the case of China, and principally so in the case of Pakistan.

How Neighbours View India

This author's interviews with several of India's policymakers and defence experts, however, reveal a more nuanced picture. There seemed to be a consensus on India being viewed as overbearing by its neighbours. The reasons are, once again, many. For one, there are divided people on the borders throughout South Asia—the Nagas, Bengalis, Nepalis, Tamils, Sindhis, Punjabis, Kashmiris, to name a few. It is very difficult for the Indian state not to get dragged into issues concerning the divided people, for reasons of both state security and electoral compulsion. Again, India seems confused about its own responsibility and identity. A classic example is the failure to build Indo-Nepalese cooperation over hydro-electricity generation, although both states are tied by geography in an extraordinary relation to energy resources.

India is also seen as overbearing by virtue of its size, growth rates, and vibrancy. It is often looked upon as uncaring towards the aspirations of its neighbours. India carries the historical burden of being the largest state of the subcontinent. But neither is this historically true, nor does India mean to be overbearing. There are certain parameters of policy in dealing with its neighbours. Neighbours feel neglected, and find India insensitive to their interests as they define them. However, policy analysts are of the opinion that no state other than Pakistan has a security threat vis-à-vis India. While with Pakistan the problem is real and not ephemeral, with huge military establishment on both sides and in confrontation, the smaller neighbours can only tease and harass India, without in any way threatening her vital interests.

Most strategic experts unequivocally state that Pakistan and China have successfully grabbed Indian lands and reduced Indian borders. India is a victim of a long battle of attrition through terrorism and insurgency techniques unleashed by Pakistan; it suffers from deaths and casualties because of terrorism and internal instability, resulting from a close nexus between local insurgent groups and enemy states. It still prefers a policy of 'forbearance and stoicism' to active, punitive action. Brahma Chellaney epitomizes this sentiment more than anybody else among India's defence analysts. 'At the dawn of the new millennium, India faces major challenges that can be effectively met only if it overhauls its approach to national security, focuses clearly on identifying and advancing its vital interests, display[s] the political determination to punish those seeking to undermine its security, and behaves as a responsible, reliable and confident state' (Chellaney 1999b: xx).

Linking Internal and External Security

India's security, therefore, requires insulation and surveillance, appropriate military capabilities and force postures, measured aggression in the face of threats, a policy of effective border control to stop infiltrators and terrorists from crossing over into the state, and punishment of the collaborators and agents of enemy states. The connection between India's external and internal security is thus closely linked. As L.P. Singh explains, 'In our case, there is often a link between internal and external security.... Both in the north-east and the north-west, their efforts to deal justly and sympathetically with our people are to an extent nullified by the hostile and uncooperative attitude of a neighbouring country' (Singh 1999: 6).

The problem with Pakistan is thought to be fundamental and rooted in history. Chellaney (1999: 315), for instance, believes that Pakistan's inexorable charge towards extremism and Talibanization is a logical corollary to its defective creation as a nation-state, and that its Kashmir mania is only the outcome of the monstrosity of its birth, which made it congenitally antipodal to what India is and stands for. It is doubly so for India because it is the essence of its territorial disputes with Pakistan and China, and the fountainhead of externally-sponsored terrorism (1999: 321).

Noted foreign policy experts in India believe that the Indo-Pak conflict is an intractable issue. Thus, Sumit Ganguly, in his review of the history of peace-making potentials of CBMs in South Asia, commented, 'Each of the four wars [1948, 1965, 1971, 1962] was the result of deliberate design and not of accident. Consequently, better understanding, better crisis communication, or more information, would not have restrained the losing side' (Ganguly 1997: 83). Similarly, J.N. Dixit, though not specifically referring to Pakistan, seems to generate the same impression in his critique of the conciliatory Gujral doctrine. Dixit laments, 'That Gujral made these gestures without demanding any reciprocity is not the point. The point is that this unilateralism had as its objective the growth of cooperativeness and trust from India's neighbours. This has not happened' (Dixit 2003: 372). T.V. Paul and Baldev Raj Nayar also express comparable views. In their words, 'As long as Pakistan aims at strategic parity with India and remains organized on a sectarian basis, the only possible option open to India seems to be, unfortunately, to proceed on the assumption of a permanent hostility on the part of Pakistan, and to take the resulting consequences as they come. Minor adjustments are unlikely to end this conflict any time soon …' (Nayar and Paul 2003: 258).

India's Strategic Culture

Strategic experts lament the absence of a strong tradition of strategic culture in India, a deficiency that has cost the South Asian security architecture dearly.[14] According to most mainstream analysts, India's lack of strategic vision is a direct result of Nehru's pacifist foreign policy and the legacy of Gandhi's non-violence. In a penetrating analysis, Jaswant Singh develops the point succinctly. In his words:

> India's strategic culture got internalized, remained fixated upon curbing within, rather than combating the external, and created a yawning

charm of mutual suspicion between the state and the citizen. In the process it has prevented India from developing its true power. The ethos of the Indian state was crippled by ... [an] ersatz pacifism, both internal and external.... Many influences have contributed to this: an accommodating and forgiving Hindu milieu; successive Jain, Buddhist, and Later Vaishnav-Bhakti influences ... [there] has been a near total emasculation of the concept of state power, also its proper employment as an instrument of state policy, in service of national interests. (Singh 1999: 13)

The absence of any self-conscious strategic culture is also borne out by this author's interviews with ex-policymakers. The majority of respondents seemed to agree that India does not have a self-conscious strategic culture. In the last fifteen years, however, the leadership has shown a far improved capacity to understand security in comprehensive terms, particularly the linkages between traditional and non-traditional security issues. The general consensus seems to be that, while India cannot pride herself of having a clearly defined strategic culture, the political leadership had a good vision of what the nation's strategic interests were, though they differed widely over the choice of means to realize these objectives.

The absence of a clear strategic orientation has apparently complicated India's position with the neighbouring states. As Stephen Cohen (1987: 45) argues, '[there has been a] restoration of a strategic perspective that reaches beyond India's immediate borders. This does not imply expansionism but recognition that India's strategic frontier may not be coterminous with its political borders.... Instead of accommodating the weaker Pakistan and recognizing the stronger China, Nehru pursued an excessively firm line toward Islamabad and too soft a line toward the Chinese.' J.N. Dixit points out that we have not been able to strike the necessary balance to meet the academic 'amorality' characterizing IR. Our moral professions and our civilizational claims result in our assuming a hectoring, pontificating, and sometimes insensitive stance in negotiations and exchanges of views, which offends our foreign interlocutors (Dixit 2003: 379). A similar pessimism is echoed in the writings of Baldev Raj Nayar and T.V. Paul:; 'There has been a marked reluctance as well in the employment of violence; India has lacked the killer instinct in inter-state conflict' (Nayar and Paul 2003: 258).

India's Internal Insecurity

Internal security remains the more chronic and perhaps debilitating aspect of India's overall security architecture. Although the sources of threats to India's internal security are diverse, the most serious, long-sustained threat consists of ethnic insurgencies that are mostly violent. The mainstream security analysts consider the internal security problem as a consequence of the break-up of the subcontinent. Witness, for example, the comment made by L.P. Singh (1999: 7):

> Even when there is no external instigation, the law and order and political problems in some of the north-eastern states, for instance in Assam, Meghalaya and Tripura, are the delayed demographic and economic consequences of Partition, and the disorganization of communications caused by it. The security problem in Kashmir ... is essentially the result of the Partition; it is in fact the outcome of the 'two-nation theory' which led to Partition.

In all these movements, whether in Kashmir, Punjab or in the northeast, the role of external actors (particularly that of India's neighbouring states) is vital. As Ved Marwah (1999: 290) insists, 'It is easy for a hostile country to sponsor terrorism in India. It simply has to exploit the competition and conflicts between the many groups that claim distinct identities along religious, ethnic, linguistic or cultural lines.'

These movements are materially supplied, and at times politically and morally rehabilitated by India's neighbours. Pakistan's intelligence service (ISI) has played a key role in encouraging and sustaining various insurgencies in different parts of India, directly in Kashmir and Punjab, and through Bangladesh in the northeast. The spread of insurgency in the Northeast is alarming. This is substantially due to the geo-strategic significance of the region in the post-Partition period, with Myanmar emerging as a sovereign state. Thus, the externalization of India's ethnic conflict(s), whose roots lay primarily in the domestic configuration of forces, is primarily responsible for the intensity and sustainability of such conflicts. Ved Marwah (1999: 291) explains:

> Once open conflict begins between a minority group and the state, any foreign assistance that enhances the groups fighting capacity becomes critical.... The availability of sanctuaries in neighbouring countries provides an essentially important strategic advantage to armed rebels. The dispersion of a people across international boundaries [make them] ... far more likely than others to be drawn

into regional conflicts are to be both beneficiaries and targets of foreign intervention.... External threats and propaganda can also activate latent group identities and interests. By contributing to their sense of common identity, cohesion, organization and capacity for political action, external forces can prompt aggrieved groups to 'mobilize' in self-defence.

***

What can we derive from these evolving trends? Is there any continuity to India's understanding of South Asia?

For the elites, who have so far governed India since its journey began as a sovereign state, the spatial imagination has been unmistakably couched in realist terms. While there are innumerable instances of India deploying the metaphors of economic cooperation and some variant of functionalism, the political logic underlying its vision of South Asia is underpinned by a cast-iron commitment to the principles of sovereign territoriality. On this reading, India's South Asia policy displays an intense territorializing effect. India's foreign policy thus struggles to balance its aspirations of being a premier global power on the one hand, and finding a solution to its legitimacy deficit in its immediate backyard on the other. No great power can emerge without negotiating its immediate neighbourhood. Though in the post–Cold War world India adopted certain measures like the 'Look East' policy in 1991 to generate stronger economic interdependence, and offered more concessions to its smaller neighbours in South Asia, India's rise unfortunately is not met by legitimacy within the South Asian context. The accusations point to India's insensitivity and arrogance borne of power. As Mitra and Schottli (2007: 30–1) point out, the lack of regional trade, the traditional ganging-up of the smaller countries against the perceived bully, India, and the involvement of 'external actors' such as China and the USA, have long been obstacles to Indian hegemony in the subcontinent, real or perceived. As a consequence, the brand recognition of Indian foreign policy oscillates between that of a regional bully and a regional push-over. Moreover, the question of legitimacy is two-fold here, which complicates matters in South Asia. Indian foreign policy is susceptible to federal concerns, and as coalition politics becomes the entrenched norm of the polity, national policies are therefore difficult to sell from the capital. They require provincial endorsement on critical matters, and the demand for domestic legitimacy often trumps its external counterpart. At the turn of the new century, for example, with tensions with Pakistan getting heightened over Kashmir, Western observers showed scepticism of India's ability to take hard decisions (Anderson 2001: 773–4). Even when political trends in neighbouring states are to India's interest, the incentive to redefine the terms of engagement is insignificant. The intense power and security-driven mindset of the elites rule out radical alternatives in space-making.

I argue that the constitution of South Asia as a region has never been very strong. Unlike more united or coherent regions of the world, South Asians have by and large failed to evolve a regional identity. In essence, territoriality trumped regional identity in South Asia, with inter-state borders becoming far more existentially demanding than the outer borders of the region. In a sense, South Asia was unable to emerge because its definition was predicated along strategic lines. Like many other regions of the world, South Asia was constituted by the needs of the geopolitics of a failing empire, and took shape in the shadow of the bipolar Cold War confrontation of the two superpowers. Thus, South Asia was, and remained, a geopolitical construct, and the failure of the region to evolve a strong regional identity was primarily due to the logic of its birth. As a geopolitical construct, South Asia could never assume selfhood, as the strategic thinking of India and most of the other South Asian states remain fundamentally opposed or discordant. While India sought a strategic unity of the region by immunizing it from extraneous military interventions of all kinds, the other states, most notably Pakistan, wanted the strategic assimilation of the region through the active involvement of great powers, particularly China and the USA. The intense geopolitical rivalry between the two most powerful states of the region ruled out the possibility of a strong regional identity for the subcontinent. However, the strategic rivalry is the result of deeper sociological and political trends, which sought to territorialize a meta-community, with all the attendant complications resulting from it.

Notes

1. The contradiction between cooperative security and realism-inspired national security is very aptly summarized by Wagner. The change in India's South Asia policy, which views the region toady more as a part of India's market and less

as a challenge to its national security, has contributed to a change in perspective that has resulted in unilateral trade concessions and in compromises on bilateral issues. The collaboration is characterized by several features. First, it is more bilateral (between India and its neighbours) than regional or multilateral (for instance, on the SAARC level). Second, security cooperation is still dependent on the overall context of bilateral relations and is therefore prone to setbacks. (Wagner 2014: 22).

2. While Buzan finds little change at the regional level, he does mention changes at the inter-regional and global levels that have impacted India's policy. In his words, 'Even though India is a huge fish in a small bowl in South Asia, it has not been able or perhaps even willing to settle its region either by force or by legitimate leadership. Instead, it looks to swim in the larger bowl of East Asia and the Indian Ocean' (Buzan 2011: 17).

3. It would be prudent to argue that unless interaction capacity as a process variable is interposed between the structure and the units, neither the so-called structural effect—that shoves and pushes the units—nor the variations in the distribution of power can be properly explained. To get to the matter more directly, a structural theory of world policies explains why different states behave similarly, while foreign policy theory reasons out why similarly placed states behave differently. As oligopolistic firms cannot wish away the fact of a competitive market but can manipulate the latter to advance its cause, similarly, powerful states cannot be immune to structural (systemic) effects, through they can work their ways through them. This is broadly the argument of Kenneth Waltz ([1979] 2010).

4. While recognizing the attractions of realism for the official elites, I do not in any way absolve realism of its many fallacies and limitations. This is not the place to advance a theoretical critique of political realism. However, two general limitations need to be stated upfront. First, the realist case for 'anarchy problematic' has been challenged by constructivists like Wendt. While many scholars agree that the international realm is without a legitimate body of authority, the meaning and consequences of such a fact are not necessarily based on realist injunctions. Countering neo-realist ideas, Wendt argues that self-help does not follow logically or causally from the principle of anarchy. It is socially constructed. Wendt, therefore, says, '[S]elf-help and power politics are institutions and not essential features of anarchy. Anarchy is what states make of it' (Wendt 1987: 395). Anarchy is a form of social culture which is constituted by agents, and whose meaning varies across time and space. Thus, anarchy of enemies is different from the anarchy of rivals or friends. Second, the realist reification of the statist ontology is false. The problem is that the state must be understood inside out; it can hardly be as a sociological void. Foreign policy is also a socio-political act. Those who enact these policies are located somewhere. Realism's refusal to

entertain domestic structures is, therefore, both shallow and naïve. My argument of geopolitical space making is mindful of these limitations. I only make the case that there is no evidence of the foreign policymakers operating with ideas vis-à-vis India's neighbourhood that can be consistently located in any alternative paradigm, India's traditional embarrassment with realism notwithstanding.

5. The strategic understanding of modern India is a distinctly colonial heritage. The centrality of India in British geo-economic and geopolitical interests can be traced to many renowned statesmen, including Lord Curzon. One of the most influential architects of modern South Asia as a geopolitical construct was Sir Olaf Caroe, who served as the foreign secretary for the British India from 1939 to 1945. For a fascinating account of his role, see Brobst (2005).

6. The Indira Doctrine is summed up as follows:

India has no intention of intervening in the internal conflicts of a South Asian country and it strongly opposes intervention by any country in the internal affairs of any other.

India will not tolerate external intervention in a conflict situation in any South Asian country, if the intervention has any implicit or explicit anti-Indian implication. No South Asian government must therefore ask for external military assistance with an anti-Indian bias from any country.

If a South Asian country genuinely needs external help to deal with a serious internal conflict situation, or with an intolerable threat to a government legitimately established, it should ask help from a number of neighboring countries including India. The exclusion of India from such a contingency will be considered to be an anti-Indian move on the part of the government concerned. (Sengupta 1983: 20–1)

7. For details, see the analysis in Hagerty (1991).

8. For an incisive treatment, see Brewster (2014).

9. Government of India 1977.

10. Vajpayee argued:

Pakistan has taken no significant action against training camps and infrastructural support to terrorism. This questions its claim to participate in the international struggle against terrorism…. The Pakistani establishment does not appear to be interested in establishing tension-free and good-neighborly relations with India by ending its proxy war against our country…. Available reports suggest that the territories of Nepal and Bangladesh are now being used by the ISI to pursue its anti-India agenda. Therefore, we have to intensify our efforts to counter terrorism in Jammu & Kashmir and subversive activities both in those States that border these two countries and elsewhere. (Vajpayee 2003)

11. India's National Security Advisor during the UPA-II regime, Mr Shivshankar Menon, had also toed the same line. In Menon's (2012) words:

But all this economics ignores the real political and security issues that enable outsiders to call this one of the most dangerous places on earth, I sense you saying to yourselves. We may have got the economics right recently, but can we get the politics right? Perhaps, would be my answer. South Asia has more than its fair share of issues with insurgencies, radicalism, terrorism, and extremism. But none of these issues has prevented this from being one of the fastest growing sub-regions in the world in the last decade, and outperforming other sub-regions. But it is an open question whether we in South Asia have the institutions and habits of working together to address the real issues of political instability and the security challenges that we face…. Empirically speaking, there has been an improvement in the security situation in important parts of South Asia. The elimination of the LTTE's armed forces in Sri Lanka, Bangladesh's successful actions against terrorists and extremist elements in the last three years, and Nepal's steady progress in its double transition to multi-party democracy and mainstreaming the Maoists are some practical examples. But overall one would have to conclude that our politics have lagged behind our economics.

12. Sri Lanka's success is truly remarkable. In the words of Peter Layton (2015), 'Few succeed, with one major exception being Sri Lanka where after 25 years of civil war the government decisively defeated the Liberation Tigers of Tamil Eelam (LTTE) and created a peace that appears lasting. This victory stands in stark contrast to the conflicts fought by well-funded Western forces in Iraq and Afghanistan over the last decade.'

13. See Press Trust of India (2014b).

14. There is a considerable body of literature on India's official strategic thinking. The best compilation is Bajpai, Basit, and Krishnappa (2014).

4 | India and the SAARC

Security, Commerce, and Community

THIS CHAPTER DISCUSSES INDIA's approach to SAARC, and finds that the region's refusal to part with hard borders is singularly responsible for a dismal record in successful regionalism.

Regionalism is primarily a space-making game; it has multiple triggers. Security, economic development, and identity considerations are all crucial to how regions shape up. Two factors are important here. First is that regions are constructs of order. Such orders may be explained either as zones of tranquillity achieved under a dominant power, or as zones that strike an effective balance of power arrangement. They may also be explained as the literature on functionalism and neo-functionalism has shown in the past and Adler's exciting use of norms has recently suggested, a powerful precondition of a regional organization is the making of a security community, a concept which is remarkably flexible, and therefore, adaptable by both constructivist and liberal paradigms.[1] This means a regional order can be constructed through functional cooperation and innovative combinations of statist and civil societal elites. Free trade and liberal policies and institutions may also bind a region together by creating a nexus between mutual cooperation and interdependence, such that the political or militaristic conflicts would eventually become obsolete and be discarded as counterproductive to the peace and prosperity of the region as a whole.

The second issue concerns the 'constitutive identity' of a region. A region could also be formed by forging a community over and above the distinctive national identities of its members. We find that the SAARC has remained a virtual non-starter, since none of these frames of regional identity formation and cooperation seem powerful or effective in the subcontinent. The idea of a security community is trumped by the strategic disunity of the subcontinent, owing both to the generic conflict between India and Pakistan, as well as India's disputes with other South Asian states on various issues. The idea of redefining South Asia as a cooperative free market area flounders due to the economic asymmetry between India and the other members on the one hand, and the pull of globalization on the other. Finally, South Asia has failed to evolve a new regional identity based on community, as its colonial past, which prioritized the idea of citizenship and territoriality over the idea of an overarching community, still dominates the elite imagination in the subcontinent. Unconditional allegiance to the norm of sovereign territoriality has trumped the notion of a South Asian citizenship in the region.

Why SAARC?

The South Asian regional experiment under SAARC commenced with certain structural limitations. For analytical clarity, it is imperative to highlight these underpinnings of the organization. First and foremost, the SAARC Charter, since its inception, was a compromise, a testimony to the reluctance of its actors to engage in forging South Asia as either a strategic, economic, or a communitarian space. Thus, the basis for cooperation under SAARC was conceived along the most generalized terms of 'promoting peace, stability, amity, and progress in the region through strict adherence to the principles of the UNITED NATIONS CHARTER and NON-ALIGNMENT, particularly respect for the principles of sovereign equality, territorial integrity, national independence, non-use of force and non-interference in the internal affairs of other States and peaceful settlement of all disputes.'[2] With the New Cold War in its backyard failing to provide any compelling converging agenda for cooperation among the seven South Asian nations, SAARC envisaged to engage itself with promoting welfare, development, all-round collaboration, fostering cooperation, and building mutual trust and understanding, so that a life of dignity and freedom might become possible for the millions.[3] The goal was to encourage a shared vision of economic development and collective action to end the long-standing problems, like poverty and underdevelopment, which have plagued the subcontinent since its inception. SAARC was to pave the way to link up with similar collective organizations that espoused common aims and purposes. It was a move to refashion the identity of the region, so that nations could get their acts together instead of remaining perennially hostage to the perils of petty squabbles.[4]

However, a complementary set of mechanisms to realize these SAARC objectives was conspicuous in its absence. Ironically, it sought to promote mutual trust and understanding, but intentionally precluded deliberations on all contentious and bilateral issues of the region by the notorious Article X of the Charter. Second, by excluding Afghanistan and Myanmar, the organization did not, in its initial stages, incorporate the entire geographical space denoted by the term South Asia. This has been rectified to a certain extent with Afghanistan joining the organization at its fourteenth summit (New Delhi) in April 2007. Myanmar is still not a core member of SAARC, which is an anomaly that exposes the cartographic limits of the organization are political, social, economic, and infrastructural terms. Thus, SAARC was envisaged as a platform based on the lowest common denominator to accommodate the major regional actors. In this sense, SAARC was an attempt to initiate cooperative mechanisms in a region torn by historical feuds, contested territorial and resource entitlements, and divergent tacit Cold War allegiances, on certain pervasive humanitarian and developmental issues that plagued one-fourth of the humankind inhabiting South Asia.

Deprived of a compelling agenda and specific timeline, with a serious 'trust deficit' among its actors, devoid of binding principles of unanimity, and with the exclusion of contentious issues, it is no surprise that the growth of SAARC has been slow and painful. At birth, SAARC members identified five common areas of interest, namely, agriculture, rural development, telecommunications, meteorology, and health and population. The organization established its secretariat in 1986. The scope of SAARC was expanded at the Kathmandu summit (1987) to include wider economic cooperation. Subsequently, SAPTA was ratified in 1995 at New Delhi, and eventually advanced towards achieving a South Asian Free Trade Area (SAFTA) (Colombo summit 1998). The Colombo summit also gave SAARC a mandate to build extra-regional dialogues. Eventually, the articulation of a joint SAARC 'voice' at the international fora was also desired (Chatterjee and Maitra 2009).

While these agreements remain on paper as landmarks in South Asian cooperation, achieving these goals has proved to be an uphill task. SAARC and its action-list has been hostage to the region's volatile peace and security quotient. Ironically, the organization itself has remained incapable of making any significant positive contributions to this end.

Why could not SAARC, now over thirty-one years and nineteen summits old, transgress its endemic deficits in favour of forging a political space that may lead to long lasting peace and development? This chapter finds that the Indian vision of graduating into a major power is a crippling detriment to the idea of a thriving SAARC. Since the unresolved problems of its immediate neighbourhood are largely held responsible for sapping India's vitality, she is increasingly becoming receptive to the idea of an extended community, which involves a conscious process of transcending its South Asian identity. Unless the idea of SAARC attaches more meaningfully to a wider frame of both geopolitical and commercial interests, its prospects do not appear to be salvageable from its current state of in/significance.

Order, Regionalism, and the Geopolitics of Space

IR Theories on Order

The attempt to build a regional organization in South Asia reveals a fundamental contradiction right from the start. What led to the making of the SAARC? In a way, the motivation was to build order at the regional level, create institutions that would foster peace and stability, and perhaps most crucially, bring the concerns of welfare and power together. What does the IR scholarship offer here? The problem of order can be addressed in two fundamentally opposed ways. The first is the realist argument, which describes the international order as a union of nation-states. This order is anarchical, and the states fend for their own security through mechanisms like internal mobilization of capabilities or alliances. Most realists agree that order depends on the efficacy of the balance of power among great powers. This means that the order holds if no state becomes too dominant to underwrite the norms of the order unilaterally, or impose its preferences on others. In contrast, a group of realists that belongs to the hegemonic stability theory, power cycle theory, and a few related approaches, envisages the international order as hierarchical and prefers hegemony over the balance of power as a precondition for order and stability. In both the versions, the aim is to reinforce the system on the basis of territorial sovereignty, and there is little autonomous contribution that extra-territorial institutions can make to the order. Realists have several arguments in their support. First, they believe that such organizations reflect the nature of the distribution of power within the international system, and are inconsequential to the nature of power competition that marks such an order. Second, some realists argue that states are motivated by relative gains, rather than absolute benefits, thereby making regional cooperation difficult to sustain. Third, realists remain deeply pessimistic with regard to the transformative potentials of such institutions.[5]

In contrast, approaches like functionalism, neo-functionalism, and integration theories, among others, have rejected this statist and power-centric vision of order-making.[6] These approaches talk about the role of international and regional institutions, the role played by technical experts as against professional politicians, and a gradual, though unmistakable, change in the character of challenges and problems afflicting states as some of the prime movers of order-making.

The relation among the federalist, functionalist, and neo-functionalist approaches is complex. However, it is essential to capture the primary points of contrast between functionalism and neo-functionalism to understand what a regional organization can hope to achieve to create a version of order which would be different from the realist alternative. In the words of A.J.R. Groom (1980: 94–5):

> The functionalist argument starts from the basic notion that form should follow function. In other words, a particular functional system of endeavour delineates itself through transaction patterns, and a suitable organizational frame for that system is determined by the needs of the function being performed. Functionalists argue that there is no need for a fixed constitution written in advance because the framework is developed and [ideally] modified as the function being fulfilled changes.... Thus, the functionalists argue, a 'working peace system' will evolve that will tend to diminish conflict by allowing cross-cutting loyalties and by creating a sense of security through fulfilling a necessary function rather than through a threat system. The development of a 'working peace system' is thus contingent upon a learning process in which successful co-operation in one dimension spills over into other spheres.

Neo-functionalists were far more ambitious; they claimed that it was necessary to bring the softer (non-political) and the harder (political) sectors together to transform regional spaces, and perhaps even the nature of world politics over time. According to Pentland (1975: 20–1), functionalism is preferred over neo-functionalism, as in the latter, the

> integration progresses 'spill-overs' lead the participants into increasingly political sectors, where the stakes of bargaining and the resources of each side are considerable. Crises, then, are an inevitable, indeed essential, part of the integrative process. Functionalism, however, sees the political effect of co-operation as occurring in the attitudes of participants and beneficiaries, slowly eroding the vestiges of particularism from within, rather than attacking them direct in increasingly long and bitter bargaining sessions ...

Neo-functionalism was an attempt to subtract the distance between functionalism and federalism. As Joseph Nye (1971: 51) writes:

> Basically, the neo-functionalists were federalists in functional clothing, pursuing federal ends through what appeared to be functional means. Thus, while the Schuman Plan looked rather functionalist, it was functionalist with two important innovations. First, the neo-functionalists avoided the [functional] approach of quiet technical self-determination that seemed to lead to political irrelevance. Rather, they deliberately chose a sector that was politically important, yet that could be planned by technocrats and did not demand immediate commitment to federal institutions. They also retained some of the federalist attack on sovereignty.

Nye further contrasted the two approaches by arguing:

> A second important neo-functionalist departure from classical functionalism was in its deliberate design of institutions that would lead to further integration, not merely in the classical functionalist sense of the transfer of 'lessons of benefit' of technical self-determination from on field to another, but through ... 'the expansive logic of sector integration'. By meshing the smaller gears of the society and getting them to turn, eventually, one could hope to turn the larger wheels. In short the neo-functionalists argue that power and welfare cannot be kept radically separate and that true technical self-determination on non-controversial topics will be condemned to triviality. The political game must be played, but played with a functionally oriented strategy

rather than a legalistic or constitutional one. On the other hand, the classical functionalists remained skeptical of the political, regional, and federal ends of the neo-functionalists.... (1971: 52–3)

The two contrasting approaches to order explain all successful examples of regional organization in radically opposed ways. The realists have grudgingly acknowledged the success of regionalism in post–World War II Western Europe and in Southeast Asia. However, their narrative makes no concession to welfare-based integrationist models. The realists say that it is the presence of extraordinary security threats that unites a region, and creates what Buzan described as 'positive security interdependence' among the leading states (Buzan 1991). Without a shared vision of security, the path to evolve a regional community of order is doomed. In contrast, the functional arguments are about the limitations of coerced unity, the success of technocrats over generalists, and the role of a myriad of civil societal actors, rather than statist politicians, in ultimately shifting the bases of political allegiance of a population socialized in a culture of exclusivist sovereignty and state-oriented models of economic growth. The broad argument is not about redundancy of politics altogether, but that the economic function based on the needs of welfare trumps the political function of separation and order as tenuous coalitions of shifting balances.

Theorizing Order in the Post-Colonial World

The problem is that the functional and neo-functional regime and integration literature came up in the context of European experiments in space-making, which hardly paid any attention to the vastly dissimilar conditions prevailing in the post-colonial world. Like the ahistorical universalism of realists, this alternative approach was shot through with a Western ontology that had no cognitive interest in engaging with the 'other'. In other words, both standard realist discourses and their alternatives neglected the historical and socio-economic specificities of the non-Western world, and were loath to accommodate departures for a long time to come. Hence, order is not a simple and innocent category. Neither is there any guarantee that successful examples of order making in a handful of contexts would unproblematically translate into other cases. Realists, on their part, neglected the differential trajectories of state making in the West and the post-colonial worlds. They paid little attention to the 'domestic' constitution of the post-colonial states, and the vastly different challenges of nation building that convulsed most of these newly independent entities. They also hardly got into the role of colonial economic forces, which had historically determined the contours of state-making, labour migration, and the politics of citizenship in the colonies, which would continue to cast their long shadows on the post-independence political trajectories of these states. The functional school, on their part, was equally gullible in thinking that the European experiments could be grafted onto dissimilar societies; they endorsed a one-size-fits-all modernity–modernization–welfare mantra as the panacea to the perils of the post-colonial (dis)order. There was scant attention paid in the order literature to the pivotal roles of community and culture in the territorialized projects of state-based nation building. The fact that shared cultural markers can be liabilities, rather than assets in an imagination to fashion a new order-based region easily passed underneath the radar of both these schools, which thought that Western experiences were universal, as a nation state–based international order had consummated the whole of humanity for the first time in history. The inability to address the overwhelming significance of domestic political conflicts in most post-colonial states in their difficult ties with their neighbours make both standard realism and the functionalist alternatives poor analytical categories to explain the trials and tribulations of a regional organization like the SAARC.

Security Community

Regional identities can be transformed if states can create a security community among themselves. There is a formidable corpus of literature on security community and regional identity formation. In simplest terms, security community connotes a shared 'perceptional' space that betrays a broad agreement amongst partners that all differences would be resolved short of armed conflict, or use of threat and violence. The concretization of the perceptional space depends on an incremental growth of the institutions and practices that build on the available body of trust in the region. Institutions formalize expectations, rewards, and sanctions. Strong institutions are thus the most powerful investments to peace.

The making of a security community is a direct affront to the theoretical claims of realism in two senses. First, a security community espouses the idea of cooperative security, whose actors define security with, rather than against, others. Second, the idea of the security community is critically anchored in perceptional or ideational considerations rather than material factors. Both these attributes are unacceptable to standard realist theories, which define security in competitive and material terms.

The making of a security community is a historical rarity, with Western Europe being the classical paradigmatic case, and ASEAN, as originally constituted, being its closest approximation. In the case of the former, the unprecedented wreckage and devastation of the two world wars provided a strong impetus to create a security community as a basic precondition for self-sustaining growth and the redemption of its civilizational heritage. The ideological polarization of Europe and the brooding shadow of a war between the Soviet Union and the USA that fell on the continent vastly contributed to the making of a security community. In the case of Southeast Asian states, it was the threat of communism that united the ruling elites in their commitment to forge the regional organization as an engine of growth in a condition of peace and stability. In the case of South Asia, the idea of a regional organization took shape in conscious separation from the idea of security and power, since contentious bilateral issues are by definition kept outside the frame of operations.

Lack of Security Community in South Asia

In brief, the idea of a security community never caught the imagination of the South Asian elites. The absence of a consensual idea of security in the subcontinent undoubtedly limits the scope of SAARC as a regional organization. It explains the inability of SAARC to develop as a security community, one that could transcend the recursive, competitive security dynamics by a cooperative framework, which could encourage peaceful modes of conflict resolution at thresholds far below from direct mobilization. The absence of war in the subcontinent since 1971 is no evidence that would dispute the aforesaid proposition; despite the lack of 'declared' wars, the South Asian states have deliberately decided to stay away from developing regional conflict resolution mechanisms and security institutions that would ameliorate the sources of conflict persisting between them.

The central realist argument is that the prevailing geopolitical dynamics of South Asia still continues to be the chief component of the region's make-up, and the continuity of that dynamic is primarily responsible for trumping the macro-transformational consequences of globalization in the subcontinent. Unlike most other regions of the world, military expenditure, in both absolute terms and as percentage of the GDP, increased in South Asia between 1990 and 2000; there is no sign of any drastic alteration in this trend. In more specific terms, realists offer three reasons as to why South Asia is unable to transcend its self-identity, or rather fails to evolve an identity at the regional level, which is commensurate with the needs of a security community, particularly in terms of evolving apposite institutions and practices. In the words of A.P. Rana (2003: 20):

> In any case, the state, caught up in its priority task of nation and state-building, within boundaries now deemed sacrosanct, gets into conflicts and difficulties related to such issues with other states of the region; such conflicts inevitably cut the ground from beneath the feet of any regional cooperative enterprise, unless it is relatively perfunctory, or carries no possibly adverse implications for the priority of the political enterprise.

Is South Asia a Political Community?

What is the vision of the South Asian community that undergirds the stronger proponents of SAARC? This is undoubtedly the most complex issue which bedevils the regional integration process in South Asia. There are three major strands here that need some attention. The first of these draws attention to the historical anomaly between British India, with its integrated labour and capital markets, and the territorialized independent states of South Asia, which have failed to achieve this integration of labour and capital. The second alludes to the natural tendency in South Asia for the local people to cross borders surreptitiously and in clandestine ways, as the economic logic of capitalism runs counter to the political discourse of territorial control. Despite security alerts and tight border control, labour migration is a constant fact in modern South Asia, which needs to be recognized and regularized by the ruling elites, rather than being disowned and hushed up. The argument here is that no matter how hard the political elites want, the economic logic will find a way out for itself. While there is recognition that issues of human security and connectivity tend to be arrogated and appropriated by the territorial dynamic of national sovereignty, there is hope nevertheless that the politics of materiality will ultimately prevail over that of denial. Rehman Sobhan articulates this most categorically in his prose:

> There is some reason to believe that what remained an ongoing movement of people ever since provincial boundaries were converted into national borders, is once again transforming South Asia into a seamless region. This progressive erosion in the restraining capacity of national boundaries, is contributing to a rapid and uncontrolled integration of labour markets within South Asia and indeed at a global level. (Sobhan 1998: 11)

The third argument is broadly about the redundancy of national solutions to extra-territorial challenges, be it economic, environmental, or infrastructural. As Raja Mohan puts it, 'Borders in the subcontinent need not necessarily remain political barriers. They need to be transformed into zones of economic cooperation among regions that once were part of the same cultural and political space' (Raja Mohan 2003: 269).

Potential of South Asia as a Regional Community

The great hope of transforming South Asia into a regional community inheres in the liberating potentials of its civil society. At least three imaginations are recognizable here. The first is the neo-liberal hope of market economics trumping the political diffidence and negativity. We have discussed this in details in Chapter 2. The fact is that there is no hard evidence to conclude that economic forces will operate in a seamless way. Two factors were identified. First, the structural imbalance in the economies may run counter to a greater economic partnership and openness. The smaller states are naturally wary of India's economic weight, and protectionist elements often ally with political forces hostile to stronger regional cooperation. India has, however, achieved greater economic success with Sri Lanka and Bangladesh in recent years. However, the reason for such a positive tendency remains unclear. Is such economic success, the result of the activities of private business actors who have found ways to negotiate hard borders of the state or does it originate in regimes that value friendship with New Delhi for their own survival? Perhaps there is a mutually reinforcing dynamic between business interests and state officials. While a synergy is ruled out, this author's interviews in Bangladesh in early 2015 found a number of Bangladeshi entrepreneurs unhappy with the state bureaucracy on both sides of the border. Second, globalization creates opportunity to reap benefits of scale for the upwardly mobile technocratic professional groups by going beyond the subcontinent. It remains to be seen what tendencies might unfold when the relatively depressed sections and classes began to respond to these opportunities more vigorously. Till now, there is little incontrovertible evidence that supports the neo-liberal case within the subcontinent.

The second line of hope concerns democratization and the apparent empowerment of the masses. The optimistic thesis rests along following lines. Although the South Asian states began their journey with distinctive national projects, their unity lay in their commitment to become strong states with consummate national identities. This commitment, however, had to be worked out through complex social structures, which got inevitably intertwined with the political dynamic itself. All South Asian states had three goals in common: (*a*) to achieve rapid economic development; (*b*) to create a strong national identity; and (*c*) to preserve territorial integration in the face of myriad challenges to state authority, including threats of secession (Shastri and Wilson 2001: 2). The nature of social elites who came to dominate these South Asian states decided the character of the political rule. In all South Asian states, the weaker and the marginal sections of the people have become politically more visible and vocal. How democratic orders transform this visibility and voice into meaningful political participation remains a major challenge. Further, new political forces would invariably put pressure on central authorities to deliver better and fairly. Federal tendencies are, therefore, growing throughout the region, complicating the democratic process in many ways. Finally, like any other part of the world, the South Asian democracies are now subject to massive expansion in information processing capacities and communications facilities that cannot be nationally regulated as before. While states retain the right and possess the power to filter information in the virtual space, they can ill afford to stop such flows indefinitely. How these macro transformations are negotiated by the South Asian political systems would largely determine what happens to their democratic projects in the future.

Problems in Building Regional Community

However, while the subcontinent may gain in democratization in the future, this may not result in any alternative discourse on regionalism. The uncertainty remains over whether the democratic forces in each of the South Asian countries can consolidate their gains despite challenges, like steering the economy through global economic recession, curbing the extremist forces in the fringes of the country, integrating alienated communities within the national mainstream, and not compromising, at least in popular perception, the nation's sovereignty or territory in the face of external or internal aggression. Another worrying trend is that the installation of democratic governments has not remedied, and in some cases has increased, the human rights violations and the level of violence. This has raised questions about the efficacy of the elected governments. These issues are relevant for each and every country in South Asia, especially those who have recently adopted democratically elected governments, like Nepal, Bangladesh, Pakistan, and Bhutan. While most South Asian states have enjoyed a rich democratic dividend since 2005, this has not necessarily transformed their fundamental social and political challenges. Democratization thus far has not changed Pakistan's abnormal security dilemma, reduced ethnic domination in Sri Lanka, or repaired political fractures in Bangladesh. Moreover, this study has also shown that democratization and violence are not antithetical entities in South Asia. The state has, therefore, often acted with a heavy hand, and detractors have also taken up arms to realize their aims. Religious extremism has grown in Pakistan. Bangladesh remains fractured in its political imagination, as it is predicated upon the dual basis of its national identity. Nepal struggles in its transition to parliamentary democracy, and the need for an equitable social contract among its numerous ethnic groups. India is besieged by a new politics of cultural nationalism, which seriously questions its tenuous liberal framework of rights. Such trends can take place alongside functional electoral democratic politics. More significantly, democratic politics has neither propelled peace nor promoted regionalism in the subcontinent.

Democracy, most unfortunately, has seldom articulated the language of community in South Asia, which would require courageous forays into the past. In other words, this prompts us to ask if South Asian politics can at all create a translatable normative language that summons its shared past in imaginative ways by building on common ties of civilization and culture. This argument has already been discussed at length in Chapter 1. Civilizational ties and shared cultural idioms may not be the ideal ingredients for a regional imagination in a context where sovereign territoriality is valourized above all else. Modern South Asia has relentlessly debated the meaning/s of sharing. The states have undeniably become more communitarian in their political practices over time. However, this communitarianism is deeply territorial in essence. Hence, the political elites across the South Asian states fear the image of community, which, once unleashed, might fundamentally challenge the politics of territorial nationalism across the subcontinent. The shared forms of music, art, literature, films, and all artefacts of culture are spaces of lived experience no doubt, but they have not so far created a political narrative of common social morality that might meaningfully challenge the reality of artificial borders and exclusive national space-making projects in South Asia. Anthropologists like van Schendel (2002) have bequeathed rich ethnographies of border transcendence by ordinary people in India despite the elaborate and intrusive institutions of surveillance and security. However, this neither disproves the materiality of territoriality, nor explains the growing narcissism over immigration throughout northeastern India, where historically, the fuzziness and indeterminacy of frontiers and linear political boundaries was once the norm (Murayama 2006: 1357).

While human beings are largely territorial, the idea of territory and boundary are not fixed or immutable categories. It is a well-known fact that modern South Asia, like most other regions of the world, is a geo-strategic construct, which the Americans took over from the British colonial strategists. The historical complexities of name making of the subcontinent are very well-researched, and need not detain us here (for representative examples, see Bose and Jalal [(1997) 2011] and Goswami [2004]). For us, it is important to note that the term South Asia is alien to the history of the subcontinent. The British used the term 'Indian subcontinent' or plain 'India'. The idea of a territorialized subcontinent is also a distinctively modern phenomenon, inextricably intertwined with the many projects and imaginations of nationhood in a colonial context. As Bose and Jalal ([1997] 2011: 3–4) argue:

> The term India, as we have seen, is of much older origin. What South Asia lacks in historical depth, it makes up for in political neutrality. The terms South Asia and India refer in the first instance to a vast geographical space stretching from the Himalayan mountain ranges in the north to the Indian Ocean in the south, and from the valley of the Indus in the west to the plains of the Brahmaputra in the east.

Or as Rehman Sobhan puts it, 'South Asia is unique amongst the other regions of the world insofar as it entered the twentieth century as a community and leaves this century as seven nation states divided by their historical inheritance which, over the course of the last half century, sundered its sense of community' (Sobhan 1998: 4).

This means that South Asia is an empty, vacuous category, a convenient geographical expression to gloss over the vicissitudes of both the bloody vivisection of the subcontinent in 1947, and the glaring contradictions between the meanings of this space in its primeval incarnations, and the distinctiveness of its modern image rooted in Western colonial experience, which introduced the forces of modernity and capitalism to the region for the first time.

The British rule not only led to the creation of several modern nation-states when colonialism ended, but also destroyed the manifold meanings of borders that had historically inhabited the place. What began as a careful mixture of fuzzy frontier zones and fixed linearity, gradually hardened into secured borders, as economic hardships of the colonial rulers warranted tighter territorial control under uniform hierarchical political control of the territory. Territoriality was thus the crucible of the restrictive projects of exclusionary citizenship in South Asia. Political elites were obsessed with keeping borders sanitized, so that the preferred logic of demographics, unleashed by the colonial project of divide and rule that culminated in the partition of 1947, remained largely intact. A fear of community underlay the making of modern South Asia. Not only is this anxiety peculiarly modern and opposed to the older historical trajectories of the subcontinent, it also prevents the fruition of any meaningful articulation of regional identity that may be capable of resolving the manifest tension between artificial political constructs and the natural tendency towards connectivity of all factors of production. While the logic of globalization and the growing ascension of market forces demand relaxation of borders and a steady capitalization of space, the states remain paranoid over human flows, migration, and refugee influx. As Mayumi Murayama's work suggests, the category of migrants is perhaps the most appropriate site for testing the consequences of territoriality. It shows how Partition led to territorial control and assertiveness, and cultivated the attendant exclusionary vocabulary of 'foreigners' and 'outsiders', which were unknown to this land. In other words, there is a clear contradiction between the spatial imageries of modern South Asia. There is a prevalent intellectual rejection of the suffocating reality of settled hard borders, and the strategic space making qua territoriality, within the civil societies of South Asian states. However, this imagination runs counter to the dominant political vision, which remains perennially inhibitive of free movement across fixed lines. In Murayama's (2006: 1351) words, 'In South Asia in particular, the artificiality of borders has been continuously challenged, not only by intellectual exercises but also by the movement of people across the borders. Nevertheless, the political significance of borders remains as strong, or even stronger today, as the "illegality" of people's movement has become a relentless concern of governments.'

Security Asymmetries

The asymmetric power relations in the subcontinent evoke a fractured perception of security, which, in the absence of a common external threat, prohibits the growth of a security community. In other words, security is not a shared project in South Asia. On the one hand, India, the evidently major power in the region, defines security of the subcontinent as the absence of any external influence in the region, which could potentially upset the status quo. On the other hand, the rest of the members seek to define their security in the region through external power intervention to thwart any potential hegemonic ambitions of India (Pasha 1996). In fact, Pakistan has always consciously weighed its commitments to South Asia with its obligations in West Asia. The statement of Pakistan president, General Zia, made prior to the first SAARC summit, outlines his views regarding SAARC and Pakistan's relations with West Asia. He said that Pakistan's participation in the summit would not in any way affect its relations with the Muslim countries, and that it would maintain its national identity at all costs, and continue to play a positive role in the Middle East, since Pakistan enjoyed an important place in the South Asian region as well as in Western Asia. Further, according to an observer from Pakistan, the regional advantage of participating in the SAARC was that the arrangement could, if the need arose, 'come to deflect the weight of India' vis-à-vis its smaller South Asian partners (Murthy 2000: 1782–3). It was emphasized that Pakistan, Bangladesh, Sri Lanka, Maldives, Bhutan, and Nepal had few direct conflicts with each other. However, none of the six states could be said to be enjoying tension-free relations with New Delhi. Previously, Nepal faced internal unrest, led by movements which evoked some sympathy in India. While the former entered into a Treaty of Peace and Friendship with India in 1950, it has made conscious attempts to increase its manoeuvrability, especially with respect to security affairs. Bangladesh, on the other hand, has problems with India regarding its Chakma ethnic group in the Chittagong hill areas. The issues of illegal immigration into India, terrorism, and border disputes have been sore points of Indo-Bangladesh relations.

The second issue that encourages security asymmetry is the principle of bilateralism, which is championed by India. As the most powerful nation in the region, the country also has the dubious distinction of being involved in maximum number of inter-state conflicts with its neighbours. However, India has steadfastly refused to evolve a multilateral conflict resolution mechanism with the SAARC, choosing instead to deal with the issues bilaterally. This arrangement in the SAARC is unique, considering the dispute resolution mechanism adopted in the neighbouring ASEAN. Thus, India has refused to discuss its political conflicts with its neighbours at the SAARC forum, despite the best efforts of the other member states. Nevertheless, these issues have cast a dark cloud over cooperation within the SAARC itself.

The former external affairs minister, Yashwant Sinha, eloquently defended the Indian doctrine of bilateralism in the following words:

> Will the UN General Assembly session not be held because there is a situation between India and Pakistan? We will both be there. Similarly, we can be there anywhere in the world, including in South Asia, and not allow, with a little wisdom on our part, to let bilateral issues cloud the SAARC process ... India is fully committed to the SAARC process. We want SAARC to prosper and become a powerful instrument of regional cooperation. It has been our endeavour not to allow bilateral contentious issues to thwart or cloud the SAARC process.[7]

On another occasion, former external affairs minister, Jaswant Singh, conveyed to visiting Bangladesh foreign minister, M. Murshid Khan, that India categorically rejected Bangladesh's suggestion to involve the SAARC in the Indo-Pak conflict, saying that there was no room for any regional grouping to play any role in settling the dispute between the two countries.

However, the remaining member states point out the impossibility of the growth of South Asian regionalism without resolving the bilateral issues. The obvious example is of course the Indo-Pak conflict centring on Kashmir, which has sabotaged, officially as well as unofficially, numerous summit deliberations. The Islamabad SAARC summit is one of the instances where the summit took on a bilateral colour, with India and Pakistan deciding to hold a composite dialogue in India to take the peace process forward. SAARC, in other words, has remained a victim of India–Pakistan conflicts on a host of issues. The popular charge is to view India as dominant while Pakistan does not seem to be interested in the project in a major way. The Indian action of air-dropping food and relief, and sending the Indian Peace Keeping Force (IPKF) to Sri Lanka to combat the LTTE crisis in 1987 presented an additional dimension to the problem of evolving a security community in South Asia. India's action under former Prime Minister Rajiv Gandhi was seen as hegemonic, and in many ways, antithetical to the doctrine of non-interference in domestic matters. Eventually, the act spurned fears of interventionism among the smaller nation-states of the region. While India has subsequently sought to allay such fears by propounding the Gujral Doctrine, the latter has done little to facilitate confidence-building in the region.

Liberalism, Free Trade, and Regionalism

Can South Asia be conceived as a market space? Apparently, the spurt of new regionalism, occurring along with globalization, is based on the logic of free trade-induced cooperation, leading to a thick web of interdependence within a region configured in conventional geographical terms.

There is a considerable number of manifest contradictions involved in this process. First, the configuration of the idea of a region along conventional geographical lines is clearly problematic, given the revolutionary changes in the technologies of communication, which have sought to redefine the meaning of space and time across the globe. Given the fluidity of technology and the increasing irrelevance of settled borders to the transaction of a whole series of goods and services, the region, as conventionally understood, is not necessarily the most productive site for trade, commerce, and economic exchanges. Modern technology has revolutionized the notion of scale, and the idea of the region as a geographical category cannot be considered immune to its effects. Second, the whole idea of liberal institutionalism hinges on the logic of Pareto optimality, where states are willing to forgo relative differences in their benefits if all gain in absolute terms.

The problem with this idea is not merely its apparent simplicity—the belief that economic calculations are necessarily independent of security and political considerations—but also its inability to factor in grossly asymmetric situations, where the larger party lacks incentive to engage the lesser counterparts, while the latter lacks the capability to reciprocate the former in terms of both positive benefits and negative penalties. The South Asian case is a classic representation of this anomaly. India demonstrates lukewarm interest in SAFTA, since it has little incentive to dismantle the tariff structures all at once, and prefers bilateral free trade agreements instead. The structural asymmetry between India's economy and the rest of South Asia quite naturally makes multilateral arrangements more favourable to the smaller states, but their deep-set fear of being swamped by Indian goods holds them back. Reviewing the poor record of SAARC after three decades of non-performance, Narendra Modi (2014) lamented:

> Yet, when we speak of SAARC, we usually hear two reactions—cynicism and scepticism. This, sadly, is in a region throbbing with the optimism of our youth…. Today, less than 5% of the region's global trade takes place between us. Even at this modest level, less than 10% of the region's internal trade takes place under SAARC Free Trade Area. Indian companies are investing billions abroad, but less than 1% flows into our region. It is still harder to travel within our region, than to Bangkok or Singapore; and, more expensive to speak to each other. How much have we done in SAARC to turn our natural wealth into shared prosperity; or, our borders into bridgeheads to a shared future?

Why does the economic logic fail to operate in South Asia? The conventional appeal of Pareto optimality fails to satisfy the weaker South Asian states, or to assuage their fears of being overwhelmed by the stronger economy of India, despite assurances of far higher yields arising out of free trade to the contrary. Pure free trade considerations have little purchase in expanding the width or depth of regional cooperation in South Asia; the very dynamic of globalization and the scale of expansion of the Indian economy rules out unconstrained economic expansion within the region. On the contrary, it brings into being the logic of transcendence, the spatial extension of the organization to link it with Southeast Asia and Asia-Pacific states, by way of India's 'Look East' initiative. The very idea of deepening the SAARC qua the liberal route is erroneous, since it does not sufficiently take the structural disparity within the region into account, which remains a major argumentative blind spot of the whole liberal or neo-liberal thesis.

The inability of member states to cooperate along the lines of Pareto optimality, coupled with the disassociation of economic regionalism from the concept of territoriality by the virtue of new technology, have reinforced each other, and hindered the growth of economic cooperation. The neo-liberal logic of regional economic communitarization, or fragmentation of the global trading system (as seen by the World Trade Organization [WTO] regime), has failed in South Asia on account of certain specificities.

Limitations of Neo-liberal Logic

First, almost all the nations carved out from the region's British colonial empire since the 1940s have abided by policies of protectionism, and promoted import substitution to advance self-reliance and development. In effect, these measures promoted both trade diversion from South Asia and duplication of commodities (like jute and rubber) across the region, thereby limiting intraregional trade. Until 1990, when South Asia, notably India, introduced systematic economic liberalization, average intraregional trade constituted only 2 per cent of the region's total trade. Thus, the growth of trade in the region has not coincided with a corresponding increase in intraregional trade. SAARC ranks very low in terms of intra-regional trade, which remains below 5 per cent of South Asia's total trade with the world. This is in comparison to intra-bloc trade in the EU, which stands at a robust 55 per cent, or at about 20 per cent within ASEAN. According to a study conducted by the World Bank:

> Intra-regional trade accounts for only 5 percent of South Asia's total trade, compared to 25 percent in ASEAN. Intra-regional investment is smaller than 1 percent of overall investment. Due to limited transport connectivity, onerous logistics and regulatory impediments, it costs more to trade within South Asia than between South Asia and the world's other regions. Finally, there is little cooperation within the region on managing shared natural resources and disaster risks that threaten sustainable growth.[8]

At the 37th SAARC Council of Ministers held at Pokhara, Bhutan, India's foreign minister, Sushma Swaraj, clearly articulated the prevailing pessimistic trends. 'The statistics are telling: our region accounts for merely 2 per cent of world trade and 1.7 per cent of world FDI [Foreign Direct Investment]. Our intra-regional trade is less than 6 per cent of our global trade and intra-regional FDI accounts for only 3 per cent of total FDI inflows', she said. She lamented, 'We continue to face significant challenges in delivering food security, health, nutrition, and education to our peoples. All this goes to show that while we are doing well individually, we have not been able to unleash our collective strength effectively' (NDTV 2016).

Furthermore, intra-SAARC trade is also skewed heavily in favour of bilateral trade between India and the other member countries. Bilateral trade between the member states excluding India is negligible (Singh 2012). The available official figures till 2012 did not show any qualitative change in this trend. However, there is an alternative perspective here that deserves attention. As Shivshankar Menon, the former national security advisor of India, argued in 2012:

> The other caveat that we should bear in mind is the fact that official figures certainly underestimate the real magnitude of trade that is taking place between South Asian countries, whether clandestinely or through third countries. Anecdotal evidence suggests that the real figure for India–Pakistan trade could be almost three times greater than the official trade figures of almost $ 3 billion. It is an open secret that most India–Bangladesh trade is not reflected in the official figures. South Asia has the dubious distinction of a relatively high level of informal trade flows unrecorded and unreflected in official trade statistics. This suggests that natural complementarities do exist between South Asian economies and have already been identified and acted upon. (Menon 2012)

Nevertheless, South Asia, being essentially a developing region, suffers from some of the common problems that many other post-colonial states face in their mutual ties with their neighbours. The 'direction of trade' illustrates that most nations in South Asia, especially in India and Pakistan, trade primarily with the developed countries. It is only Bangladesh and Sri Lanka that import a substantial proportion from South Asia, primarily India. Ironically, these form only a small fraction of India's exports. Further, the countries have chosen to behave as competitors in the international export market, rather than as a comprehensive bargaining group, like ASEAN.

Moreover, intra-regional trade has also been held hostage to inadequate infrastructural facilities in terms of road, rail, and air services. Despite being geographically contiguous, the region is one of the least integrated in terms of existing rail/road/air infrastructure and safe passage. Further growths in the logistics sector over the past decades in these countries have been uncoordinated, with no effort to promote compatibility of the various transport systems, especially the railways. Eventually, it has inhibited intra-regional trade movement by increasing costs and security of delivery. The lack of infrastructure is a major blind spot in the SAARC initiatives that launched SAFTA. Further, despite the apparent enthusiasm for a free trade area, the SAARC nations have failed to provide transit facilities through their territory for goods coming from neighbouring countries. The critical importance of transport in facilitating economic integration has been admitted by the SAARC leaders. To quote the former Indian prime minister, Manmohan Singh,

> We all know when we talk of great integration, the transport costs, transaction costs, can become a problem to closer trade integration. So, it is quite obvious that in this region we have to ensure that means of transport and communication do not become a bottleneck to expanding mutually beneficial economic cooperation. We want trade expansion to become a win-win game. Therefore, easier transit rights, access to each other's transportation and communication systems can facilitate that process and that is what I was referring to. (Singh 2005b)

There has been no perceptible change on ground since the Indian prime minister outlined the promise. Sushma Swaraj in 2016 said that connectivity is central to regional development, and will determine how 'we meet our goals of growth, employment and prosperity'. In her words, 'As we seek to overcome basic problems of physical connectivity, it is important for us to move forward quickly on pending agreements on rail and motor vehicles. Economic activities, cultural connections, and people to people contacts will flow naturally from such connectivity' (NDTV 2016).[9]

The commitment to establish a South Asian Economic Union (SAEU) was articulated in 1998 in a report drafted by the SAARC Group of Eminent Persons (SGEP). The SGEP report proposed, among other things, a South Asian Customs Union (SACU), which would be an ideal forerunner to SAEU; it hoped that the SACU would be ready by 2015. As it happens with customs unions within accepted economic models of regional economic integration, all South Asian countries were expected to move on to uniform tariff and non-tariff barriers on imports vis-à-vis non-member states. The SAFTA came along the same path, and was put into effect in 2006. It was understood to constitute a major landmark in achieving the ambitious SAEU. However, SAFTA's contribution to intra-SAARC trade has been passable at best. It required that member states assign a number of products to what came to be called a 'sensitive list', which would be kept out of tariff liberalization. The hurdles faced by the SAARC's flagship programmes like SAFTA seem predictable. Even during its inception, despite obvious benefits accruing to all states, scepticism seemed palpable. During the first phase, India put as many as 884 items on the aforementioned 'sensitive list'. Complicating matters further, Pakistan implemented the SAFTA with India only along the lines of the existing bilateral trade policy. In the words of Prabhash Ranjan (2016):

> In 2012, under phase two of tariff liberalisation under SAFTA, countries agreed to prune their sensitive lists. However, this trimming was not significant. For example, while India brought down the number of products in its sensitive list by 95 per cent for least developed countries (LDCs) of South Asia (Nepal, Bhutan, Bangladesh, and Afghanistan), it reduced its sensitive list for non-LDC countries only by around 30 per cent. Pakistan shortened its sensitive list for all countries by about 20 per cent.

The most disappointing aspect of SAPTA remains the India–Pakistan conflict in general, and Pakistan's refusal to reciprocate the most favoured nation (MFN) status to India. Economists Nasir Iqbal and Saima Nawaz (2016) have argued that this is hardly unnatural. As they put it candidly, 'Contrary to standard economic theory, the common border has a negative and significant impact on Pakistan's bilateral trade in the region. Common borders are a barrier to, not a facilitator of, trade with Pakistan.'

Political Conflicts

Further trade liberalization in the region has been a prisoner of political conflicts. Pakistan's refusal to implement the norms of the SAFTA fully is based on the argument that liberalization of trade has to be linked to progress on the resolution of long-standing disputes between the two countries, the core issue being that of Kashmir (Pillalamarri 2014). Co-operation at the SAARC has often been held hostage to such differences between member states, especially India and Pakistan. Writing in 2007, the former Indian foreign secretary, Muchkund Dubey, had warned that by the time the SAFTA goal of reduced tariff of 0 to 5 per cent is finally realized by 2016, it may well become irrelevant, on account of multilateral FTAs negotiated under the WTO regime and bilateral free trade agreements (Dubey 2007: 1238). Another major omission of SAFTA is the trade in services, despite the fact that South Asia is fast emerging as a major exporter of services to the developed world. In addition, SAFTA pays little attention to non-tariff and quasi-tariff barriers imposed by member countries. While South Asia's share in the world FDI inflows in 2015 stood at a dismal 2.9 per cent, East and Southeast Asia could woo 25 per cent of the world FDI flows. According to World Investment Report 2015, 'FDI Inflows to South Asia increased to $41 billion in 2014, primarily owing to growth in India, the dominant FDI recipient in the region' (United Nations Conference on Trade and Development [UNCTAD] 2015: 48). However, much to India's chagrin, the growth in FDI in South Asia is propelled by Chinese investment in a number of countries of this region, particularly Pakistan and Sri Lanka.[10] The overwhelming evidence thus reveals that the negative trends have held sway. Pakistan and the smaller countries within SAARC have refused to remove the non-tariff barriers. Analysts attribute this inability as much to economic maladies—like the absence of appropriate institutional frameworks to control non-tariff barriers, corruption, and clandestine and undocumented underground trade—as to the persistence of political differences which refuse to counter the positive benefits of open-horizon trade.

Most scholars opine that the onus for triggering regional integration lies heavily with India, owing to its physical prominence, economic predominance, and potential strategic aspirations in the region. It is argued that just as intra-regional trade has been circumscribed by political misgivings in the region, India's leadership in announcing unilateral trade liberalization vis-à-vis its neighbours could infuse trust and reap strategic dividends. Further, it would also facilitate economic integration of India's geographical fringes, like the northeastern states. The issue of energy security also provides a point of convergence among the SAARC members. While these factors are likely to prompt greater economic linkages, it may be a while before they crystallize into economic integration. This is reflected by the hurdles in securing the oil pipeline from Iran through Pakistan. Ironically, while SAARC remains the most prominent regional organization, crucial economic projects have seldom taken the SAARC route, and have crystallized overwhelmingly through bilateral or multilateral agreements.

Community, Space, and Regionalism

Another way to build a regional organization is to understand where it could take the form of a 'community', by encouraging cultural bonds that dilute the coarseness of territoriality. But such community-making requires a politics of reflexivity and a constant accumulation of trust, which in turn demands the growth of social power structures bequeathed to such a radical redefinition of the identity of the region. Community-making is the most demanding of regional imaginations, for it requires a denaturalization of the conventional wisdom prevalent for decades together. Communities require the denaturalization of settled borders and a denial of the politics of exclusivity, which the post-colonial national states breed. The nation as a spatial imagination is remarkably strong in South Asia, despite innumerable contestations to its specific claims or privileges. One need not, however, misread the nature of such contestations, no matter how strong they appear. Threats to real nations do not threaten the imagination of the nation in modular forms. Each contestation encapsulates new claims to nationhood, with little political imagination to the contrary. All South Asian states are beset with serious legitimacy claims, and states like India, Pakistan, and Sri Lanka suffer from endemic secessionist movements which are ethno-nationalist in inspiration. The inherent weaknesses of the nation-building projects have turned the South Asian states increasingly xenophobic towards each other when it comes to the definition of citizenship and the articulation of political community. South Asia continues to build on the statist model of 'otherization', where the secured, progressive domain of the rights-bearing and duty-bound citizen is contrasted with the regressive and necessitous realm of the external, reflected in the kid-glove treatment meted out to neighbours in a climate of mistrust and fear. Tight border control mechanisms, rigid and effective differentiation between the insiders and outsiders, the citizen and the outsider, and the hysteria over migration and people's movement still continue to define the normative and cultural architecture of the South Asian subcontinent. The politics of difference remains an existential necessity for the autonomy of South Asian states. Exclusions are, thus, compulsions for these states. Such exclusionary practices tend to undermine the alternative community-making of the subcontinent, a fringe project that lingers on margins. Given the modular compulsions of nationalism in South Asia, its regional identity is hostage to the politics of will, as exemplified by each of its member state. The idea of an overarching community threatens the very articulation of the subcontinent along the principles of sovereignty, territoriality, and citizenship; community-making, therefore, confronts both memory and the present, at once. While it seeks to deny the legitimacy of difference as a condition of the historical possibility of separate nation-states, the transcendence of these differences in a new political project of late modernity threatens the sovereignty of particularity as expressed in the body of the nation. The weakness of the idea of a regional peoplehood, one that rises above citizenship and the implied distinction between 'us' and 'they', explains the superficiality of SAARC as a regional organization. Its inability to espouse any alternative identity remains its primary weakness, a failure that further strengthens the logic of transcendence.

Unable to resist the pull of territoriality, the political elite in South Asia have problematized their ties with immigrant populations living abroad—mainland India has embraced a diverse diaspora, a practice emulated by Pakistan, Bangladesh, and Sri Lanka all over the globe. The imagination is indeed fuelled by economic considerations. If, during colonial times, diaspora-based themes were largely dictated by political and identity considerations, often going against economic interests, the same tendency seems to be perpetuated in post-colonial South Asia, where developing diasporic linkages seem safer when away from the neighbourhood.

South Asia as Community

The community imagination of South Asia as a theatre of cooperation continues to be fragile, owing to the legacy of state-centric configuration of the subcontinent. There are several reasons why South Asia has not evolved as a community. The foremost of these is most certainly the unexceptional tenacity of the nation-state as a container for the political community. Successful territorial nationalism requires the neat binaries of inside/outside, rights/force, community/outsiders, order/anarchy, and so on, to be maintained. The configuration of a political community within a specific territorial container would, therefore, require harsh differences with others. The orderly, rightful, and prosperous life of a body of citizens enjoying the protection of a legitimate sovereign requires the others to be defined as opposites. This, however, is a myth, a dangerously false representation, for,

> [w]hile political boundaries may be continuously readjusted and redrawn, social boundaries are taken to be sacrosanct and immutable. The right to live in one's community, an indispensable plank in the agenda of human rights, is both self-evident and an evil-in-itself. I want to live in my community not because it delivers certain goods, but because it defines my identity.... Insofar as the state appropriates the social space of community, it forces the latter to come into conflict with itself. (Das 2003: 41)

Given the complexity (if not complete untruth) of each of these attributes that threatens to subvert the political project of nation-building from within, the oppositional character assumes even more ferocity, for the national security imaginary is required to make the states what they are not. The dominant discourse is, above all, a silencing strategy, a move to configure the territorial nation, despite its ethnic incompatibility. Borders become crucial for the consolidation of this artifice, despite the routine transcendence and historical abnormality. The South Asian states, therefore, display the obvious distortion of a coercive construction, a perverse tendency to define identity at the margin. As Samaddar (1998a: 58) alleges:

> Whatever may be the actual figures of migration across the border, the reality of transborder human flow has been so perennial and persistent and hence so overwhelming and real that the state has had to succumb to it. The state realizes that this is not only the territorial border, but the margin of the nation too. Either the glorious nation is today a thing of the past along the border, or this is a border village, thana, subdivision, district and province which does not respect the nation.

Moreover, to desperately preserve the stability effects of territoriality and nationalism in the face of multifarious struggles within, scapegoating the neighbour has become an indispensable aid. Referring to the state strategies pursued in the northeastern states, Das (2003: 87) argues, 'It becomes possible for the state to argue that any doubt expressed in this regard is externally engineered and manipulated by a foreign country.... This also makes it possible for the state to treat the internal "enemy" much in the same manner as it treats an external enemy.' Surveillance, counter-insurgency techniques, superior intelligence, augmented military capacity, and so on, perpetuate the problem rather than settling it. But even such routine tactics are believed to be insufficient or ineffective. They fail to divide and keep the lines intact. They compromise the flow, and deflate and succumb. Hence, the national security imaginary in South Asia invests in a strategy of total negation, an attempt to deny communication to people on the plea of security, order and identity. Samaddar (1998a: 59) fears:

> Out of this lament has come a reluctant acknowledgement that people on the border cannot be prevented [from] interacting with each other, that trade will continue, that brutal methods against the migrants will incur great displeasure on this side. Hence a method more than merely policing the border has to be found to tackle the problem. The state has indeed decided on such a policy: not on one policy, in fact, but three: *total demarcation of the border, issuing of photo-identity cards to villagers near the border, and border fencing.* Truly, a deadly combination. (emphasis added)

The imagination of the region as community demands transcending the identity of the state and its politics of territoriality by a new politics of reflexivity, for modernity cannot heal the psychology of fear. The promise of modernity and its 'exorcism of the demon of tradition', the reification of the state as the embodiment of the heroic man and a sacred site of his 'mancraft', the incessant homogenization of identities and the denial of differences are problems and not solutions for security. Samaddar (1998a: 63) cautions, 'States in South Asia have gone mad over migration, refugees, exiles and migrants. The state system is being subverted at will along the Indo-Bangladesh border, Bhutan–India–Nepal border, IndoPak border in Kashmir, IndoBurma border, and Burma–Bangladesh border.... It is said, "whom the gods would destroy, they first make mad".'

The promise of security lies in tapping the forces that ignore, subvert, and defy the territorial markers of control and power, and refuse to accept the received wisdom of the familiar historical narrative that silences any possibility for change. South Asia remains a theatre of conflicts, being hostage to a maximalist model of accommodation, one that requires total friendship from the other. Differences and asymmetries have no role here. The reflectivist model of accommodation, on the contrary, accepts, allows, and accommodates differences, by negating the normative desirability and practical feasibility of total friendship. Total friendship is the convenient ploy to defer 'real' friendship, one that allows meaningful differences to be negotiated without any arbitrary affirmation/negation based on a mythical idea of a common good. Reflexivity, in contrast, defines the self by some element of the other, thereby sublating both the rigid distinction between the subject and the object, and identity and difference (such dichotomies being deliberately biased towards specific categories). India's security then lies in its conscious recovery of a contra-history—a history that goes against the received narrative of territoriality, arms race, alliances, and crippling force postures. Only a politics that redefines the neighbourhood and reconfigures the innate pessimism of frontiers and margins can provide meaningful security to the people and communities. Democratization and 'heterologue', pluralism and communication, rather than balance of power, border surveillance, and deterrence, are the real investments to South Asian peace.[11]

Contrary to the expectations of radical visionaries like Samaddar or communitarian scholars like Ashis Nandy, the peculiar historical configuration of the subcontinent tends to rule out trust or community as models of cooperative regionalism in South Asia. The subcontinent remains one of the most territorialized parts of the world, with all states aspiring for exclusive models of nationhood and ruling out the idea of extended neighbourhood that may melt the distinction between right-bearing citizens and the outsiders.[12] The contrasting responsibility of the citizens towards each other and the South Asian people spells out the problem of evolving a regional identity that can transcend the modular or territorial notion of state-based identity in the subcontinent. The South Asian region is, thus, premised on a paradox: extraordinary sensitivity of state leaders to any intervention to domestic affairs from the neighbours persists alongside routine abrogation of the non-interventionist norm. Given the intensity of the citizen/non-citizen divide in the subcontinent, the definition of space as community does not even appear to be a remote possibility within a meaningful time-horizon.

Sub-regional Cooperation in South Asia

While economic cooperation at the SAARC remains hostage to bilateral, political, and historical issues, India and other member states have sought to redefine the South Asian economic space in a manner that facilitates transcendence to adjacent economic zones, and avoids the inter-state conflicts that besiege the SAARC. Thus, the Bay of Bengal Initiative for Multi-Sectoral Technical and Economic Corporation (BIMSTEC) has been conceived of as a bridge between South and Southeast Asia, and also to foster economic consolidation by avoiding the rhetoric of the Indo-Pak conflict. BIMSTEC, involving Bangladesh, India, Myanmar, Sri Lanka, Thailand, Nepal, and Bhutan, is an attempt to reap the benefits of higher economic growth outside the formal framework of SAARC. India's political differences with Bangladesh and Burma (Myanmar) have thwarted the anticipated gains of this initiative. As political relations are improving, however, better infrastructure and connectivity may change this scenario. While SAARC remains bedevilled by controversies over multilateralism and bilateralism, such initiatives will only gain ground in the future. This would, on the one hand, help further problematize the notions of neighbourhood, and, on the other, tend to bypass the political blind spots of the subcontinent. As China becomes more involved in South Asia, India's desire to move into Southeast and East Asia will increase.

India is not averse to sub-regional cooperation involving China, as in evident from the evolution of the Bangladesh–China–India–Myanmar Forum for Regional Cooperation (BCIM) out of the Kunming Initiative, a Track II sub-regional organization, formed in 1999 (Basu 2013). While BCIM gained a Track I status in 2011, the mutual conflict between the two Asian giants have impacted the experiment, as is also the case with the Shanghai Cooperation Organization (SCO), which admitted India and Pakistan as full-fledged members in 2015. Many strategic developments in the last two decades have rendered the fate of the BCIM precariously balanced at the moment. This region was seen as the converging point of the major markets in Asia—China, Southeast Asia, and South Asia. Dual objectives were prominent in driving the BCIM initiative since its inception: economic integration of the sub-region that would also enable integration in Asia; and the development of the border regions. The BCIM agenda evolved from trade, transport, and tourism to include energy cooperation. The idea of multi-modal transportation was also added with the focus on Inland Water Transportation and the promotion of port development and coastal shipping. In October 2013, during Indian Prime Minister Manmohan Singh's visit to China, Kolkata, and Kunming were identified as sister cities. The first meeting of the BCIM-EC joint study group was held in December 2013 in Kunming, thus officially setting up the mechanism to promote cooperation. These developments clearly indicated that India and China are prepared to work together in their common peripheries. The current BJP government has also expressed enthusiasm in the BCIM as an integral part of its 'Act East' policy. However, with the announcement of the 'One Belt One Road' (OBOR) initiative by China, the BCIM-EC has become largely encumbered as a sub-regional initiative. In 2017, China released a white paper titled the 'Vision for Maritime Cooperation under the Belt and Road Initiative', which talks about joining the China–Pakistan Economic Corridor (CPEC) with the Bangladesh–China–India–Myanmar corridor. The document envisages linking the two projects under Beijing's OBOR initiative through maritime routes. The plan is to link the South China Sea with the India Ocean. Beijing also calls the Bangladesh–China–India–Myanmar corridor as part of the ambitious design (Firstpost 2017).

But New Delhi is fundamentally opposed to the OBOR and the CPEC for its strategic implications, and weary of its policy-level integration with the BCIM. The CPEC cuts through those parts of Kashmir that are directly disputed by India and Pakistan. India skipped 'China's Belt and Road' forum in May 2017, making its opposition to CPEC clear. However, Beijing has continued building the controversial project, saying it has nothing to do with a bilateral dispute between India and Pakistan. The CPEC corridor, that cost over $50 billion to build, stretches 3,000 km, from Kashgar in western China to Gwadar port in Pakistan on the Arabian Sea. China is also funding and building several mega infrastructure projects, including road, railway networks, and power plants. China is looking for immediate action and commitment to the initiative (Firstpost 2017).

In the third meeting of the BCIM Joint Study Group held on 26 April 2017 in Kolkata, the differing agendas, purposes, and viewpoints between India and China became palpable. Indian external affairs ministry additional secretary, A. Gitesh Sarma, cautioned, 'We should be mindful of different domestic circumstances and developmental aspirations in our respective countries.' Sarma added, 'While we focus on expanding trade volumes, equal attention should also be paid to its sustainability. Greater access to each other's markets is desirable to achieve more viable and sustainable trade cooperation in our region' (Iyer 2017).

India is worried that the BCIM would only be instrumental in facilitating Chinese imports of natural resources and exports of processed goods to this region. India also suffers from a substantial trade deficit with China that continues to mar its engagement with the BCIM. However, India acknowledges the importance of development of its North Eastern Region and eastern neighbours as part of its 'Act East' policy, and its engagement with BCIM and the multiple other fora that all deliberately exclude China, such as the Bangladesh–Bhutan–India–Nepal Initiative, the Bay of Bengal Initiative for Multi-sectoral Technical and Economic Cooperation, and the Mekong–Ganga Cooperation. It might be prudent for India to critically examine China's grand strategy of trans-boundary connectivity before deepening its sub-regional commitments.

Given the geopolitical stakes involved, gains will not be easy to consolidate, particularly when it comes to extending sub-regional co-operation in India's northwest. However, the trend is towards encouraging such cooperative ventures, which admits to India's growing reluctance to limit itself as a South Asian power. Such efforts, while paving the way to India's rise, would further weaken the regional identity of South Asia.

***

The problems with SAARC as a regional organization are multifarious. But the point remains that India has a structural asymmetry vis-à-vis its South Asian neighbours. Indian role conceptions of power, wealth, and community are at variance with the present material parameters of South Asia. India's aspired power projection goes beyond South Asia, and it clearly wants liberation from the South Asian quagmire to play a more assertive role in Asian, if not global, affairs. Indian security thinking is clearly dominated by a status quoist vision of unifying the South Asian subcontinent strategically as a precondition to expand its influence elsewhere.

When it comes to commercial policies and the economic imagination underlying it, the logic of transcendence assumes even more clarity. South Asia as an economic space is too claustrophobic for a growing Indian economy, and the logic of scale, more than anything else, demands rapid integration of India with Southeast Asia and the Asia-Pacific, with or without the existing South Asian states. The structural difference between the Indian economy and those of its neighbouring states of South Asia is a strong impediment in the way of establishing a free trade regime in South Asia that would be truly remunerative and economically attractive for all the states of the region. India clearly prefers bilateral economic deals with its South Asian neighbours, rather than genuine economic multilateralism, for obvious reasons. The relatively weak and smaller neighbours want just the opposite. The pull of globalization has further compromised the chances of success for a liberal regional economic arrangement. The logic of the market, to which the liberal imagination and the present direction of India's foreign and domestic economic policies are inextricably wedded, militates against the idea of suboptimal gains in the interest of altruistic considerations. There is yet to be any compelling counter-economic reasoning which makes regionalism at the level of the SAARC, as it is presently constituted, an attractive option for India, in keeping with the meta-assumption of self-interest, or egoism as the driver of the liberalization policies, pursued in the different spheres of the economy as a whole.

Finally, the SAARC is structurally and historically incapable of transcending its self-image as a collective of sovereign nation-states, where the latter is deemed to be the only form of community that has a claim to being a legitimate political arrangement. The fixity and the exclusionary nature of South Asian borders rules out its transmogrification into a looser form of political community, which would radically question the inside/outside, or the citizen/other distinctions. India suffers from grave difficulties in its capacity for identity-transformation within the subcontinent, since the principle of territoriality as a container of national specificity trumps attempts at redefinition over and above the state. The neighbours have problems of community vis-à-vis India, and these cannot be ignored in fashioning a vision for regional cooperation along communitarian lines. In simple words, South Asia remains too state-centric to allow itself to be redefined as a community of people. India arguably has little incentive in such a move, since its existing conflicts over community remain intense and often violent, and any attempt by New Delhi to espouse a vision of a community is liable to be translated as socially hegemonic by the neighbours. The dilation of the state and the contested nature of community-state ties trump the community imagination of South Asia. Given the centrality of India in the subcontinent and the unsettled claims of nationhood in virtually all South Asian states, there is little realistic possibility of curving out a new South Asian identity at the level of a community that might provide a fresh conceptual basis to build a strong regional organization here. At least, India's unsettled historical residues of conflicts over community, vis-à-vis its neighbours, rule out such a vision as serious paradigm for regionalism in South Asia.

Notes

1. The most exciting work in this field spans over forty years and involves the two path-breaking publications by Deutsch et al. and Adler and Barnett (Adler and Barnett 1998; Deutsch et al. 1957).

2. See the SAARC Charter, point 1. Available at http://www.saarc-sec.org/ SAARC-Charter/5/, accessed 12 May 2017.

3. The New Cold War was a period of renewed superpower rivalry after Ronald Reagan took over as the American President in 1981, that continued till 1985. It was primarily triggered by the Soviet invasion of Afghanistan in 1979. It also involved the Central American crisis that saw a string of communist inspired rebellions breaking out in this zone, turning it into a major flashpoint of global politics. The New Cold War also saw war and tension in Angola and Mozambique in Africa between forces supported by the two rival super powers. For a lucid account, see Mann (2009).

4. For a detailed account, see the SAARC Charter, particularly, the 'Objectives' outlined in Article I.

5. For a very useful analysis, see Mearsheimer (1994). The most robust liberal counter-argument can be found in Keohane and Martin (1995). However, the functionalist and neo-functional literature remains the standard-bearer in setting the primary theoretical bets against realists, who reject the case for regional organizations.

6. See Mitrany (1948, 1965, 1966, 1976), Haas (1958, 1964), and Keohane (1991) in particular.

7. See *The Tribune* (2002).

8. See The World Bank (n.d.).

9. Sushma Swaraj described the problem in 2016 exhaustively. To quote her:

> The 'characteristic features' of South Asian economic relations like restrictive trade policies, lack of information, resource constraint and

dependence on external aid also contradict the idea of cooperation for absolute gains. Regional economic integration has already achieved remarkable successes in Europe, South East Asia, and elsewhere. Then why has our region been left behind? The problem is that our land, air and maritime connectivity is still very tenuous. Weak transport connectivity, complex procedures of customs clearances at the border, limited crossing points for entry of goods, onerous and costly trans-shipment requirements, and inefficiencies in the payment systems, all inhibit smooth cross-border movement of goods and seriously undermine the competitiveness of businesses and overall economies in the region. South Asia has the second highest intra-regional trade costs. (NDTV 2016)

10. According to the 2015 Report:

Inflows to Pakistan increased by 31 per cent to $1.7 billion as a result of rising Chinese FDI flows in services, in particular a large investment made by China Mobile in telecommunications. In addition, Pakistan will benefit significantly from the China Pakistan Industrial Corridor, (*WIR14*, box II.3) and the associated Chinese investment in infrastructure and manufacturing in the overall context of implementing China's 'One Belt, One Road' strategy. (UNCTAD 2015: 48)

The report also noted, 'If the implementation of the 21st Century "Maritime Silk Road" gains ground, an increasing amount of Chinese investment will flow to Sri Lanka, particularly in large infrastructure projects, including another port planned in Hambantota, as well as highways and an airport' (2015: 48).

11. Samaddar has written extensively along these lines. See particularly, Samaddar (2001a).

12. As the recent developments in the Western world, both in Europe and in the USA show, it is not uncommon for states to turn xenophobic, particularly when migration and refugees start flooding in from places that may not be culturally or socially congruous to the host societies.

5   Imageries of Space

Looking East and the Indo-Pacific

Southeast and east asia have been crucial to Indian foreign policy for a long time, though the articulation of the 'Look East' policy happened only in 1991. According to Pranab Mukherjee, who was then the foreign minister of India, 'The essential philosophy of our "Look East" strategy, which is now well-established, is that India must find its destiny by linking itself more and more with its Asian partners and the rest of the world. We believe that India's future and our own best economic interests are served by greater integration with East Asia' (Press Trust of India 2012). The 'Look East' policy is the first consciously articulated form of the idea of an extended neighbourhood, which has a much older pedigree in India's foreign policy discourses (Scott 2009).

One of the drivers of India's 'Look East' policy has been the need to overcome the fatality of geography. It is, therefore, primarily an experiment in space-making. It was originally born out of the need to transcend the constrictions of the given territorial borders at India's eastern front, to overcome the increasing obsolescence of the geographical contours of South Asia, and to revive India's historic ties with the Southeast Asian nations. However, it assumed over time both, a new strategic valence, and further spatial extension by opening up to the Asia-Pacific. Further, with the increasing assertiveness of China in the South China Sea, and Beijing's efforts to checkmate New Delhi in the Indian Ocean, the 'Look East'/'Act East' policy has assumed greater strategic depth. The articulation of the concept of the 'Indo-Pacific' coincided with the American efforts at re-balancing the Asia-Pacific, inasmuch as both shared the objective of resisting the growing powers of People's Republic of China (PRC) in this zone. National security has thus come to firmly undergird India's 'Look East'/'Act East' policy, and a plethora of government statements and actions, too, readily confirm the imperatives of maritime security of India's growing commerce in this region. In this silent transformation, the alternative spatial imaginations have been pushed below. The fact that India's northeastern states have always been a fluid construct of several cartographies was lost on the national elite, whose visions of national development took shape within fixed territorial lines.

This chapter looks into the various possible articulations India's 'Look East' policy may gather over time. I argue that there are three ways of looking at India's 'Look East' initiative, each underpinned by a certain conceptual orientation. The first is that 'Look East' policy might be conceived as an extended security trajectory, whereby India would develop a sophisticated array of security relations in Southeast and East Asia, with an eye to project India's legitimate power, and resist the growing Chinese domination of the region. The momentum of this policy would thus hinge on India's strategic interests, and the reward of this initiative would primarily translate in terms of India's security interests.

The second vision of the 'Look East' drive sees it primarily as a strategy of economic cooperation, undergirded by liberal or neoliberal trade theories. The rationale here is that there are prospects of large mutual gains to be derived from extensive trade and commercial relations between India and the Southeast and East Asian nations, extending up to Japan, and including Australia in the south. This vision is based on an optimism born out of globalization, and the pursuit of similar liberal policies by all the major states of the region. This vision is more robust compared to the realist, power-based understanding, and builds on the logic of absolute gains. Thus, the pace of cooperation between India and East Asia is not to be decided by how these states divide or share their respective gains, but by the actual volume of gains accruing from a much-extended level of transaction between the actors concerned. The security metaphors are either sidestepped or abhorred by the proponents of this view. They believe that the promise of India's 'Look East' diplomacy lies in multiplying the level of prosperity of the state.

The third and final vision argues for a communitarian reading of the 'Look East' venture. This argument links up India's 'Look East' policy with the Indian Northeast in general, and the issue of subnationalism in particular. India's Northeast policy has so far faltered as a spatial imagination. The 'Look East' policy provides an excellent opportunity for the Indian state to overcome the legacy of parochial territoriality. The integration of the Indian Northeast within a dense economic maze, stretching from Myanmar to Korea through Bangladesh, Thailand, and the new ASEAN states, might ultimately help this marginalized region to transcend the historical tyranny of fixed borders and allow its inhabitants fullest possible benefits in the process of economic exchanges qua the 'Look East' move. This view interprets the positive dividends of the 'Look East' policy in terms of investments into community building and soft-border exercises. It differs from the second vision in making its communitarian pledges a vital precondition to a successful economic transformation of the northeast region. In other words, the key to successful economic relations lies in effective community formations.

Which of the three conceptions of space surveyed in this chapter will ultimately shape India's 'Look East' policy cannot be speculated upon at the moment. It seems that the Indian government wants the 'best-of-all' kind of an approach, resulting in easy compromises, awkward bottlenecks, and policy indecisions. This trend is expected to continue till there is a conscious articulation of the underlying conceptual map, which may guide India's 'Look East' policy to its desired destination.

Power, prosperity, and community can be desired in equal measures, but their policy implications are expected to be distinctive, rather than coeval. Each of these frames is reducible to precise cost-benefit analysis in terms of Indian national interests, provided there is a prior unity over what these interests consist of. Till these decisions are consciously made, the power, market, and community visions of the 'Look East' initiative would keep playing against each other, generating complementarities as well as frictions. It is only hoped that with more vigorous involvement in the 'Look East' experiment, the battle of ideas would throw up a winner.

Redefining Neighbourhood

The region to the east of India has had varying degrees of salience in Indian foreign policy perspective. Historically, the ties between India and many of the present countries of South and Southeast Asia date back to over two millennia. The two regions were linked with India by virtue of ethnic similarity, through trade, political expansion by Indian kings (during the great era of South Indian empire-building in the eighth century CE), and due to the strong presence of the Indian diaspora in these countries. British imperialism forged this region into an 'India-centered strategic system' (Cohen 2005: 245). After independence, by virtue of its geopolitical location and historical position, India was expected to play the role of a stabilizer and peacemaker in this part of Asia. However, it was unable to play this critical role in shaping the destiny of Asia as envisioned by Nehru (the main architect of Indian foreign policy), primarily due to Cold War constraints. During this period, India's relation with the Southeast Asian countries, except for Vietnam, was strained. According to Cohen, while India dismissed Southeast Asia's economic capabilities, and was scornful towards the pro-West policies of countries like Singapore, the latter looked upon India as a potential major power that failed to come to terms with economic reforms (2005: 255). As the Cold War moulds were broken, India's foreign policy displayed a major concern about carving out a strategic place for itself in an increasingly globalized and dynamic Asia. It was in this context that India's 'Look East' policy (conceived by the former prime minister, P.V. Narasimha Rao, in the 1990s) was designed to repair relations with her eastern neighbours. It provided the much-required opportunities for furthering her national interest. Eventually, it also proved to be a getaway from the stagnant regionalism and economic cooperation, which was attempted in South Asia through the creation of the SAARC.

Positive engagement with Southeast Asia in the post–Cold War era began in the 1990s, when India became a full-dialogue partner (1995) and then a member of the ASEAN Regional Forum (ARF; 1996). Since then, India has regularly, though not always effectively, participated in the deliberations of the forum in both the capacities. Despite some initial setbacks, such as the Asian financial crisis (1997), the Pokhran nuclear tests (1998), and so on, positive factors, such as the pursuit of a simultaneous 'Look West' policy by ASEAN, have registered impressive progress in strengthening Indo-ASEAN relations during the initial stages of cooperation. The twenty-first century has seen more comprehensive engagement between India and the ASEAN countries. This new 'phase' in bilateral cooperation is based on a certain calculation of geo-strategic and economic interests.

According to G.V.C. Naidu, India has certain disadvantages, as well as advantages, if it was to be a power of consequence in the Asia-Pacific region. The first major disadvantage is that, unlike the other three great powers, namely, the USA, China, and Japan, India's involvement in the region has been minimal. Second, India is geographically on the periphery of the traditional Southeast Asian space. Third, India's political, economic, and strategic linkages with the rest of the Asia-Pacific are rather weak. Fourth, India's 'Look East' policy of engagement with the region has not been satisfactory: more often, it appears tentative rather than rooted in long-term strategy and planning. Fifth, India has failed to spell out its interests, concerns, and strategic stakes lucidly, which often results in considerable confusion, especially in Southeast Asia. Finally, India has failed to dispel the perception that it is obsessed with Pakistan.

On the other hand, India's advantageous position is because its involvement (however insignificant it may be) in the region has always been benign. Unlike China and Japan, it does not have to worry about its past. Moreover, India has always supported any regional move that was aimed at peace and stability—the creation of ASEAN, for instance—and opposed Cold War alliance politics. India never perceived a threat emanating from the Asia-Pacific (except China), nor did it ever pose a threat to any country. India's defence capabilities are formidable (its navy is the largest in the Indian Ocean littoral), and its economy is one of the fastest growing. It is the only country in the region that can match China in terms of size and military power. In a major shift, India acquiesced to support the ARF, a multilateral initiative. Because of these reasons, India is uniquely placed to play a significant role in the Asia-Pacific's balance of power. The recent period has witnessed a rapid growth in Indian interests—economic, political, and strategic—in the region, and there is a growing realization that developments in the Asia-Pacific do impinge upon Indian interests (Naidu 2000).

In a vital speech given at Harvard University in 2003, Yaswant Sinha, who was India's external affairs minister during the 1998–2002 period, outlined India's new inflection towards the Southeast Asian states:

> In the past, India's engagement with much of Asia, including South East and East Asia, was built on an idealistic conception of Asian

brotherhood, based on shared experiences of colonialism and of cultural ties. The rhythm of the region today is determined, however, as much by trade, investment and production as by history and culture. That is what motivates our decade-old 'Look East' policy. (Sinha 2003)

The policy was, therefore, both continuity and change. While recognizing the cultural approach as a way of rebuilding bridges with the ASEAN nations, Amitav Acharya emphasizes the departure. In his words:

But it is important to recognize that the 'Look East' policy was also supported by strategic and diplomatic developments, which changed the outlook of both India's and South-East Asian neighbours in engaging each other. These developments included the end of the Cold War, the settlement of the Cambodia conflict, the rise of China, and the emergence of new multilateral institutions in the Asia Pacific region. (Acharya 2015: 456)

In this chapter, I want to argue that India's definition of South Asia as a region would determine to a large extent its concomitant idea of a neighbourhood, extended or otherwise. According to the practitioners and experts, the problems of India's foreign policy with regard to the 'Look East' initiative stems from the apparent dissonance between its spatial conceptualizations of South Asia (as a geo-strategic space) and Southeast Asia/Asia-Pacific (as spaces of economic interdependence and liberal economic policies, or as spaces of market operations). While the geopolitical imperatives of India demand the prioritization of the power-based conceptualization of space in the subcontinent, the need for rapid economic development presses the other horn of the dilemma—to dilute geopolitical rigidities in the interests of economic benefits qua free trade and market liberalization. All the phases of India's 'Look East' Policy have emphasized the synergy between economics and security interests. However, this conceals an inbuilt tension in space making along power and prosperity terms, as what maximizes the interests of one may not necessarily be good for the other. In other words, the consideration of power and market/wealth might pull in different directions, which is contrary to the readings of the votaries of the complementarity thesis—one that sees economic gains and politico-military gains as mutually reinforcing, and that each must be used to further the cause of the other. In India's policy documents, and amidst expert opinion, one clearly witnesses both sets of arguments pertaining to the debate.

Space as Power

That security is an important consideration for the new strategy of 'Look East' was amply borne out by the speeches of India's former prime minister, Atal Bihari Vajpayee. Speaking on the subject in an address to the Institute of Diplomatic and Foreign Relations in Kuala Lumpur, Malaysia, on 16 May 2001, Vajpayee (2001) articulated his vision of a new Southeast Asian security structure that harped on the virtues of cooperative security in the region. Vajpayee recognized the enmeshing of a myriad of security threats that required extra-territorial solutions. However, his vision of security interdependence that liberally dealt with challenges of food and energy security, spread of global diseases, and environmental degradation was about expanding India's ambit of security in its extended neighbourhood in the near east. It was largely about non-traditional security threats that had to be addressed collectively. It also underlined the necessity of tapping economic and business opportunities so that some of India's structural problems like poverty and underdevelopment could be resolved. Yet, this vision smuggled in the idea of the military security of vital sea lanes of communication in Southeast Asia, through which vital supplies moved among a host of states. Security dialogue was sought not only to accommodate India to the already existing framework of cooperative security architecture in this region, but was also necessary to fight the scourges of state-sponsored and cross-border terrorism.[1]

A Security Discourse

The 'Look East' policy gradually evolved into a security discourse. In a sense, this was hardly a conscious shift. Security interests were always paramount for the state, even when it was seeking greater economic benefits by opening up to the East. While it hardly outlined this shift, there was a widespread belief that the two objectives of security and prosperity were largely complementary and required close coordination. For instance, Yashwant Sinha (2003) maintained:

> India's 'Look East' policy has now entered its Phase-II. Phase-I was focused primarily on the ASEAN countries and on trade and investment linkages. Phase-II is characterised by an expanded definition of 'East' extending from Australia to China and East Asia with ASEAN as its core. Phase-II *marks a shift in focus from exclusively economic issues to*

economic and security issues including joint efforts to protect sea-lanes, coordination on counter-terrorism etc.... (emphasis added)

Security and Economic Development

In reality, however, these two interests could hardly be completely at peace with each other. In other words, the logic of security, and the logic of development are not necessarily identical. While security can very well be conceived as a precondition for development, and economic prosperity can improve security by making available more resources to the state, these goals may very well be divergent as well. For instance, military security may require insulation and deterrence from great power policies that may be inimical to national security interests, as well as the long term geopolitical goals of a state that looked upon itself as a major power destined to fulfil its power potential. In contrast, economic prosperity might require close cooperation and flexible responses with a number of big powers that may not entertain similar security interests with India. Slowly but decidedly, the logic of India's 'Look East' policy hardened into a national security discourse that required a spatial imagination of power over economic prosperity.[2]

In an address on 'India's Foreign Policy Priorities for the 21st Century', the external affairs minister, S.M. Krishna (2012), said, 'While our Look East Policy began with a strong economic emphasis and content, it *has expanded to encompass strategic and security engagement* in the region' (emphasis added). The turn towards a narrative of security was complemented by a change in ASEAN's thinking on its own maritime concerns. As the Cold War ended and the USA began to withdraw its bases from the Asia-Pacific, a new multilateralism came to replace the earlier emphasis on inclusivity. This laid to the floating of the ARF, an umbrella security organization of the group, which ultimately accepted India as a member.[3] The ASEAN states realized that its preferred security multilateralism coincided with India's growing concerns about maritime security in the region. A security partnership has thus naturally formed over time.

This shift is ultimately the result of India's determination to stand up to increasing Chinese domination, which its mainstream political elites and the security community unhesitatingly believe threatens India's vital geo-strategic interests. As one of India's leading experts on Southeast Asia puts it, 'As Beijing extends its presence in the

Indian Ocean through its cooperation with countries like Sri Lanka, Bangladesh, Maldives, and Myanmar, naval presence in the Pacific Ocean becomes critical for New Delhi, for strategic deterrence against Beijing' (Ghoshal 2016: 159).[4]

Extending the Power Imagery: From 'Look East' to the Indo-Pacific

The idea of the Indo-Pacific is the latest space-making exercise by the Indian foreign policy community. Priya Chacko has shown the multiple positions on the concept, ranging from a muscular counter-hegemonic and strategic vision that seeks to checkmate the growing Chinese power in a region vital to India's rise; one that rejects this orientation to security and prefers genuine multilateralism, to one based on 'plural, open and inclusive' security architecture (Chacko 2012: 2–3). India has been participating in joint naval exercises (Malabar) with the USA, Japan, Singapore, and Australia. The maritime doctrines released by the Indian Navy also articulate an ambitious Asia-Pacific reach to India's naval capabilities. While the USA has welcomed India's role as a 'net security provider' to preserve maritime transportation routes and global commons in the Indian Ocean (Scott 2012: 89), both New Delhi and Washington, DC have refrained from institutionalizing security roles in a manner that might send overtly provocative signals to China.

Manmohan Singh saw India's relation with the ASEAN as a gateway to the Indo-Pacific.[5] The official imprimatur to a security-centric turn to India's engagement in the Asia-Pacific qua 'Look East' policy thus started before Modi assumed office. However, during his several visits to Japan and the USA, Modi had intensified the security dynamic that underlies the loose Indo-Pacific construct. Increasingly harassed by the Chinese, and with relations souring with Pakistan, Modi sensed that states like Japan and South Korea were too happy to welcome Indian navy to sail in Pacific waters. With a dithering USA, Modi took a gamble. According to Patrick M. Cronin and Darshana M. Baruah (2014), India's 'Act East' policy was a natural corollary of the Modi Doctrine that entailed heightened security collaboration with Japan, Australia, and the USA. It also involved investing in fledging security ties with the ASEAN, seeking a more vigorous role in the ARF, and bringing in the far away islands in Indian Ocean and the Pacific into India's security parameter.

Modi, in fact, worked hard to elevate Indo-Japanese relations to a new strategic partnership as the fulcrum of this doctrine. In his latest state visit to Tokyo, the Indian prime minister pointed out:

> Our strategic partnership is not only for the good and security of our own societies. It also brings peace, stability and balance to the region. It is alive and responsive to emerging opportunities and challenges in Asia-Pacific ... The successful Malabar naval exercise has underscored the convergence in our strategic interests in the broad expanse of the waters of the Indo-Pacific. As democracies, we support openness, transparency and the rule of law. We are also united in our resolve to combat the menace of terrorism, especially cross-border terrorism. (Press Trust of India 2015)[6]

At the banquet speech on 11 November 2016, the Indian prime minister put emphasis on the virtues of open societies, and their role in changing the prevailing atmosphere in this region (See Press Trust of India 2015). To read between these lines, the emphasis put on democracy, rule of law, dialogue, and good neighbourliness indicates an alliance based on values that include some categories of states but not others. According to analysts like Raja Mohan (2013), this proactive stance on the part of India meant that East Asia was now central to India's political and geo-strategic imagination. India's role was to counter expansionist designs that threatened peace and stability of this zone. His language was couched in metaphors that cautioned against the fallibilities of territorial conflicts that may destroy the developmental potential inherent in the region.

However, not all security partnership is about balancing out China. Security cooperation between India and the ASEAN states includes anti-piracy activities, anti-terrorism, narcotics prevention, climate, and food and energy security-related issues. India and the ten ASEAN countries signed a partnership pact for peace, progress, and shared prosperity in November 2005. The agreement outlines a multi-pronged action plan for boosting trade, investment, tourism, culture, sports, and people-to-people contacts. The leaders agreed to intensify efforts to combat international terrorism and other transnational crimes, such as drug trafficking, arms smuggling, human trafficking, particularly of women and children, sea piracy, and money laundering. Prime Minister Manmohan Singh, who inked the ASEAN-India Partnership for Peace, Progress and Shared Prosperity pact with leaders of ASEAN countries at their third annual summit on 30 November 2004, said that if the twenty-first century is to be the Asian century, India and the regional grouping must work together for a future of shared prosperity. Significantly, Singh quoted Jawaharlal Nehru's speech at the Asian Relations Conference in 1947, where he said that Asian leaders must work jointly to draft a new future. Further, the leaders agreed to foster closer cooperation in reforming and democratising the United Nations and institutions under it by making them 'more reflective of the contemporary realities' (Outlook India 2004). The four-page partnership accord and the nine-page action plan envisages their cooperation in multilateral fora, particularly the World Trade Organisation, and in addressing common challenges of economic, food, human, and energy security.

The ASEAN nations also sought India's help for training their forces in anti-terrorism operations. Despite essentially being a trade-promotion document, there is a strong anti-terror tenor to the agreement. Thus, for the first time, the security relationship with ASEAN included active training and joint exercises with an ASEAN group of anti-terror operatives, though at bilateral levels, India has joint working groups on counter-terrorism with many of the individual members. India and ASEAN also pledged to 'build institutional linkages for intelligence and information sharing, exchange of information and cooperation in legal and enforcement matters'. The agreement also seeks to 'explore developing anti-terrorism cooperation' (Outlook India 2004). Counter-terrorism has emerged as a cardinal aspect of India–ASEAN partnership in non-traditional security issues. At the 2016 ASEAN–India summit meeting, the Indian prime minister urged all member-states to evolve specific plans for cooperation in key areas of maritime security, counter-piracy, and humanitarian and disaster relief. In his opening remarks, Modi argued, 'Terrorism has emerged as a major global challenge that affects us all here. We have excellent bilateral cooperation with ASEAN members. And, we should see how we can enhance our cooperation at the regional and international level, including through support for adoption of Comprehensive Convention on International Terrorism' (Press Trust of India 2015).

India's emergence in the Southeast Asian strategic scenario is seen by the ASEAN in the context of the active interest of the USA in the region, the strategic partnership between the US and India in the region, and in the changing strategic relations between major Asian powers like China and Japan. The ASEAN looks at India as a countervailing force vis-à-vis China. In the event of China's resorting to impinging upon US military expansion, India will emerge as a force to reckon with. India's size, defence capabilities, and economic strength makes it a potential competitor of China. Thus, India's role as a key player is expected to be strengthened in the regional balance of the twenty-first century. On the other hand, closer cooperation between India and ASEAN hinges, to a considerable extent, on India's capacity to manage its immediate security environment in South Asia.

Most scholars stress on India's participation in the multilateral efforts of Southeast Asia to gain a proper foothold in the region. They see India's active participation in the ARF's practice of preventive diplomacy as vital to India–ASEAN cooperation in reducing friction and enhancing trust. India's induction into the Council for Security Cooperation in Asia Pacific (CSCAP) may be regarded as something symbolizing the understanding and thus, constituting an important step taken toward increasing bilateral cooperation with Asia-Pacific region.

However, the enthusiasm over the ARF-led multilateralism has not overwritten India's security policies in terms of traditional balance of power. Analysts like G.V.C. Naidu (2000) maintained that India's policy in this area was always predicated on a balance of power. In fact, there was no necessary contradiction between balancing policies and co-operative multilateral security mechanisms, though, in the long run, these approaches might become lopsided and may require extensive revision in the light of regional and global events on one hand, and India's security and national interests on the other.

India's 'Look East' policy has given India an opportunity to see its security interests beyond the Straits of Malacca. Indian naval co-operation with the USA broadens India's access to East Asia. Further, India's involvement in the sea lane security of the East Asian countries acts as a challenge to China's vested interests in the Indian Ocean region. The strategic importance accorded to India by the USA. was understood when the Indian Navy was involved by the Bush administration in the 'Team Challenge', a multinational navy exercise held in the Philippines in the summer of 2002. The USA invited the Multinational Planning Augmentation Team (MPAT) of observers from Australia, Brunei, Indonesia, Japan, Korea, Malaysia, Mongolia, Singapore, Thailand, and India. It was the first ever exercise by the Indian Navy in the East Asian security zone, especially in China's primary security domain.

India's foray into East Asia is a response to China's strategy of encircling India with a ring of weapon-client states, which included Myanmar, Bangladesh, Sri Lanka, and Pakistan, all of whom have been supplied with Chinese weapons. China has bases and facilities on the Hainggyi Island at the mouth of the Bassein river, communications facility on the Cocos Island (to the north of Andaman and Nicobar), and is modernising its existing base facilities at Akyab, Mergui, and Sittwe. The Indian navy released its major maritime doctrine in 2007, which articulated its vision of guarding the Indian Ocean and undertaking requisite modernization initiatives to play a more meaningful role in India's naval security. The new report published in 2015 reflected a more realist shift. It reiterated the need to carve out a role commensurate with the new global economic and military shifts to bring the Indian Ocean and the Western Pacific Ocean sectors into closer synergy and within a single strategic arc and to sail beyond Indian Ocean to 'Southeast Indian Ocean, including sea routes to the Pacific Ocean and littoral regions in the vicinity, the Mediterranean Sea, the West Coast of Africa, and their littoral regions' (Baruah 2015) to protect the sea lanes of communication and ward off various threats.

In its maritime doctrine released in 2007, the Indian navy shifted from defending the country's coastline from its rival, Pakistan, to declaring the entire Indian Ocean Region (IOR), ranging from the Persian Gulf to the Malacca Straits, as being its 'legitimate area of interest'. India plays a major role in policing the international sea lanes through the Indian Ocean. New Delhi started to expand its maritime reach by signing agreements with Malaysia and Indonesia regarding naval patrolling of the western end of the strategically important Straits of Malacca. The Indian government exploited the 26 December 2004 Asian tsunami disaster to flex its naval muscles in the region. In its largest ever peacetime operation, the Indian navy dispatched thirty-two ships, twenty-two helicopters, eight aircraft, and 8,300 troops to distribute food, medicine, and other relief supplies to Sri Lanka, Maldives, and Indonesia. India's strategic interests have increased as its footprint as a power has expanded. The new maritime policy of 2015 reflects the need to counter the growing complexity in its extended neighbourhood in the context of China's rise and the fraught situation in South China Sea. A successful 'Look East' policy promised much needed firepower to thwart China's projection of power into a region that is conceived as vital for India's national interests. Such a balance-of-power reading is not inimical to economic and other forms of cooperation. But the latter is invariably subordinated to the grand objective of India's acquisition of a much-needed strategic depth.[7]

The idea of connectivity is consistently appropriated by geopolitics when it comes to spatial imaginations and the extended neighbourhood. Nothing conveys this better than India's reticence and steadfast refusal to hitch its bandwagon to China's initiatives of the Silk Road Economic Belt, and the 21st Century Maritime Silk Road. India's foreign secretary, Jaishankar, unambiguously alluded to China's efforts in building roads and bridges as a tool to constrain India by sneaking into its neighbourhood. In 2016, at the International Institute for Strategic Studies Fullerton Lecture in Singapore, he commented that the 'One Belt, One Road' initiative was China's own unilateral effort, and that India would not commit to buy in without significant consultation. The Indian spokesperson of Ministry of External Affairs explained the Indian position along the following lines:

> We are of firm belief that connectivity initiatives must be based on universally recognized international norms, good governance, rule of law, openness, transparency and equality.... Expansion and strengthening of connectivity is an integral part of India's economic and diplomatic initiatives. Regarding the so-called 'China-Pakistan Economic Corridor', which is being projected as the flagship project of the BRI/OBOR, the international community is well aware of India's position. No country can accept a project that ignores its core concerns on sovereignty and territorial integrity.[8]

A careful reading of this and many other statements by India show that the strategic and geopolitical logic underlying a realist concept of space has come to dominate alternative spatial imaginations. While not opposing the role of connectivity, which is firmly located in a paradigm of interdependence and economic prosperity, the Indian position unhesitatingly prioritizes the claims of sovereign territoriality. Jaishankar took pains to contrast the new silk route from the old, describing the latter as a connectivity initiative for trade and cultural exchanges that had little political connotations. In contrast, he described the new Silk Road as a geopolitical tool designed to project China's growing influence in Asia. Hence, far from being an imagination of commerce or culture, the OBOR and New Silk Route are geopolitical constructs to either deter or hedge against American power in the Asia-Pacific. India, therefore, sees the Chinese connectivity projects as strategic ploys that would ultimately contain and limit India's rise as a power. Unresolved territorial disputes with Beijing and Pakistan's all-weather geo-strategic partnership with China have further reinforced this geopolitical framing of connectivity.

In fact, as rising powers, both India and China are investing in connectivity projects that are invariably tension ridden. There is an increasing balance-of-power orientation to India's thinking in this regard, which is best reflected in India's eagerness to partner with Japan to craft an alternative to China's OBOR initiative. Darshana Baruah of Carnegie India wrote in a recent paper, 'China plans to build a corridor of infrastructure projects across both land and sea routes connecting Southeast Asia to Europe … As China extends its influence and reach throughout Asia, Japan and India naturally are seeking to do the same' (quoted in Dipanjan Roy Chaudhury 2018). India's warming up to the USA also fits in here, as many analysts see the USA attempting to redraw the geopolitical map of Eurasia and resisting China's ascension as an economic and military power by courting powers like India and Japan, with which Beijing has long term differences and rivalry. India's policymaking elites and commentators see the OBOR and New Silk Route as both an opportunity and challenge. While there is debate on relative costs, the discourse is firmly laid in a geopolitical matrix. Whether imagining its neighbourhood in its immediate vicinity or far off, the Indian policymaking elites have remained committed to a conception of space as power, and notions of connectivity, infrastructure, culture, community, material, and symbolic capital are ultimately read invariably in broad geopolitical terms.

Space as Market

Against this power-based reading of space in India's 'Look East' initiative comes a body of research that is distinctively neo-liberal in orientation, and deploys the market notion of space to define India's extended neighbourhood as the ambit of her 'Look East' policy. This is indeed the highlight of the policy in the eyes of India's national elite. Here, economic needs trump hard geopolitics. The vision builds on varied models of globalization, some weak, some strong. The stronger version urges that owing to deterritorialization, interconnectedness, and an unprecedented increase in the velocity of social activities, the traditional or classical idea of state-led development has become impossible, both empirically and theoretically. Borders have therefore become meaningless—they are barriers to the free movement of (most) factors of production, and hence, they should be substantially diluted in the interest of trade and free-market activities.

'Look East' here emerges as a potential source and destination of huge investment opportunities, economic cooperation, and business initiatives, emanating from the same are what is claimed to be India's best chance to catch up with the global powers, particularly China. Prime Minister Atal Bihari Vajpayee, while addressing the ASEAN–India summit, declared that India was working towards eliminating trade and investment barriers, and advocated a trade turnover of $30 billion with the ASEAN by 2007, as well as the establishment of a free trade area in a timeframe of ten years. He listed the strong points of the Indian economy, which included a rich pool of English-speaking human resource, information technology, the Indian financial services industry, pharmaceutical industry, entertainment business, and the infrastructure sector. These strong points would help enhance India–ASEAN trade and investment. The then current trade between India and the ASEAN, which was at less than $10 billion, did not do justice to the combined population of 1.5 billion that produced a $1.5 trillion worth of goods and services annually. Laying stress on better connectivity between India and the ASEAN, Vajpayee said, 'We could see how close we can get with an open skies arrangement' (quoted in Shahin 2003). He announced India's unilateral decision to connect all the ten ASEAN capitals with four metropolises in India through daily flights, without further bilateral discussions. The framework agreement spelled out a programme for free trade agreements in goods, services, investment, areas of economic cooperation, and an early harvest programme. Taken together, these steps promised considerable improvement in economic and political co-operation between India and its Southeast Asian neighbours, extending from Myanmar to the Philippines. India and the ASEAN agreed to create the eastern equivalent of the European Union in the coming two decades. The Bali Concord II envisioned a single Southeast Asian market, and called for the creation of an ASEAN Economic Community modelled on the EU by 2020 (Hew 2006).

The Congress-led UPA government, which came to replace the first NDA regime, did not make any sharp breaks with previous policies. On 4 November 2004, at the third ASEAN–India Summit, K. Natwar Singh, the then foreign minister under the UPA-I regime, enthusiastically proposed exploring the possibilities of a broad 'Asian Economic Community', and signed an agreement for an ASEAN-India Partnership for Peace Progress and Shared Prosperity. The UPA-II maintained this trend. In the words of Manmohan Singh (2013):

> India stands ready for the signature of the India-ASEAN Free Trade Agreement on Services and Investment by the end of this year and its early implementation. This will complement our Agreement on Goods and bolster our economic partnership ... I also welcome efforts by the Federation of Indian Chambers of Commerce and Industry to revitalize the ASEAN-India Business Council, and to set up an ASEAN-India Trade and Investment Centre. These measures will contribute to stronger trade and investment flows between us ... India-ASEAN trade stood at 76 billion US dollars last year. I remain confident that we can meet our target of 100 billion US dollars by 2015 and double that volume by 2022.

The UPA government repeatedly emphasized greater connectivity as the way forward to economic ties. Singh took the ASEAN to be the cornerstone of India's 'Look East' policy, and repeatedly harped on greater physical connectivity between India and the ASEAN group of states to be the primary 'strategic objective' of New Delhi.

Economic cooperation between India and the ASEAN states have grown steadily, though the figures fade into relative inconsequence in comparison to China. India–ASEAN trade and investment relations have been mostly encouraging, with the ASEAN emerging as India's fourth largest trading partner. The annual trade between India and the ASEAN reached approximately US$ 76.53 billion in 2014–15. Though it declined to US$ 65.04 billion in 2015–16, the factors responsible were not peculiar to their economic ties, but concerned declining commodity prices caused by yet another slowing down of the global economy. Two-way investment flows have expanded rapidly, with the ASEAN contributing approximately 12.5 per cent of investment flows into India since 2000. FDI inflows into India from the ASEAN, from April 2000 to May 2016, amounted to about US$ 49.40 billion, while FDI outflows from India to ASEAN countries was about US$ 38.672

billion for the period from April 2007 to March 2015 (Press Trust of India 2015).

However, the prosperity model emphasizes the need to obtain Chinese cooperation in a whole range of economic processes and activities, and to use China to penetrate the Southeast Asian economies. As C.S. Kuppuswamy (2003) argues:

> Some political pundits are of the view that since India and ASEAN have a common aim of Chinese containment in the region, India should strengthen its relations with this grouping. There is no point in creating an impression that India is in competition with China. This is unnecessary and counter-productive. The economic potential of this region should be a more compelling factor than this subsidiary political aim.

Even the extended 'Look East' policy builds on the same idea: there is no gain in antagonizing China. Japan and Korea (and Australia) are additional (complementary) investment sources; they are not tactical choices to reign in an increasing assertive China. Thus, quite in contrast to the geo-strategic attempts to counter Chinese influence, there has been a simultaneous effort to normalize relations with China and explore the possibilities of cooperation. Bilateral trade between India and China stands at around US$ 4.5 billon. When compared to the US$ 3.5 billion trade with Japan, it illustrates the progress in efforts to normalise bilateral relations.

The strategic dimension, however, has cast its shadow on trade, commerce, and economic cooperation involving all actors. Thus, Zhao Hong (2007), a noted Chinese expert, concedes: in sum, ASEAN's economic success and mutual unease over China's rapid rise are among key factors that bring India and ASEAN closer to each other. Indeed, it is arguable that India's effort to enhance its economic linkages with ASEAN is part of its overall strategy to work with ASEAN to balance the increasing influence that China might wield in its free trade agreement (FTA) with Southeast Asia. The fact of the matter is that, while trade and commerce is on the rise among India, China, and the ASEAN states, there is no independent economic trigger at work which is impervious to fundamental strategic undercurrents.

Engagement with Japan is based on economic complementarities, as well as developing strategic convergences. In August 2002, both countries agreed on a global partnership in the twenty-first century, at a time when

economic sanctions imposed by Japan on India following the nuclear tests
of May 1998 were still in force. During her recent visit, Japanese Foreign
Minister Kawaguchi spoke of Japan's strategic partnership with India,
and India's pivotal role in the vision to create a pan-Asian economic area,
extending from East to South Asia. Energy security features as another
area of convergence among Japan, Korea, China, and India, as they
were by 2002, the second, fourth, sixth, and eighth largest importers
of oil in the world. Cooperation among these countries to ensure the
security of the sea lanes constitutes another priority. Under Prime
Minister Modi, India–Japan relations have increasingly assumed a geo-
strategic dimension. While, India remains the biggest recipient of Japan's
official development assistance (ODA), expansion of trade has been slow.
According to the data released by the Embassy of India in Tokyo, India–
Japan bilateral trade (in US$ billion) increased from 10.18 in 2007–8
to 18.61 in 2011–12, but had declined to 15.51 by 2014–15. The latest
figure (April 2015–March 2016) is 14.51 (Embassy of India, Japan n.d.).
In contrast to pure economic cooperation, both states seem to be co-
operating under the growing shadow of China, and prioritizing the logic
of security over that of liberal economic cooperation. Jayadeva Ranade
(2016) has crisply summed up the dynamics evinced during Modi's
November visit to Japan.

> Modi's visit to Tokyo not only emphasised the commonalities
> between the two countries and strengthened bilateral ties, but
> underlined the growing convergence of strategic interests. Maritime
> cooperation is a potential major area of cooperation. In the context
> of China's unrelenting claim over 3 million square kilometres of the
> South China Sea, both countries have a vital interest in ensuring the
> neutrality of air and sea navigation lanes in the South China Sea, and
> keeping them open.

India's achievements in the software sector, and those of the East
Asian countries in the hardware sector, offer natural synergies, which
are currently in the process of being jointly exploited to mutual benefit.
Here, the sub-regional initiatives for greater economic linkages may be
mentioned. BIMSTEC, Mekong–Ganga Cooperation, Bay of Bengal
Community (BOBCOM), and the Bangladesh, Bhutan, India, and Nepal
Growth Quadrangle (BBIN) have been forged for optimal utilization of
the region's resources, enhancing linkages within the region, and thereby,
serving as a bridge between the SAARC and the ASEAN. The BIMSTEC

has grown as a bridgehead between South Asia and Southeast Asia, and India had sought to derive benefits from the dual exclusions of Pakistan (South Asia) and China (Southeast Asia). It is noteworthy that all the sub-regional initiatives initiated by India have consciously excluded China. Thus, clearly, the overt normalization of relation with China has not dispelled India's fears of a dominant China's constant thrust towards the Bay of Bengal. The greater linkages with the countries of the Bay of Bengal region are to counter the growing influence of China in these countries. If India's extended neighbourhood is really about reaping the benefits of free trade, the exclusion of China makes little economic sense.

Space as Community: The Failed Cartography of 'Look East' Policy through Northeast India

Contrary to such realist and neo-liberal conceptions of space, there can also be a third spatial imagination of the region in terms of community. One can argue in fact that the best period in India's Southeast Asian relations was the one that witnessed the conscious deployment of a historically narrativized, cultural imagery of space. Nehru's exhortation of Asian values as the real motivational force unifying the two graphical zones in a dynamic cultural embrace was largely a cultural imagery. In the changed context of present times, the cultural argument requires a voluntarist account, whereby the participants—particularly the people of India's northeastern states, from where the 'Look East' vision should be actively launched—are neither to be understood as blind supporters of the policy, nor as the uncritical recipients of oddly invisible benefits of statist wisdom, but as actors legally and politically empowered to look east for and of themselves.

This section is an attempt to analyze how the 'Look East' policy has appropriated a certain understanding of the Northeast. The past attempts to integrate the Northeast with the Indian mainstream, economically at least, have yielded no tangible results. The focus has now shifted to transnational and sub-regional cooperation between India and Southeast Asian countries, as it is seen as the only way to bail out the region from its state of underdevelopment and political crisis. India can thus ill afford to bypass the Northeast in its 'Look East' imagination. The optimality of the said policy, in fact, critically hinges upon how the entire region is transformed by the innovative blending of a series of subnationalisms that straddle the sensitive parts of India's Northeast, Bangladesh, Myanmar, and Thailand. As visions, the community imagination is diametrically opposed to the realist reading. Unlike the realist discourses, it is non-statist, and hostile to mainstream security considerations. It is not fundamentally opposed to the market-based conception of space, as espoused by the liberals, but it puts the claims of community prior to those of the market.

There are historical and communal/ethnic linkages between India's Northeast and Southeast Asia. The Ahoms of Assam migrated several centuries ago from the Shan state of Burma, and also have close linguistic bonds with Laos and Thailand. The Chins from Myanmar migrated over the past centuries to Manipur; the Meities of Manipur have had kinship ties for over 2,000 years with the Burmans of Myanmar. Similar migrations have also occurred in India's Northeast from the Yunnan province of China. Connectivity here is thus not merely about creating physical infrastructure; it is also about connecting people by reviving shared links. Expanding ties with Southeast Asia can be facilitated by making the people of the Northeast a stakeholder in this dialogue.

The Indian government was prompted to change its course when it realized that India's northeastern states have long remained underdeveloped partly because of the inability of the Indian state to think beyond policy options embedded in static geographical frames. While the necessity of the rapid economic development of the region is unexceptionable, it is equally evident that traditional recipes will not do. Over the decades, the centre has invested enormous sums in this area, with little development to show. The argument for economic discrimination does not hold, as the central government's per capita expenditure in the Northeast has been one of the highest since independence. A quick glance at the map suggests that the whole region has a tenuous physical link with the rest of India through the Chicken's Neck corridor of north Bengal.

Many Indian policymakers recognize the need to refashion a new cartography of development in this region. Noted economist and Rajya Sabha member, Jairam Ramesh is of the opinion that the region requires political integration with rest of the country and economic integration with Southeast Asian countries. He argued that the different models of development adopted in the past four to five decades in the region—the latest being the heavy doses of public expenditure—had failed to work: 'If the initiatives to forge regional trading arrangements with East and South-East Asian countries through Myanmar bear fruit, that will integrate India and South Asia economically with the newly industrialized eastern bloc' (Ramesh, quoted in Talukdar 2004). But the share of benefits for the northeastern region from such integration will depend on how much of the trade traffic will move through the land routes via northeastern India, and who benefits from the economies of scale.

By mechanically investing capital in the region, no meaningful development can take place in this area. A large part of the money invested in the region is thus lost to spillage. The Indian state's developmental thinking was shaped by the existence of about 4,500 kilometres of borders with China, Myanmar, Bangladesh, Bhutan, and Nepal. The popular belief is that the constraints imposed by security concerns, illegal migration, and closed economies have blocked the circulation of international capital in the region. 'Look East' policy challenges these set practices in a number of ways. 'The economic integration of the Northeast with South East Asia', according to Das (2003: 347), will enable her to

1. 'liberate' the Northeast from its presently landlocked and peripheral status by way of opening it to the port of Chittagong and connecting it to the proposed Trans-Asian highway passing through such places as Guwahati, Ledo, Jiribam, Yangon, Bangkok, Kuala Lumpur, Hanoi, and Laos.

2. reap the economic and political advantages that will follow on its being linked up with the 'powerhouses' of the South East Asian economies.

Accordingly, India has undertaken numerous bilateral and multilateral projects for boosting connectivity between its Northeast, and Southeast Asia. The important ongoing and potential infrastructure projects in this regards are the Moreh–Tamu–Kalewa Road, the India–Myanmar–Thailand Trilateral Highway, the Trans-Asian Highway,[9] India–Myanmar rail linkages, the Kaladan Multi-Modal Transit Transport Project, the Stilwell road, the Myanmar–India–Bangladesh gas/oil pipeline, the Tamanthi hydroelectricity project, and the optical fibre network between Northeast India and Southeast Asia, which has been operational since 2009 (Levesque 2008). While work is underway on these projects, the pace is sluggish, due to bureaucratic inefficiencies and infrastructural bottlenecks.

The Kaladan Multi-Modal Transit Transport Project (hereafter the Kaladan Project) is a major landmark, which will connect India's eastern seaport of Kolkata with its landlocked northeastern state of Mizoram, by traversing Arakan and the Chin state in Myanmar through a newly constructed river-and-highway transport system. The project was conceived by the Indian government as a means to develop a trade route between its mainland and the Northeast, as an essential element of the 'Look East' policy. The Indian government expects the Kaladan Project to lead to increased economic linkages with Myanmar and the rest of Southeast Asia. The original plan conceptualized the Kaladan Project as a precursor to establishing a gas pipeline along the same route. It promises to provide an alternative route for the transport of goods to northeast India (Kaladan Movement n.d.). India has made substantial investments in the road infrastructure, for instance, at the second India–Myanmar border trade point at Rih–Zowkhathar in the Mizoram sector by upgrading the Rih–Tidim and Rih–Falam road segments in Myanmar. Apart from developing road links, the Northeast is on the map of the Indian Railways, which is constructing a track from Jiribam in Manipur, passing through the border town of Moreh, to Hanoi in Vietnam via Myanmar. Through these efforts, the Government of India has demonstrated its keenness to develop the Northeast (Haokip 2011: 4).

Land or Sea?

How may the Northeast benefit from the 'Look East' policy? Policy analysts argue that the region has to be physically connected to Southeast Asia, so that it can transcend the geographic constrictions of being a landlocked periphery of India and benefit from the robust economic growth of Southeast Asian states. But the northeastern states do not have direct physical access to the more advanced Southeast Asian states, for the region opens to Myanmar and southern China. Myanmar, with which India shares a 1,643 km-long land border, is the most critical gateway for the region to Southeast Asia. But Myanmar has proved to be an exceedingly difficult foreign policy challenge for India. It was, for an extended period of time, under military rule, and witness to a protracted and violent pro-democracy movement that had isolated it internationally. China took full advantage of its international isolation, and cultivated the military junta to the fullest extent. While India had sought to pursue a pragmatic policy vis-à-vis Myanmar, it could neither balance the Chinese influence and massive economic investments, nor provide the kind of moral and political support that the pro-democratic forces wanted from it. Myanmar became a safe haven for a number of anti-Indian insurgent outfits, and given India's vulnerability in its northeastern frontier, it could not pursue a robust policy against the junta-led government. However, with the return of democracy to Myanmar, no matter how large the shadow of the military over it, India's more restrained policy of non-commitment to Myanmar's domestic affairs seemed to be paying dividends.

The Indian policy towards Myanmar has always been a delicate balance between a refusal to renege on her prior commitment to democracy and democratic ideals, and maintaining good relations all the while with the government of Myanmar, since it decided to warm up to the Southeast Asian economies through 'Look East' policy. India's foreign policy objectives in Myanmar include balancing against China's growing economic and strategic footprints in this region, exploring the possibility of tapping Myanmar's abundant hydrocarbon reserves, convincing the Myanmar government to flush out insurgents from their shelters, and obtaining guarantees of smooth passage for goods and services moving between India and other Southeast Asian countries (Das 2010: 348–9). Reconciliation between Thein Sein's government in Myanmar and the Western democracies has augured well for New Delhi's foreign policy towards Myanmar, producing tangible benefits by way of much-increased investment in Myanmar's infrastructure. Myanmar's role is pivotal if India's Northeast is to take advantage of the 'Look East' policy. This benefit demands massive investments in Myanmar's infrastructure, so that the Northeast can connect physically with more prosperous markets of Southeast Asia.

Myanmar is important to India not only for much needed natural gas, precious metals, minerals, and critical physical connectivity with the ASEAN economies, but is also one of the major theatres for its strategic interests vis-à-vis China, which, in the words of one of India's leading defence analysts, 'has endeavored for centuries to bind Burma to itself, mostly in search of a southern route to India and the Indian Ocean' (J. Singh 2012). Both India and China have high stakes in Myanmar, and their competitive nationalisms have often clashed in this geo-strategically important state. In recent decades, China had a clear upper hand in this competition, as it took full advantage of the international community's isolation of Myanmar to advance its own strategic interests, investing handsomely in infrastructure and in building pipelines, connecting southern and western China to the Indian Ocean.

Both India and China see Myanmar as vital to their security interests, and India's 'Look East' policy is a conscious attempt to checkmate China's quest for regional expansion of its power. India took time to come to terms with the military though. With Myanmar becoming a democratic state, however, India's ties with this vital eastern neighbour have improved steadily. The significance of this relationship is not limited to the economic benefits flowing to the northeastern states; the attraction for Myanmar is that India could well become its gateway to the west.

However, there are challenges in the way. If Myanmar is uneasy about China's tendency to suppress minority groups and individual liberties, they are also aware of India's manifestly poor record in dealing with its own minorities and dissenters in the Northeast. Moreover, while China has invested in business and infrastructure development in Myanmar in a big way, India's parallel policy has been sluggish and lacklustre. Thus, while underscoring the significance of the strategic subtext of India's 'Look East' policy in Myanmar, one must also acknowledge that the competition between the Asian giants over Myanmar may prove counterproductive for all the stakeholders in the long run. A noted Burmese historian, Thant Myint-U, has also urged for more nuanced cooperation among China, India, and Burma that is expected to benefit all the parties. In his words, 'There doesn't need to be a new "Great Game" over Myanmar. Myanmar doesn't need to choose between India and China, and instead should seek to be the best of friends with both countries. This will be to the advantage of the entire region' (quoted in Naing 2016). Hence, empowering ethnic communities holds the key to success in this battle of ideas for Myanmar's support. Along with business and strategic competition, ingenuous political engineering in regions of unparalleled ethnic and linguistic diversity is crucial to India's success in Myanmar.

This, however, depends on India's foreign policy success in Myanmar, something that is never guaranteed, given the economic, political, and strategic stakes involved. Peace and stability on the Indian side of the frontier are also vital preconditions for this. While the political situation in the Northeast, barring a few isolated pockets, has shown much improvement compared to past disturbances, the costs of peace are exorbitant for all the stakeholders in the process.

Another variation of the continental approach will be to integrate the Northeast with Southeast Asia via Bangladesh. A noted exponent of this view is Renaud Egreteau, who wants India to move more through Bangladesh rather than through Myanmar. In his words:

> If we were to take a somewhat provocative view, we would consider the possibility of solving India's problems with Bangladesh by opening up the Northeast southwards rather than eastwards to Myanmar.... India has to think twice before planning a very close partnership with Burma/Myanmar through the northeast and, for the time being it would be more advantageous for the Northeast to remain a territorial boundary and not a gateway to the East. (Egreteau 2006: 160–1)

Egreteau's argument hinges upon the political uncertainties in Myanmar and India's longstanding difficulties in the neighbouring northeastern states. There is a lingering unease that investments in infrastructure will strengthen insurgencies and breed more corruption, rather than usher in the economic development of the region through improved connectivity with the neighbouring Southeast Asian states.

There is a second model of India's 'Look East' policy, which does not move through either Myanmar or Bangladesh. Instead, it seeks to go through the more conventional maritime route via the Bay of Bengal. This is historically the path taken by the Indian rulers to expand cultural influence in the region. Even the colonial encounter with the region saw vast migration of indentured Indian labour travel across this sea route. This, however, is not merely the view of a handful of scholars and policy intellectuals. As Sanjib Baruah (2005: 23–4) cautions:

> As it has been in the past, even in modern times it is cheaper and less troublesome for India to trade with Southeast Asia by sea rather than by land. The land route not only goes through a difficult physical terrain, there is a perception that the route is full of danger. It may be tempting therefore for India to build relationships with Southeast Asia that are primarily maritime rather than continentally oriented.

A maritime 'Look East' policy will bypass the Northeast, and connect with Vietnam across the Bay of Bengal through Thailand. Vietnam has been traditionally one of India's closest partners. In recent times, however, India's engagement with Vietnam has been elevated to a strategic level. Robust institutional mechanisms of foreign office consultation and strategic dialogue between the two countries are underway, accompanied by regular visits between the two nations' defence personnel. Naval co-operation is on the rise, and the Indian Navy has been supplying critical spare parts to Hanoi for its Russian-origin ships and boats. India's foray into the South China Sea has indeed given a new twist to its engagement with Vietnam as part of its 'Look East' policy, as it offers a firm geo-strategic foundation to a policy conventionally modelled on cooperation based on free trade arrangements. India's increasing presence in the troubled waters of the South China Sea further encourages this route. The Andaman and Nicobar Islands offer excellent operational advantages in this regard. As Indian President Pranab Mukherjee commented, 'These islands have the potential to be a springboard for India's engagement with South East Asia and the Indo-Pacific region. They can be developed as a significant trading, shipping and tourist hub' (Press Trust of India 2014a). This vision is attractive, because it involves less investment and fewer hazards, but will completely bypass the Northeast.

Power, Territoriality, and the Northeast: An Assessment

There is a built-in tension in India's 'Look East' policy. The first component of this tension is the official and statist position, which has remained the dominant discourse. The other is the people-centric alternative, which sometimes surfaces to remind us of the inadequacy of the official discourse in the context of the Northeast. The official discourse is based on the need for facilitating human movements between South and Southeast Asia, using 'Look East' policy to earn high dividends in a liberal economy, and satisfying India's interests in a vital strategic theatre. The official policy, nevertheless, invokes the commonalities and continuities of 'cultural heritage' as an integral part of the trade, tourism, and cultural exchanges in Southeast Asia. As former Prime Minister Manmohan Singh (2005a) puts it, 'Full advantage may be taken of the Look East policy of the Government of India. ASEAN markets provide significant opportunities for NER [North Eastern Region], particularly in the promotion of horticulture, floriculture, and medicinal herbs. Affinity in the cultural background will make our products acceptable and saleable once the connectivity is improved.' Jairam Ramesh (2005) had also taken a similar position, and advocated that the Northeast requires political integration with the rest of the country, and economic integration with the Southeast Asian states. But the share of benefits for the region from such integration will depend on how much of the trade traffic will move through the land routes via northeast India. While there are possibilities for the entire Northeast to seize upon its place as India's eastern *entrepôt*, it remains a conveyor belt in this imagination, carrying goods both ways, and dressing up smartly to perform this exchange. Further, these 'benefits' are decided by the Indian state, and there is apparently little that the local imagination contributes to in this exercise. This is a remarkably functionalist view of the role of the Northeast in India's 'Look East' policy, which uses cultural connections for economic benefits, and urges the region to be developed accordingly. Apparently, the Northeast's value lies in its capacity to serve expanding foreign markets in these countries. 'Cultural affinities', argues Das, 'are seen only as a means to an end that add to the "acceptability" and "saleability" of Northeast's products' (Das 2010: 351–2).

Not surprisingly, these state-led initiatives have not yet changed the fate of the Northeast. Attempts to increase road and rail linkages in the Northeast remain a prisoner to fears of insurgency, terrorism, and Chinese expansion. Thus, despite its potential, trade through the Manipur–Myanmar route has remained small and insignificant, with little impact on the regional economy. Trade with Tibet and the Yunnan province of China has not started yet, though India and China have agreed to initiate border trade through the Himalayan pass at Nathu La between Tibet and Sikkim. It needs to be noted that the trade routes between Arunachal Pradesh and Tibet are still closed in the absence of a border agreement, and links to Yunnan through Manipur, Mizoram, or via Myanmar, are yet to materialize.

The economic condition of the region remains generally unchanged. In most states of the region, the local population has not become an effective stakeholder in this newly-laid infrastructure, nor is there any qualitative shift in the way the state conceives of development as a whole. The 'Look East' policy remains as much state-driven as the more insular and differentiated approaches have been in the past. The 'Look East' policy is not seen as something that empowers the Northeast and makes its residents stakeholders in the process. As Thongkholal Haokip (2011: 5) puts it:

> Before meaningful trading activities can take place, the region needs to prepare itself, starting from agriculture, in terms of productivity. Processing industries have to be set up to manufacture quality goods which can be offered in international markets at acceptable prices.

The entire infrastructure of roads, railways, communication and air transport will have to be completely revamped... If this cannot be achieved, the Look East Policy will not benefit the region and in that case it will only act as a corridor between mainland India and Southeast Asia.

Sanjib Baruah aims to break down the notion that the lack of access to the ocean is the main reason for the region's persisting underdevelopment. He points out that historically, India's Northeast was placed along the Silk Road, which was in use as late as the nineteenth century. Along with trade of silk and other commodities, this route also facilitated the spread of Buddhism from India to across Asia. Assamese towns, such as Hajo and Sualkuchi, were important pilgrimage spots for Hindus, Muslims, and Buddhists, as well as trading centres (Baruah 2005: 213–4). Thus, Baruah says, 'Northeast India's place in trade along the southern Silk Road serves as a reminder that the region's recent history as a remote, underdeveloped, and troubled hinterland is neither inevitable nor unchangeable' (2005: 214). He calls for initiating serious discussions with regards to the opportunities and risks for the region from different kinds of transnational and sub-regional cooperation, which were being forged at a time when Indian policy was 'looking east'. Baruah has developed a strong case for a new continental perspective for the region in the context of the 'Look East' initiatives. He says that the political boundaries have often worked against border areas, and quotes Sushil Khanna, an economist: '[T]here is no doubt that the disruption of trade and commerce and communication due to partition of the country, as well as India's import substitution strategy of industrialization and gradual erection of barriers to international trade have disrupted economies that till 59 years ago were well integrated, and deprived the region of gain from trade based on comparative advantage' (2005: 219). Baruah cautions that downplaying the continental dimension may have adverse effect on region-building efforts, and may also frustrate India's diplomatic ambition of being a major power (2005: 225). He thinks, 'economic integration of the Northeast India with surrounding neighbouring countries ... is bound to open new economic opportunities' (2005: 220). Further 'transnational region building' can bring important dividends in terms of India's political troubles (2005: 221). Thus, a successful 'Look East' policy should have both a maritime as well as a continental thrust.

Scholars like Baruah, who are sympathetic to the people's perspective, urge that sub-regional initiatives are crucial to the economic regeneration of this cross-border region by bringing together the Northeast and the adjacent transnational areas on its east, like the Ganga–Mekong sub-region, the Bangladesh, India, Myanmar, Sri Lanka, Thailand Economic Cooperation, and an exercise in second track diplomacy, the BCIM Regional Economic Forum—a product of the Kunming Initiative of 1999. India, however, remains wary of China's entry into these groupings. There is, in other words, considerable variance in the political and economic resources committed to these initiatives. For instance, India is not enthusiastic about being involved with China multilaterally, even while it is working hard to improve bilateral relations. At the multilateral level, India prefers the Ganga–Mekong sub-region, and the BIMSTEC, which does not include China, to the BCIM forum. Thus, on the road-building front, while there has been movement in the building of the road through Myanmar across Moreh in Manipur—expected eventually to connect India to Thailand—there is less enthusiasm for rebuilding the Stilwell Road that could connect the Northeast to the Yunnan–Northern Myanmar–Southeast Asia corridor. As long as China is kept at a distance, and we remain blind to the long-term uncertainties inherent in Burmese politics, steps towards cross-border region-building cannot gain momentum.

The people-centric approach advocates a continental orientation to the 'Look East' policy, which provides a direct role to the northeastern states. Baruah claims that China has taken full advantage of Yunnan's geographical location and of its cultural affinities with its neighbours in its efforts to strengthen ties with Southeast Asia. India could do the same with the Northeast, and take advantage of the Northeast's history and culture as a soft-power resource. If the cultural heritage of Buddhism, Angkor Vat, and the Ramayana bind India and Southeast Asia, so do the community and ethnic roots of the Tai Ahoms or the Khasis. There is little official acknowledgement in the statist imagery that Balinese Hinduism and art forms are probably closer to Manipur's than to those of the Hindi heartland. While Southeast Asia's awareness of the Northeast is growing, the official narrative of New Delhi has no eye for it.

The 'Look East' policy was an attempt to resuscitate the ailing northeast India. It sought to do this by opening up the region. However, what does 'opening up' mean? Does it mean allowing free movement of all factors of production across manmade artificial borders? Or, is it about allowing local communities figure out for themselves how they wish to connect and open up to the 'east'? As Samir Das (2010: 345) argues:

> In simple terms, new policy rethinking has opened up many a possibility that breaks open the given contours of the Northeast as a region. More often than not, as we will argue, it contests—if not subverts—the official imagination. In a sense, Look East aims at 'liberating' the region not only from its presently landlocked and peripheral status but also from the governmentalized modes of imagining it.

While Das is right in exposing the tension, such subversion has not happened. The discourse of territoriality and national security has managed to silence the alternative voices.

In a sense, the 'Look East' policy was an attempt to liberate the spatial constraints of the landlocked Northeast. The thinking was to let the region grow economically by connecting with Southeast Asian economies. Connectivity and economic enterprise were expected to ultimately break the shackles of poverty and insurgency. However, this official discourse was, like all previous developmental models had tried in this region, a national construction that had little understanding of local traditions, and more crucially, no patience for alternatives discourses based on different cartographic imaginations.[10] The fact that this region had always enjoyed deep communitarian connectivity prior to the spatial transformation of the colonial period is kept outside the radar of the national policymakers. Every official discourse that talked about the 'Look East' policy in terms of benefits accruing to the Northeast took the lines on the map for granted, and was unable to take the necessary political risks for radical shifts in the spatial imagery of the region.[11] The Northeast was transformed into a space of national security foremost, with ever-tightening border control mechanisms practised by all the states within the region. Sovereign territoriality had to be secured against both internal disruptions and external conspiracies that fed on close kin-group ties. Thus, internally challenged nation-states cannot trust lowering their guard on borders.

The community imagination of borders, space and connectivity is radically at odds with the national security discourses of the state. As Karin Dean (2005) argues:

> The conceptual nexus of the political map can control, dominate, and submerge the life-world but it cannot phase it out. The naturally

connected lived space has nowhere to disappear. It can only become more resistant when suppressed or submerged.... The society has over a short time come to be associated only with the territorial state, and the territorial definition of 'society' has replaced the earlier domination of the social definition. The state through its territory, sovereignty and boundaries has in a relatively short time, particularly in South and Southeast Asia, become the all-defining arrangement for the organization of space.

Similarly, Sanjib Baruah argues that a genuine Northeast-based 'Look East' policy needs to be risk-taking, and cannot fall hostage to a narrow security mentality, which seems completely out of step with the demands of the contemporary global economic forces (Baruah 2005: 37–8).

Security analysts have rejected such a bold no-holds-barred approach to borders and movements. Thus, they securitize connectivity and mobility. While praising the Modi government's decision to link up the India–Myanmar–Thailand trilateral highway with 'a grid of 27 East–West and North–South four-lane corridors', an army officer cautions, 'While economic cooperation with Myanmar needs to be directed particularly to Myanmar's western region and north-western areas being adjacent to north-eastern areas of India, the IMT Highway passes through hotbeds of insurgencies; Sagaing Division in west Myanmar and Moreh in Chandel district of Manipur' (Katoch 2016). Nothing can describe the malaise better. The national-security state of India evinces little confidence in the logic of the 'habitus' as a lived social space. Its insecurity in the Northeast does not allow it to come out of the shell. The Northeast, therefore, remains the black hole of sovereign territoriality, and the unceasing desperation to master it has subverted the communitarian imagination under the jackboot.

The three cartographies operating in the region are distinct in their operational codes. The economic logic of the 'Look East' policy demands mobility, the security imperative calls for surveillance and regulation of flows, while the community imagination wishes to rescue the social space from the clutches of the territorial state. If the 'Look East' policy is to live up to its potential of becoming the Northeast's road to peace and prosperity, it has to have a robust continental thrust and include a clear vision of a transnational region-building project. That can only be done with greater synchronization of our foreign policies towards China, Myanmar, and the ASEAN, and our domestic policies towards northeast India. In short, a genuinely radical 'Look East' policy demands a re-articulation of the settled parameters of space by redefining it as habitus and as flow. This, however, seems to be beyond the capacity of the Indian state to deliver. Hence, India's 'Look East' policy, in its imaginative best, would most likely vacillate between the conventional spatial idioms of geopolitics and a form of liberalism coexistent with the cartographic certainties of our times.

The Indo-Pacific

India's 'Look East'/'Act East' policy has gradually assumed a new maritime shape where oceans have become vital to India's national interests. The concept of the Indo-Pacific will have to be understood in the light of India's manifold maritime interests in the Indian Ocean that now extends well into the Pacific. The Bay of Bengal region is in fact the gateway to this newly extended maritime space. Crucially, oceans are also spaces, and therefore, subject to meanings and constructions. Dennis Rumley, Timothy Doyle, and Sanjay Chaturvedi indicated that there were distinct connotations to the IOR and Indo-Pacific as constructs. One related to the ocean and its littoral states, where concerns of human security, economic development, ecology, and sea bed usage made it a fit case to be placed under the Indian Ocean Rim Association that seeks to demilitarize security, without derecognizing the valence of safety. Accordingly, the Indian Ocean Rim Association has taken a more holistic vision of ocean security, development, and connectivity, involving both and state and civil society representatives, and emphasized the civilian aspects of security against a military-centric one.[12] The 'Indo-Pacific' idea, in contrast, refers to a 'strategic system' covering 'the trade routes and sea lanes that cross the Indian Ocean itself, but also extend past the Straits of Malacca and the Sunda and Lombok Straits into the South China Sea and north to China, Taiwan, Korea, and Japan, and indeed on the west coast of North America. As trade highways, these routes are arguably the most important in the world today, and the "choke points" and contested waterways along the highway attract critical attention of the "hard security" kind'. (Rumley, Doyle, and Chaturvedi 2013: 2–3). For Bisley and Phillips, likewise, Indo-Pacific is the result of the growing commercial and naval ambitions of China and India, and the resultant strategic competition on the one hand, and the importance of the Indian Ocean as 'an "energy superhighway", binding together the fates of societies on the littorals of both oceans and broadening the relevant strategic geography of states formerly focused only on their immediate regions' (Bisley and Phillips 2012), on the other. The strategic reading of the Indo-Pacific is particularly emphasized by Brewster who sees this as a mental map to transcend the constraints of the Indian Ocean in both strategic and commercial terms. Brewester says, 'India's Look East/Act East policy reflects an expansion of Delhi's strategic interests eastwards into the western Pacific Ocean, just as Beijing's Maritime Silk Route/One Belt One Road strategies reflect the expansion of China's area of strategic interest into the Indian Ocean' (Brewster 2017: 287–8). This is in line with his hypothesis that the Indo-Pacific connotes limits of Chinese maritime power as other littoral states are invariably gravitated towards the USA and India. The manifest Chinese vulnerability in the far flung waters strengthens India's strategic resolve to contain Beijing's growing interests in the Indian Ocean (2015: 57).

Brewester makes the vital point that the traditional understanding of the Indian Ocean as an enclosed sea having closely guarded sea lanes, stands fundamentally transformed by the security interdependence between the two oceans inherent to the idea of the Indo-Pacific, thereby making it impossible to contemplate unilateral domination of the oceanic space. (2015: 287–8). Is the Indo-Pacific a unified strategic or geopolitical space in the making, or a complex terrain marked by many differentiations? While scholars remain divided, even those critical of militarizing the oceanic space tend to agree on the geopolitical reading of the idea.[13] The increasing embrace of the concept by India marks a steady geo-political shift in its mental map of the oceanic space. This shift is brilliantly articulated by Dhruva Jaishankar. He takes the concept to indicate three things for India. First, like Brewester, he finds in the concept the idea of the two oceans making a shared geostrategic space, creating strong security interdependence between states. Second, it indicates the shift of geopolitical competition from land to the sea. This automatically makes the control of the maritime space crucial to virtually all domains. It signals an imperative for India to emerge as a naval power and act on its capabilities. Third, India's central location at the confluence of the two oceanic systems, and given its rise as a major economic and naval power with significant capabilities, it automatically becomes 'the geopolitical keystone of the Indian Ocean' (Jaishankar 2017). Moreover, India has also been playing a more active role in humanitarian and disaster relief operations. These have often focused on rescuing citizens of India from conflict zones, although India has helped citizens of many other countries in the process. A recent example in the IOR is Operation Raahat in Yemen (Sakhuja 2015). India has also extended disaster relief to other countries, including assistance to Indonesia and Sri Lanka following the 2004 tsunami, to Myanmar after Cyclone Nargis, to Bangladesh after Cyclone Sidr, and to Sri Lanka after Cyclone Roanu. Relative to other countries in the region, India has advantages in terms of capabilities. These include better maritime domain awareness, and military equipment in the form of transport aircraft, helicopters, and support vessels that can help deliver food, water, and medical supplies (Parmar 2012).

***

This chapter, in line with my basic argument, has deployed the three frames of power, market, and community to make sense of India's evolving 'Look East' to 'Act East' policy. The chapter finds that originally India sought economic dividends by opening up to the Southeast Asian states with which it shared ancient historical and cultural ties. Politics, however, drove them apart. Despite broadly comparable post-colonial experiences, India drifted away from these states as foreign policy and developmental priorities were conceived differently. India's non-alignment and the pro-market policies of the ASEAN states prevented full-scale normalization of ties for a long time. After globalization and India's economic liberalization in the early 1990s, the differences started to recede. India articulated its Look East policy as a way of redefining its neighbourhood, as Southeast Asia afforded enormous potential in terms of economic and business cooperation. Hence, the first moment of the 'Look East' drive was indeed economic. Yet, as is evident in other theatres as well, India's spatial imagination ultimately returned to its more familiar moorings, and the 'Look East' policy also took to more strategic direction. India's great power ambitions coupled with the rise of China came to script this policy. The familiar national security metaphors were increasingly deployed as the policy evolved over time and India became increasingly enmeshed in the existing strategic architecture in this region. The ambit of the policy also expanded as India started strategic negotiations with the far flung Asia-Pacific states. Ultimately, the geopolitical thrust pushed the 'Look East' policy forward. As Modi assumed office, this strategic outlook assumed greater confidence and boldness. The increasing geopolitical contest in the region over unresolved sovereignty issues further accentuated this trend. As China became more aggressive over its claims in the South China Sea, the psychology and memory of unresolved territorial conflicts between New Delhi and Beijing came to underwrite the subtext of India's power-laden imagination of its extended neighbourhood in the east. The nebulous notion of the Indo-Pacific, though apparently couched in terms of economic benefits for all stakeholders, continuously threw in geopolitical references. The narrative that took shape underscored the vital significance of power and shared strategic interests among a host of states that had unresolved tensions with China. Hence, the power imagination had trumped the market understanding of space.

If liberals prevailed, the extent of cooperation between India and East Asia was to be decided by notional benefits accruing to all actors measured in actual volume of trade resulting from transactions between the actors concerned. The security-centric understanding, however, elbowed out a full-blown liberal imagination of this policy. Rather than enhanced prosperity for everyone, the emphasis gradually shifted to hedging and relative gains, as security interests came to be regarded as paramount. This chapter also surveyed the 'communitarian' impulse underlying this new vision of neighbourhood. The 'Look East' policy could have liberated the landlocked and economically underdeveloped northeastern states from the cruel fate of closed borders that have no bearing with the logic of development. The integration of the Northeast with the neighbouring countries by moving through Burma, Bangladesh, Thailand, and the new ASEAN states, was indeed an important motivation of the policy planners. This imagination, however, requires bold initiatives, and challenging the logic of territoriality and sovereignty. It needed imaginative gambling into community building and soft border experiments. This needed the logic of economic transformation of the eastern region to work through a communitarian understanding of space. Unless communities were factored in on their own terms, the 'Look East' policy would be as alien to this region as other developmental models of the past. The success of this initiative depended on how it configured an imaginative blending of a series of subnationalisms that straddle the sensitive parts of India's northeast, Bangladesh, Myanmar, and Thailand. Community and geopolitical imaginations are contradictory imageries of space. While the logic of community is not entirely opposed to that of prosperity, the underlying drivers are distinct. This chapter concludes that the political elite who formulated this new imagination rhetorically kept playing the power, market, and community images against each other, as each brought categorical benefits to particular stakeholders. However, at the end, the strategic or security-centric vision evolved as the dominant cartography underlying India's extended neighbourhood in East and Southeast Asia. As in South Asia, the conceptions of space and politics rooted in sovereign territoriality ruled out alternatives based on market prosperity and cultural community. The alternatives retain their rhetorical purposes. The momentum, however, is undeniably strategic.

Notes

1. That security is an important consideration for the new strategy of 'Look East' was amply borne out by the speeches of India's former prime minister, Atal Bihari Vajpayee. Speaking on the subject in an address to the Institute of Diplomatic and Foreign Relations in Kuala Lumpur, Malaysia, on 16 May 2001, Vajpayee (2001) argued,

> The security dialogue between India and ASEAN is, therefore, of utmost importance. Threats like religious extremism, drug trafficking, money laundering and terrorism have cast a dark shadow over our region. India has been a victim of state-sponsored and cross-border terrorism seeking to redraw national boundaries. Such violence in the name of holy war is a grave menace, especially to pluralistic societies.

2. Anil Wadhwa, India's secretary (East), in a speech titled 'Security and Defence within the Framework of the Look East Policy', explained the shift in categorical terms:

> The dangers posed by potential flash points, the rising defence expenditure, investment in anti-access/area denial capabilities as well as other asymmetric capabilities further define the complex environment within which India has to secure its defence and strategic ties with the region.... In such a scenario, we need to see the evolving security architecture in the region through the prism of India's security and development interests. India's primary interest is to create an enabling external environment for the economic progress of the country as well as to enable it to attain its rightful place at the 'top table' of the region. This requires a peaceful periphery and a stable international environment.... India's security parameter radiates out in concentric circles, and ASEAN is part of the first circle beyond our immediate boundaries. There is, therefore, an intrinsic security dimension to our Look East Policy, and ASEAN is the first stepping stone towards it. (Wadhwa 2014)

3. According to Amitav Acharya, 'While India had to wait for two years before it was accepted into the ARF, the new framework of "cooperative security" gave it an opening to advance its "Look East" policy beyond its initial economic focus' (Acharya 2015: 458).

4. Mohan Malik (2016), a noted strategic analyst, harbours similar views. In his words:

> As part of its 'Act East' policy that dovetails with the 'U.S. rebalance' and Japan's 'Proactive Contribution to Peace', India has increased coordination, both military and diplomatic, with East and Southeast nations that also see China as a threat. New Delhi is currently negotiating the sale of the BrahMos cruise missile to Vietnam and frigates and patrol craft to the Philippines, while also forging military-to-military ties and economic and trade links with Indonesia, Malaysia, Thailand, and Singapore.

5. The then Indian Prime Minister maintained,

> We see our partnership with ASEAN not merely as a reaffirmation of ties with neighbouring countries or as an instrument of economic development, but also as an integral part of our vision of a stable, secure and prosperous Asia and its surrounding Indian Ocean and Pacific regions. Our future is inter-linked and a stable, secure and prosperous Indo–Pacific region is crucial for our own progress and prosperity. (M. Singh 2012)
>
> The Secretary East further corroborated the underlying security narrative in unambiguous terms. He spoke of India's participation in the ongoing security dialogue, New Delhi's whole-hearted commitment to build a co-operative security architecture built on security co-operation, and the need to stand up against hegemony and provocations. (Singh 2013)

6. Media statement by prime minister during his visit to Japan (11 November 2016).

7. As G.V.C. Naidu (2013: 66) points out:

> Through what began in the early 1990s as an effort to allay a few Southeast Asian countries' concerns over the Indian naval expansion, India's defence interactions with East Asian nations have witnessed remarkable transformation over the years. One can clearly see the beginning of a new activist policy that has never been seen before. In fact, defence and strategic links appear to be more robust than economic or political aspects of India's Look East policy, if one looks at the scale and degree of the agreements and interactions.

8. See Ministry of External Affairs (2017).

9. The Trans-Asian Highway is a proposed network of roads extending from Tokyo to the border with Bulgaria, to the west of Turkey, passing through North and South Koreas, China, and other countries in Southeast, Central, and South Asia. The corridor is expected to improve trade links between East Asian countries, India, and Europe.

10. In a comprehensive survey of the nexus between development and security tragedies in the northeastern region, Gurudas Das has corroborated this fundamental fallacy.

11. In the words of Robert Haokip:

> The national government, thus, largely controls this space and its people who are considered to be rebellious under the garb of national security threat, insulating them along what are considered to be very 'sensitive' international borders through border fencing and strict vigil by security forces.... This is primarily because India looks towards the 'East' but not through its 'northeast', coupled with its attachment to post-colonial territoriality which has continually placed the region in a seized situation. (Haokip 2015: 202, 203)

12. The IORA documents bear this out:

> Recognising that a safe and secure Indian Ocean is important for socio economic development, IORA assigned Maritime Safety and Security (MSS) in 2012 as the top priority area of focus. The importance of the Indian Ocean as a major transit area for international trade that carries half of the world's container ships, one third of the world's bulk cargo traffic, and two thirds of the world's oil shipments requires attention and strategies for Maritime Security, includes elements of international peace and security, sovereignty/territorial integrity/political independence, security from crimes at sea, security of resources and environmental security; while Maritime Safety is concerned with training (both technical and personnel), transport, construction and equipment related issues, assistance in distress situations, etc. (Indian Ocean Rim Association n.d.)

13. In terms of economic space, however, the Asia-Pacific has a degree of 'economic coherence'. While the Pacific and Indian Oceans should be regarded as 'strategically linked', the Indo–Pacific Region should be viewed as a strategic space that is not 'integrated', but rather one that is evolving 'gradually and partially' (Rumley, Doyle, and Chaturvedi 2013: 6).

Conclusion

THIS BOOK HAS ASKED three questions about India's spatial imagination of South Asia as a region. First, what conception of space underlies India's vision of its neighbourhood? Second, who articulates this vision? And third, what are the consequences of this dominant imagination?

In order to answer the first question, it was necessary to distil the existing literature on territorial space across a variety of traditions. Each of these adds something to our understanding of space. Thus, political theory asks the vital question of what territory means and the possible justifications available to it. Territory has both a property and a jurisdictional rationale. In modern times, states have claimed territory on the ground of jurisdiction. However, the arbitrariness of borders and their ethical justifications continue to haunt us. Can states restrict entry at borders? Whose justification must it seek if it wants such powers of regulation for itself? While popular sovereignty in an age of democracy complicates the moral basis of any claim by a state to unilaterally control borders, most states continue to abide by a Hobbesian answer, which makes sovereign territoriality the premise of a political community. On the other hand, critical geographers have questioned the cartographic imaginations of fixed boundaries and closed borders. They have not only invoked the argument of historical contingency of the modern state and territory, but have also drawn attention to the complex episteme that underlie that hegemony. They have encouraged scholars to think above, below, and beyond the national state, and have held the idea of national security to be primarily responsible for the emasculation of the alternative spatial imaginations. Most of these radical scholars draw on the works of Henri Lefebvre or Michel Foucault, among others. Lefebvre famously commented, 'An existing space may outlive its original purpose and the *raison d'être* which determines its forms, functions, and structures; it may thus in a sense become vacant, and susceptible of being diverted, reappropriated and put to a purpose quite different from its initial use' (Lefebvre [1974] 1991: 167, emphasis in original).

Something like this has happened to the contemporary state and its territorial space. The territorialized state was meant to classify populations and to create institutions to discipline them in the interests of the transformative processes of global capitalism. Over time, it has become a self-fulfilling prophesy. IR scholars have lately recognized the need to explain territoriality and borders, rather than to accept them uncritically. However, the deeper nuances of social space seldom attract the attention of the IR scholar, who remains obsessed with the geopolitical meaning/s of national space. I do not offer in this book any explanation as to why IR has such a tunnel vision of space. My objective was far more limited.

This book shows that India's understanding of its neighbourhood is informed by a certain version of realism, as South Asia remains a segregated space of power and sovereign territoriality. What explains the longevity of this imagery? A part of the answer lies in its genealogy. Modern South Asia was a territory crafted by the colonial powers that fundamentally separated the symbiotic relationship between the state and society that existed earlier. The British defined South Asia in geopolitical terms, indeed in the interests of imperial capital, and its chosen political instrumentalities of divide and rule never allowed a cohesive political community to come into being. The sociocultural basis of the meta-community that existed in the subcontinent was politically transformed by colonialism. Territoriality fixed the range of spatial imagination of the elite. However, territory by itself does not determine national identity, and South Asia's post-colonial elites have struggled perennially over their fractured national projects. In this process, territoriality became the only safe political principle, which they desperately held on to as every other marker was contested. The territorial conception came to be predicated upon power and strategic purposes. Austere realism came handy, as the external domain of threats, risks, and uncertainties were indispensable in forging a sense of national purpose within hard borders.

This conception has deep consequences for the perceptions and practices of the South Asian elites. Border control and surveillance gain primacy over free movement of people and commodities. Since territory became the basis for forging the boundaries of political community, citizenship has also become contentious. Commonalities in ethnicity and culture have paradoxical effects upon a territorialized space. On the one hand, such commonalities are socially, culturally, and artistically transgressive of borders. Yet, such easy translatability leads to insecurity and closure. Each of the five chapters of this book has demonstrated this strategic spatial orientation of India towards the neighbourhood.

All South Asian states are in fact territorial constructs. Globalization, liberalization, democratization, and long-standing social and economic insecurities have failed to transform the meanings of space here. India's evolving security doctrines have been part of a constant endeavour to keep the subcontinent under its strategic leadership, and its political elites and security experts have relentlessly reified this orientation. Geopolitical tussle between India and Pakistan have kept the region divided, and have prevented the growth of a healthy regionalism. SAARC has, therefore, done precious little to evolve a commercial or cultural framing for the subcontinent. Sub-regionalism, based on common economic interests, has been a proxy for the failed dialectics of regionalism. However, strategic concerns over the growing footprints of China in South Asia and the Indian Ocean have limited its success. Finally, India had tried to grow out of its backyard by extending its neighbourhood, particularly in Southeast Asia, through its 'Look East'/'Act East' policy since the early 1990s. However, space-as-power has come to dominate its 'Look East' imagery, as India has tugged along the rather unspecified trajectory of the 'Indo-Pacific'. Neither space as commerce nor space as community has, therefore, prevailed in India's special imagination of its neighbourhood.

This last point needs to be explained. If the idea of commerce or prosperity prevailed as an imagery of space, South Asia would have looked very different. For one, SAARC would have evolved along functional lines, and the latent economic linkages could have been fully tapped. It would have led to a far more robust infrastructure, and inter-regional trade would have flourished. More critically, it would have transformed India's Northeast by allowing freer communication of all factors of production across the Yunan Province of China in the north, Myanmar through the east, and Bangladesh border through the south. Sub-regional cooperation would have also yielded far more, as it would have been guided by economic considerations, rather than the fears of insurgency, external meddling, and the need to resist China's designs in Myanmar. The 'Look East' policy would have assumed a more robust continental thrust, and economic cooperation with China would have emerged as the primary challenge of the policy. It is a fact that South Asia is not a zone of economic complementarity, and India's overbearing economic preponderance comes in the way of a balanced economic order. However, given the economic interests of all the states involved, it makes little economic sense not to hitch with the Indian bandwagon. Further, space-as-commerce would have welcomed a more active Chinese economic presence throughout South Asia. In contrast, almost all Chinese investment in infrastructure in South Asian states makes India suspicious and critical. India's opposition is invariably couched in a language of power, for it sees Chinese investments as steps to an eventual strategy of encirclement. China has only returned the same geopolitical logic in opposing India's entry into various institutional arrangements in Southeast and Central Asia. Even a definite turn towards market economics has not led India to change its course, as China's market reforms have reinforced its nationalism and search for geopolitical prominence.

The community imagination fails due to entirely different reasons. South Asia was historically a space that had no territorialized state order. Its geography was variable, as was its history. Colonial modernity transformed the identity of the place for good. In the words of Sudipta Kaviraj, 'Through its long history what we now can call "South Asia" was a space that was intimately recognized, but formally unnamed. It was a vast expanse which contained hundreds of political formations in which neither the states made exclusive claims on its subjects, nor did the people on their states' (Kaviraj 2014: 10). South Asia was a colonial construction that defied the long-term historical and cultural trends which had defined its plural identities. In every state created out of the retreat of the British after 1947, the contradictions between the national imaginations of the statist projects, and the social culture remained endemic. Fear of the neighbours became a common ploy to strengthen national integration, which operated through strategies of 'otherization'. However, culture is not a physical entity that can be stopped at manned borders. Culture percolates under all man-made boundaries. Communities divided by states may get used to separate political existence, but cannot forget or deny their cultural roots. These connections are the brick and mortar of a social spacing that do not follow the logic of territorial nationalism. It is this malleability of culture that makes it a potentially subversive material. As Kaviraj says, 'Different socialities of space find ways of evading the brutal enforcement of state borders. State borders and efforts at containerization are frustrated as much by historical forces as by forces of the future' (2014: 11). Therefore, there is no way that the South Asian elites can take a chance with culture. South Asia, when conceived as a community space, has no political takers in any of the states. The tension over migration and the debates on the conditions of political community in all the South Asian states bear this out. Appreciating a sumptuous biryani may not be difficult for South Asians; however, this shared culinary aesthetics does not translate into any notion of fraternal political space defined by cultural commonalities and deep bonds of community.

Who imagines South Asia as a space of power? The evidence marshalled in this book incontrovertibly suggests that this spatial imagination of the region as a theatre of power is an elite political imagination. I have quoted several instances where alternative perspectives were highlighted and the futility of this territorial nationalism was exposed. However, such criticisms have happened mostly within the civil society and by people who are ideologically and conceptually opposed to state and sovereignty. My work has suggested a remarkable degree of consistency in the spatial articulation of the region across political regimes in India. Despite the central tension between secular–pluralistic and Hindu revivalist imaginations of the national project and identity, both camps unite on the territorial idea of India, and have shown broad commitment to the principles of security of borders against all threats, the need to acquire a military capacity strong enough to repel adversaries, tight border control mechanisms, and priorities of national sovereignty. The political community in India is thus a function of territoriality, rather than the other way round.

The partition of India in 1947 has survived in the collective political memory of the nation. Any prospect of further loss of territory is thus invariably securitized by the elite. Territory and borders are hence out of bounds for democratic deliberations. In sum, the answer to my second question is a straightforward one. Space-as-power is an elite articulation of space. It is, however, one of the two elite imageries. The other notion is that of a region conceived as a zone of prosperity. However, efforts to realize the market imagery have not succeeded in South Asia. There is no strong liberalism in the subcontinent. Hence, a powerful constituency to back the prosperity is missing here. Moreover, all South Asian states remain state dependent in their economic trajectories, the ascension of neo-liberal capitalism notwithstanding. Development has remained largely a prerogative of the political elite, whose chosen institutions and practices encourage the power imagination. Space-as-community is largely a civil societal imagination in India and across South Asia. However, there is a lack of clarity on what community means, and many positions are visible. I have, throughout the different chapters, examined the cognitive structure of the imagery of the space-as-community. There is no dominant political articulation of this view. Hence, what spatial practices might result from a communitarian vision cannot be empirically tested, either in India or across South Asia.

What are the results of India's spatial imagination of the South Asian region? Three consequences are readily seen. First, the power imagery has denied India flexibility in its foreign policy. Thus, its security policies have sought to hegemonize the subcontinent, but have failed. The consequences have of course been far more debilitating for Pakistan, which has increasingly got sucked into what T.V. Paul has described as a 'geo-strategic curse'. Second, space-as-power has hobbled regional cooperation with smaller neighbours as well. India's search for security makes these states wary. Hence, South Asia remains a geopolitical construct, framed in Curzonean colonial idioms, which has prevented the region from evolving a regional identity that would allow all-round development of its people. Third, this imagination has propelled a quest for an extended neighbourhood. While India has geographically broadened its reach, the spatial imagery deployed by the official elites has not changed. India has always defined its immediate neighbourhood as a geopolitical arena that must be secured against external powers. The extended neighbourhood is, likewise, a search for strategic depth in far-flung oceanic waters, to balance an increasingly assertive China. This, however, is in consonance with the view that as India's spatial imagination moves across, through, and beyond the Indian Ocean, the spatial imageries become increasingly nuanced, due to its entanglement with the logics of geopolitics, geo-economics, and geo-strategy. Yet, there is an unmistakable prioritization of the power reading amid all the nuances. While critical geographers, maritime historians, and social constructivists may have a very different story to tell, this study finds a clear muscularity to India's spatial imagination, near or afar. An extended neighbourhood could have ushered in economic benefits to frontier zones on both east and west sides, which the geographic confines of the South Asian subcontinent deny. However, space-as-power is not the appropriate idiom of such a discourse of development for outlying regions. The kind of risk taking that is necessary for such a venture demands an alternative spatial imagination, which the political elites in India and South Asia have shied away from. While this book does not invest in an argument of deterministic pessimism, it finds no empirical evidence of such an alternative vision having guided India's policies in the past, or becoming politically meaningful in the immediate future. A detailed survey of how geo-economics, climate considerations, national disaster management, the engagements with the social and political challenges of Indian diasporas living in the littoral states around India's maritime space, and a critical interrogation of the politics of social construction and transformation of spaces remain on the future research agenda. Spatial imaginations are perennially alive and evolving. My story is plotted on the valence of sovereign territoriality, where official elites are the chief characters. How their thinking may change is another story in the making.

Bibliography

Abizadeh, Arash. 2008. 'Democratic Theory and Border Coercion: No Right to Unilaterally Control Your Own Borders'. *Political Theory* 36 (1): 37–65.

Abraham, Itty. 2014. *How India Became Territorial: Foreign Policy, Diaspora, Geopolitics*. Stanford: Stanford University Press.

Acharya, Amitav. 2003. 'Regional Institutions and Asian Security Order: Norms, Power and the Prospects for Peaceful Change', in *Asian Security Order: Instrumental and Normative Features*, ed. M. Alagappa. Stanford, CA: Stanford University Press.

Acharya, Amitava. 2015. 'India's "Look East" Policy', in *The Oxford Handbook of Indian Foreign Policy*, ed. D. Malone, C. Raja Mohan, and S. Raghavan, pp. 452–65. New Delhi: Oxford University Press.

Adler, Emanuel and Michael Barnett. 1998. *Security Communities*. Cambridge: Cambridge University Press.

Agamben, Giorgio. 2005. *State of Exception*. Chicago: University of Chicago Press.

Agnew, J. 1994. 'The Territorial Trap: The Geographical Assumptions of International Relations Theory'. *Review of International Political Economy* 1 (1): 53–80.

————. 1998. *Geopolitics: Revisioning the World Politics*. London: Routledge.

Agnew, John. 2008. 'Borders on the Mind: Re-Framing Border Thinking'. *Ethics & Global Politics* 1 (4): 175–91.

Albert, Mathias and Lothar Brock. 2001. 'What Keeps Westphalia Together? Normative Differentiation in the Modern System of States', in *Identities, Borders, Orders*, ed. M. Albert. Minneapolis: Minnesota University Press.

Anderson, Malcolm. 1996. *Frontiers: Territory and State Formation in the Modern World*. Cambridge: Polity Press.

Anderson, Malcolm, Didier Bigo, and Eberhard Bort. 2000. 'Frontiers, Identity and Security in Europe: An Agenda for Research', in *Borderlands under Stress*, ed. M. Pratt and J.A. Brown, pp. 251–74. La Haye: Kluwer Law International.

Anderson, Walter. 2001. 'Recent Trends in Indian Foreign Policy'. *Asian Survey* 4 (5): 765–76.

Andreas, P. 1998–9. 'The Escalation of U.S. Immigration Control in the Post-NAFTA Era'. *Political Science Quarterly* 113 (4): 591–615.

Andreas, P. and T.J. Biersteker, eds. 2003. *The Rebordering of North America: Integration and Exclusion in a New Security Context*. London and New York: Routledge.

ASEAN. 2004. 'ASEAN–India Partnership for Peace, Progress and Shared Prosperity'. *Association of Southeast Asian Nations*. Accessed on 5 October 2017. http://asean.org/?static_post=asean-india-partnership-for-peace-progress-and-shared-prosperity-2.

Ashley, Richard K. 1987. '"The Geopolitics of Geopolitical Space": Toward a Critical Social Theory of International Politics'. *Alternatives* 12 (4): 403–34.

Ashley, Richard K. and R.B.J. Walker. 1990. 'Conclusion: Reading Dissidence/Writing the Discipline—Crisis and the Question of Sovereignty in International Studies'. *International Studies Quarterly* 34 (3; Special Issue: Speaking the Language of Exile: Dissidence in International Studies): 367–416.

Ayoob, Mohammed. 1982. 'India, Pakistan and Super-Power Rivalry'. *The World Today* 38 (5): 194–202.

————. 1990. 'India in South Asia: The Quest for Regional Predominance'. *World Policy Journal* 7 (1): 108–9.

Bajpai, Kanti. 1995. 'Introduction: International Theory, International Society, Regional Politics, and Foreign Policy', in *Interpreting World Politics: Essays for A.P. Rana*, ed. K. Bajpai and H. Shukul, pp. 31–2. New Delhi: SAGE Publications.

Bajpai, Kanti, Saira Basit, and V. Krishnappa, ed. 2014. *India's Grand Strategy: History, Theory, Cases*. London: Routledge.

Balibar, É. 1998. 'The Borders of Europe', in *Cosmopolitics: Thinking and Feeling beyond the Nation*, ed. P. Chean and B. Robbins. Minneapolis: University of Minnesota Press, pp. 216–33.

————. 1999. 'At the Border of Europe'. Lecture delivered at the Aristotle University of Thessaloniki, Greece. Accessed on 6 January 2018. http://makeworlds.org/node/80.

Bandyopadhyay, Sekhar. 2004. *From Plassey to Partition: The Making of Modern India*. Hyderabad: Orient Longman.

Banerjee, Paula. 2010. *Borders, Histories, Existences: Gender and Beyond*. New Delhi: SAGE Publications.

Baruah, Darshana M. 2015. 'India's Evolving Maritime Strategy'. *The Diplomat*. Accessed on 18 September 2016. http://thediplomat.com/2015/12/indias-evolving-maritime-strategy/.

Baruah, Sanjib. 2005. *Durable Disorder: Understanding the Politics of Northeast India*. New Delhi: Oxford University Press.

Basrur, Rajesh. 2008. *South Asia's Cold War: Nuclear Weapons and Conflict in Comparative Perspective*, as a part of Asian Security Studies. New York: Routledge.

Basrur, Rajesh M. 2001. 'Nuclear Weapons and India's Strategic Culture'. *Journal of Peace Research* 38 (2): 181–98.

Basu, Pratnashree. 2013. 'From Kunming Initiative to BCIM Corridor'. *Observer Research* Foundation. Accessed on 20 November 2016. http://www.orfonline.org/research/from-kunming-initiative-to-bcim-corridor/.

Bauder, Harald. 2011. 'Toward a Critical Geography of the Border: Engaging the Dialectic of Practice and Meaning'. *Annals of the Association of American Geographers* 101 (5): 1126–39.

Bhattacharya, Harihar. 2004. 'Internal Threats to Security: Indian Federalism and the Accommodation of Ethno-Religious Identity in India', in *Anatomy of Fear: Essays on India's Security*, ed. P. Bhattacharya, T. Chakraborti, and S. Chatterjee. New Delhi: Lancer's Books.

Biersteker, Thomas J. 2002. 'State Sovereignty and Territory', in *Handbook of International Relations*, eds, W. Carlsnaes, T. Risse, and B.A. Simmons. New York: SAGE Publications.

Bisley, Nick and Andrew Phillips. 6 October 2012. 'The Indo-Pacific: What Does It Actually Mean?'. *East Asia Forum*. Accessed on 3 February 2018. http://www.eastasiaforum.org/2012/10/06/the-indo-pacific-what-does-it-actually-mean/.

Blackwill, Robert D. and Jennifer M. Harris. 2016. *War by Other Means: Geoeconomics and Statecraft*. Cambridge, MA: Harvard University Press.

Bose, Sugata and Ayesha Jalal. [1997] 2011. *Modern South Asia: History, Culture, Political Economy*. London: Routledge.

Brecher, Michael. January 1963. 'International Relations and Asian Studies: The Subordinate State System of Southern Asia'. *World Politics* 15 (2): 213–35.

Brenner, Neil and Stuart Elden. 2009. 'Henri Lefebvre on State, Space, Territory'. *International Political Sociology* 3: 353–77.

Brewster, David. 2014. *India's Ocean: The Story of India's Bid for Regional Leadership*. New York: Routledge.

———. 2015. 'An Indian Ocean Dilemma: Sino-Indian Rivalry and China's Strategic Vulnerability in the Indian Ocean'. *Journal of the Indian Ocean Region* 11 (1): 48–59.

———. 2017. 'Silk Roads and Strings of Pearls: The Strategic Geography of China's New Pathways in the Indian Ocean'. *Geopolitics* 22 (2): 269–91.

Brobst, Peter John. 2005. *The Future of the Great Game: Sir Olaf Caroe, India's Independence, and the Defense of Asia*. Akron: University of Akron Press.

Brown, Judith. 1998. 'The Jewel without the Crown'. *The New York Times*. Accessed on 20 November 2016. http://www.nytimes.com/books/98/02/15/reviews/980215.15brownt.html.

Brown, Wendy. 2010. *Walled States, Waning Sovereignty*. New York: Zone Books.

Brubaker, Rogers and Frederick Cooper. 2000. 'Beyond Identity'. *Theory and Society* 29 (1): 1–47.

Buzan, Barry. 1991. 'New Patterns of Global Security in the Twenty-First Century'. *International Affairs (Royal Institute of International Affairs)* 67 (3): 431–51.

———. 2011. 'The South Asian Security Complex in a Decentring World Order: Reconsidering Regions and Powers Ten Years On'. *International Studies* 48 (1): 1–19.

Buzan, Barry and Gowher Rizvi. 1986. *South Asian Insecurity and the Great Powers*. London: Macmillan.

Buzan, Barry and Ole Waever. 2003. *Regions and Powers: The Structure of International Security*. Cambridge: Cambridge University Press.

Cantori, Louis J. and Steven L. Spiegel. 1970. *The International Politics of Regions: A Comparative Approach*. Englewood Cliffs: Prentice Hall.

Carens, J.H. 1987. 'Aliens and Citizens: The Case for Open Borders'. *Review of Politics* 49: 251–73.

Castells, Manuel. 1996. *The Rise of the Network Society* (Vol. I), as a part of *The Information Age: Economy, Society and Culture*. Cambridge, Mass.; Oxford, UK: Blackwell.

———. 1997. *The Power of Identity* (Vol. II), as a part of *The Information Age: Economy, Society and Culture*. Cambridge, Mass.; Oxford, UK: Blackwell.

———. 1998. *End of Millennium* (Vol. III), as a part of *The Information Age: Economy, Society and Culture*. Cambridge, Mass.; Oxford, UK: Blackwell.

Chacko, Priya. 2011. *Indian Foreign Policy: The Politics of Postcolonial Identity from 1947 to 2004*. London; New York: Routledge.

———. 2012. 'India and the Indo-Pacific: An Emerging Regional Vision'. *Indo-Pacific Governance Research Centre Policy Brief* 5: 1–7. Accessed on 20 November 2016. https://www.adelaide.edu.au/indo-pacific-governance/research/policy/Chacko_PB.pdf.

Chadda, Maya. 2000. *Building Democracy in South Asia: India, Nepal, Pakistan*. New Delhi: Vistaar Publications.

Chakrabarty, Bidyut. 2004. *The Partition of Bengal and Assam, 1932–1947: Contour of Freedom*. New York: Routledge.

Chatterji, Joya. 2007. *Spoils of Partition: Bengal and India 1947–1967*. Cambridge, UK: Cambridge University Press.

Chatterjee, Partha. 1986. *Nationalist Thought and the Colonial World: A Derivative Discourse*. University of Minnesota Press.

———. 1993. *The Nation and Its Fragments: Colonial and Postcolonial Histories*. Princeton, NJ: Princeton University Press.

———. 1994. 'Secularism and Toleration'. *Economic and Political Weekly* 29 (28): 1768–77.

———. 2008. 'Democracy and Economic Transformation in India'. *Economic and Political Weekly* 43 (16): 53–62.

Chatterjee, Shibashis. 2016. 'India–Bangladesh Relations: An Overview', in *Engaging the World: Indian Foreign Policy since 1947*, ed. S. Ganguly, pp. 76–104. New Delhi: Oxford University Press.

Chatterjee, Shibashis and Rumela Sen. 2004. 'Communialism, Internal Security and the Indian State', in *Anatomy of Fear: Essays on India's Internal Security*, ed. P. Bhattacharya, T. Chakrabarti, and S. Chatterjee, pp. 181–207. New Delhi: Lancer's Books.

Chatterjee, Shibashis and Sulagna Maitra. 2009. 'Space and Regional Cooperation: The SAARC Story', in *Envisioning a New South Asia*, ed. T. Nirmala Devi and A.S. Raju. New Delhi: Shipra Publications.

Chellaney, Brahma. 1999a. 'The Regional Strategic Triangle', in *Securing India's Future in the New Millennium*, ed. B. Chellaney, pp. 348–52. New Delhi: Orient Longman and the Centre for Policy Research.

———. 1999b. 'Preface', in *Securing India's Future in the New Millennium*, ed. B. Chellaney, pp. xviii–xxi. New Delhi: Orient Longman and the Centre for Policy Research.

———. 2014. 'Deconstructing the Modi Foreign Policy'. *The Hindu*, 4 December. http://www.thehindu.com/opinion/lead/deconstructing-the-modi-foreign-policy/article6658904.ece.

Chester, Lucy. 2007. 'The Future of the Great Game: Sir Olaf Caroe, India's Independence, and the Defense of Asia'. *Journal of Interdisciplinary History* 37 (4): 676–7.

Chibber, Bharti. 2004. *Regional Security and Regional Cooperation: A Comparative Study of ASEAN and SAARC*. New Delhi: New Century Publications.

Cohen, Stephen Philip. 1987. *Security of South Asia*. New Delhi: Vistaar Publications,.

———. 2005. *India: Emerging Power*. New Delhi: Oxford University Press.

Cronin, Patrick M. and Darshana M. Baruah. 2014. 'The Modi Doctrine for the Indo–Pacific Maritime Region'. *The Diplomatic*, 2 December. http://thediplomat.com/2014/12/the-modi-doctrine-for-the-indo-pacific-maritime-region/.

Crossette, Barbara. 2008. 'Indira Gandhi's Legacy: Vying for Mastery in South Asia'. *World Policy Journal* 25 (1): 36–44.

Dasgupta, Jyoti Bhushan. 1968. *Jammu and Kashmir*. The Hague: Martinus Nijhoff.

Das, Sumir Kumar. 2003. *Ethnicity, Nation and Security: Essays on Northeastern India*. New Delhi: South Asian Publishers.

————. 2004. 'Identity and Frontiers in International Research', in *Understanding Global Politics: Issues and Trends*, ed. A.J. Majumdar and S. Chatterjee. New Delhi: Lancer's Books.

————. 2010. 'India's Look East Policy: Imagining a New Geography of India's Northeast'. *India Quarterly: A Journal of International Affairs* 66 (4): 343–58.

Dean, Karin. 2005. 'Territorialities Yet Unaccounted'. *Seminar: Gateway to the East* (550): 50–4. Accessed on 25 July 2017. http://eprints.soas.ac.uk/17278/1/2005/550/550%20karin%20dean.htm.

Destradi, Sandra. 2010. 'India and the Civil War in Sri Lanka: On the Failures of Regional Conflict Management in South Asia'. GIGA Working Papers 154/2010, Humburg, p. 13. Accessed on 21 September 2016. http://www.giga-hamburg.de/en/system/files/publications/wp154_destradi.pdf.

Deutsch, Karl W., Sidney A. Burrell, Robert A. Kann, and Maurice Lee Jr. 1957. *Political Community and the North Atlantic Area: International Organization in the Light of Historical Experience*. Princeton: Princeton University Press.

Dirk, Nicholas. 2001. *Castes of Mind: Colonialism and the Making of Modern India*. Princeton, NJ: Princeton University Press.

Dittmer, J. and N. Gray. 2010. 'Popular Geopolitics 2.0: Towards New Methodologies of the Everyday'. *Geography Compass* 4: 1664–77.

Dixit, J.N. 2003. *India's Foreign Policy 1947–2003* (Updated Edition). New Delhi: Picus Books.

Dossani, Rafiq, Daniel Sneider, and Vikram Sood. 2009. *Does South Asia Exist?* Washington, DC: Brookings Institute.

Doyle, Michael W. 1983a. 'Kant, Liberal Legacies, and Foreign Affairs, Part 1'. *Philosophy & Public Affairs* 12 (3): 205–35.

————. 1983b. 'Kant, Liberal Legacies, and Foreign Affairs, Part 2'. *Philosophy & Public Affairs* 12 (4): 323–53.

Dubey, Muchkund. 2007. 'SAARC and South Asian Economic Integration'. *Economic and Political Weekly* 42 (14): 1238–40.

Dutta, Sujit. 2011. 'South Asian Regional Security Architecture: Between Anarchy and Order', in *South Asia: Envisioning a Regional Future*, ed. S.S. Pattanaik. New Delhi: Pentagon Press.

Eder, K. 2006. 'Europe's Borders: The Narrative Construction of the Boundaries of Europe'. *European Journal of Social Theory* 9 (2): 225–71.

Egreteau, Renaud. 2006. 'Instability at the Gate: India's Troubled Northeast and Its External Connections'. *Centre de Sciences Humaines* (16).

Elden, Stuart. 2009. *Terror and Territory: The Spatial Extent of Sovereignty*. Minneapolis: University of Minnesota Press.

———. 2013. *The Birth of Territory*. Chicago: University of Chicago Press.

Elman, Miriam Fendius. 1997. 'The Need for a Qualitative Test of the Democratic Peace Theory', in *Paths to Peace: Is Democracy the Answer?*, ed. M.F. Elman, pp. 1–57. Cambridge, MA: The MIT Press.

Fearon, James D. 1999. 'What is Identity (As We Now Use the Word)'. *Stanford University*. Accessed on 3 August 2016. https://web.stanford.edu/group/fearon-research/cgi-bin/wordpress/wp-content/uploads/2013/10/What-is-Identity-as-we-now-use-the-word-.pdf.

Firstpost. 2017. 'Linking CPEC with Bangladesh-China-India-Myanmar Corridor Will Benefit People: China'. *The Firstpost*, 27 June. https://www.firstpost.com/business/linking-cpec-with-bangladesh-china-india-myanmar-corridor-will-benefit-people-china-3749181.html.

Foucault, Michel. 1984. 'Of Other Spaces: Utopias and Heterotopias'. *Architecture/Mouvement/Continuité*. Accessed on 11 February 2018. http://web.mit.edu/allanmc/www/foucault1.pdf.

Frances, Steward and Taimur Hyat. 2002. 'Conflict in South Asia: Prevalence, Costs and Politics', in *The South Asian Challenge* by Khadija Haq. New Delhi: Oxford University Press.

Ganguly, Sumit. 1986. *The Origins of War in South Asia: Indo-Pakistani Conflicts since 1947*. Boulder, CO: Westview Press.

———. 1994. *The Origins of Wars in South Asia: The Indo-Pakistani Conflicts since 1947*. Boulder, CO: Westview Press.

———. 1997. 'Past Attempts at Mediation and Conflict Prevention in South Asia: Would CSBMs Have made a Difference?', in *Mending Fences: Confident-and-Security-Building Measures in South Asia*, ed. S. Ganguly and T. Greenwood. New Delhi: Oxford University Press.

———. 1999. 'India's Pathway to Pokhran II: The Prospects and Sources of New Delhi's Nuclear Weapons Program'. *International Security* 23 (4): 148–177.

———. 2015. 'Hindu Nationalism and the Foreign Policy of India's Bharatiya Janata Party'. Transatlantic Academy Paper Series, Washington, DC.

———. 2016. *Deadly Impasse: Indo–Pakistani Relations at the Dawn of a New Century*. Cambridge: Cambridge University Press.

Ganguly, Sumit and Devin T. Hagerty. 2006. *Fearful Symmetry: India-Pakistan Crises in the Shadow of Nuclear Weapons*. Seattle, WA: University of Washington Press.

Gelpi, Christopher F. and Michael Griesdorf. 2001. 'Winners or Losers? Democracies in International Crisis, 1918–94'. *American Political Science Review* 95 (3): 633–47.

Ghoshal, Baladas. 2016. 'China and India's Look East Policy'. *Oxford Scholarship Online*. Accessed on 18 September 2016. http://www.oxfordscholarship.com/view/10.1093/acprof:oso/9780199463800.001.0001/acprof-9780199463800-chapter-8?print=pdf.

Giri, Radhika. 2015. 'Caught between the Devil and the Deep Blue Sea, Sri Lankan Tamil Refugees Have Lost a Future'. *The Weekend Leader* 6 (3). Accessed on 4 May 2017. http://www.theweekendleader.com/Causes/2226/stuck-in-india.html.

Gordon, Sandy. 2015. *India's Rise as an Asian Power: Nation, Neighbourhood, and Region*. Washington, DC: Georgetown University Press.

Goswami, Manu. 2004. *Producing India: From Colonial Economy to National Space*. Chicago, IL: University of Chicago Press.

Government of India. 1977. *Foreign Affairs Record, Volume XXIII, No. 11*, pp. 215–16. New Delhi: Ministry of External Affairs, Government of India.

Groom, A.J.R. 1978. 'Neofunctionalism: A Case of Mistaken Identity'. *Political Science* 30 (1): 15–28.

———. 1980. 'International Organisation in World Society', in *International Organisation: A Conceptual Approach*, ed. P. Taylor and A.J.R. Groom. London: University of London Press.

Guha, Ramchandra. 2011. *The Makers of Modern India*. Cambridge, MA: Belknap Press.

Guha, Ranajit. 1997. *Dominance without Hegemony: History and Power in Colonial India*. Cambridge, MA: Harvard University Press.

Gujral, I.K. 1997. 'Aspects of India's Foreign Policy'. Speech at the Bandaranaike Centre for International Studies in Colombo, Sri Lanka, 20 January. Accessed on 17 May 2017. http://www.stimson.org/research-pages/the-gujral-doctrine/.

Haas, Ernst. 1958. *The Uniting of Europe: Political, Social, and Economic Forces, 1950–1957*, as a part of Library of World Affairs Series, No. 42. Stanford, CA: Stanford University Press.

———. 1964. *Beyond the Nation-State: Functionalism and International Organization*. Stanford, CA: Stanford University Press.

Hagerty, Devin T. April 1991. 'India's Regional Security Doctrine'. *Asian Survey* 31 (4): 351–63.

Hansen, T.B. 1996. 'Globalisation and Nationalist Imaginations: Hindutva's Promise of Equality through Difference'. *Economic and Political Weekly* 31 (10).

Haokip, Thongkholal. 2011. 'India's Look East Policy'. *Third Concept—An International Journal of Ideas* 24 (291): 7–11.

————. 2015. 'India's Look East Policy: Prospects and Challenges for Northeast India'. *Studies in Indian Politics* 3 (2): 198–211.

Harvey, David. 1989. *The Condition of Post-Modernity: An Enquiry into the Origins of Cultural Change*. Oxford: Blackwell.

Hew, Denis. 2006. 'Economic Integration in East Asia: An ASEAN Perspective'. UNISCI Discussion Papers, No. 11, pp. 49–57. Accessed on 16 October 2017. https://www.ucm.es/data/cont/media/www/pag-72530/UNISCI11Hew.pdf.

Hong, Zhao. 2007. 'India and China: Rivals or Partners in Southeast Asia?'. *Contemporary Southeast Asia* 29 (1): 121–42.

Indian Ocean Rim Association. n.d. 'Maritime Safety and Security'. *Indian Ocean Rim Association*. Accessed on 27 June 2017. http://www.iora.int/en/priorities-focus-areas/maritime-safety-and-security.

Insight IAS. 2009. 'Prime Minister Manmohan Singh's Speech in the Parliament Reiterating India's Stance Taken During NAM Summit at Sharm-Al-Sheikh in Delinking Talks From Terrorism While Dealing With Pakistan'. *Insight IAS*. Accessed on 12 January 2017. http://www.insightsonindia.com/2009/07/30/text-of-the-prime-minister-manmohan-singhs-speech-in-the-parliament-reiterating-indias-stance-taken-during-nam-summit-at-sharm-al-sheikh-in-delinking-talks-with-terrorism-while-dealing-with-pakist/.

Iqbal, Nasir and Saima Nawaz. 2016. 'Why Has SAFTA Failed to Boost Pakistan–India Trade?'. *East Asia Forum*. Accessed on 24 May 2017. http://www.eastasiaforum.org/2016/03/19/why-has-safta-failed-to-boost-pakistan-india-trade/.

Iyer, Roshan. 2017. 'Reviving the Comatose Bangladesh-China-India-Myanmar Corridor'. *The Diplomat*, 3 May. https://thediplomat.com/2017/05/reviving-the-comatose-bangladesh-china-india-myanmar-corridor/.

Jackson, Robert. 2000. *The Global Covenant. Human Conduct in a World of States*. Oxford: Oxford University Press.

Jaffrelot, Christophe. 2007. *Hindu Nationalism: A Reader*. Princeton, NJ: Princeton University Press.

Jain, Rajendra K. 2011. 'From Idealism to Pragmatism: India and Asian Regional Integration'. *Japanese Journal of Political Science* 12 (2): 213–31.

Jaishankar, Dhruva. 2017. 'Why 2017 Idea of the Year Is the "Indo-Pacific"?'. *Hindustan Times*, 29 December. https://www.hindustantimes.com/analysis/why-2017-idea-of-the-year-is-the-indo-pacific/story-A0fctWmn3s5Nc04PxZrCHO.html.

Jalal, Ayesha. 1974. 'Conjuring Pakistan: History as Official Imagining'. *International Journal of Middle East Studies* 8 (4).

_____. 1985. *The Sole Spokesman: Jinnah, the Muslim League and the Demand for Pakistan*. Cambridge: Cambridge University Press.

_____. 1995. *Democracy and Authoritarianism in South Asia: A Comparative and Historical Perspective*. New York: Cambridge University Press.

_____. 1996. 'Secularists, Subalterns, and the Stigma of "Communalism": Partition Historiography Revisited'. *Indian Economic and Social History Review* 33 (1): 93–103.

_____. 1998. 'Nation, Reason and Religion: Punjab's Role in the Partition of India'. *Economic and Political Weekly* 33 (32): 2183–90.

_____. 2014. *The Struggle for Pakistan: A Muslim Homeland and Global Politics*. Cambridge, MA: The Belknap Press of Harvard University Press.

Joshi, Shashank. 2013. 'India's Afghan Muddle'. *The Hindu*, 18 December. Accessed on 13 November 2017. http://www.thehindu.com/opinion/lead/indias-afghan-muddle/article5470772.ece.

Kaladan Movement. n.d. 'About the Kaladan Multi-Modal Transit Transport Project'. *Kaladan Movement*. Accessed on15 September 2006. http://www.kaladanmovement.org/index.php/about-the-kaladan-multi-modal-transit-transport-project.

Kapur, Ashok and A. Jeyaratnam Wilson. 1996. *Foreign Policies of India and her Neighbours*. London: Macmillan.

Katoch, Prakash. 2016. 'India-Myanmar-Thailand Highway: Strategic Dimensions'. *Indian Defence Review*. 5 November 2017. http://www.indiandefencereview.com/news/imt-highway-strategic-dimensions/.

Kaviraj, Sudipta. 2014. 'A Strange Love of the Land: Identity, Poetry and Politics in the (Un)Making of South Asia'. *Samaj South Asia Multidisciplinary Academic Journal* 10: 1–15.

Kearney, M. 1991. 'Borders and Boundaries of State and Self at the End of Empire'. *Journal of Historical Sociology* 4 (1): 52–74.

Keohane, Robert O. 1991. *The New European Community: Decisionmaking and Institutional Change*, ed. S. Hoffmann. Boulder, CO: Westview Press.

Keohane, Robert O. and Lisa L. Martin. 1995. 'The Promise of Institutionalist Theory'. *International Security* 20 (1): 39–51.

Khan, Yasmin. 2007. *The Great Partition: The Making of India and Pakistan*. New Haven, CT: Yale University Press.

Khanna, Parag. 2016. *Connectography: Mapping the Future of Global Civilization*. New York: Random House.

Khilnani, Sunil. 2003. *The Idea of India*. New York: Farrar, Straus and Giroux.

Kohn, Bernard S. 1996. *Colonialism and Its Forms of Knowledge: The British in India*. Princeton, NJ: Princeton University Press.

Krasner, Steven D. 1999. *Sovereignty: Organized Hypocrisy*. Princeton, NJ: Princeton University Press.

Krishna, Sankaran. 1999. *Postcolonial Insecurities: India, Sri Lanka, and the Question of Nationhood.* Oxford: Oxford University Press.

Krishna, S.M. 2012. 'India Will Serve as Bridge across World's Great Diversity: Krishna'. *Rediff.com.* Accessed on 23 September 2016. http://www.rediff.com/news/report/india-s-foreign-policy-priorities-in-the-21st-century/20120929.htm.

Kumar, Priya. 1999. 'Testimonies of Loss and Memory: Partition and the Haunting of a Nation'. *Interventions: International Journal of Postcolonial Studies* 1 (2): 201–15.

Kuppuswamy, C.S. 2003. 'India's Look East Policy: Gaining Momentum with the Prime Minister's Visit', Paper No. 819, South Asia Analysis Group. Accessed on 11 April 2017. http://www.saag.org/papers9/paper819.html.

Kurian, Nimmi. 2014. *India–China Borderlands: Conversations beyond the Centre.* New Delhi; London: SAGE Publications.

Laine, Jussi P. 2016. 'The Multiscalar Production of Borders'. *Geopolitics* 2 (3): 465–82.

Lattiner, Mark. 2002. 'Preface', in *Religious Minorities in Pakistan,* by Iftikhar H. Malik. London: Minority Rights Group International. Accessed on 15 September 2017. http://citeseerx.ist.psu.edu/viewdoc/download?doi=10.1.1.440.4047&rep=rep1&type=pdf.

Layton, Peter. 2015. 'How Sri Lanka Won the War: Lessons in Strategy from an Overlooked Victory'. *The Diplomat,* 9 April. http://thediplomat.com/2015/04/how-sri-lanka-won-the-war/.

Lefebvre, Henri. [1974] 1991. *The Production of Space.* Oxford: Blackwell.

———. 1976. *De l'État,* vol. II. Paris: General Union of Editions.

Levesque, Julien. 2008. 'North East in India's Look East Policy'. *Institute of Peace and Conflict Studies.* Accessed on 7 February 2017. http://www.ipcs.org/article_details.php?articleNo=2558$cID=9.

Levy, Jack S. 1988. 'Domestic Politics and War'. *The Journal of Interdisciplinary History* 18 (4): 653–73.

Malik, Mohan. 2016. 'India's Response to the South China Sea Verdict'. *The American Interest.* Accessed on 16 July 2017. https://www.the-american-interest.com/2016/07/22/indias-response-to-the-south-china-sea-verdict/.

Mann, James. 2009. *The Rebellion of Ronald Reagan: A History of the End of the Cold War.* New York: Penguin Group.

Marwah, Ved. 1999. 'Threats to Internal Security', in *Securing India's Future in the New Millennium,* ed. B. Chellaney. Hyderabad: Orient Longman.

Mathew, Liz. 2016. 'PM Modi Speaks to People of Pakistan: Let Us Go to War against Poverty, Unemployment…Let's See Who Wins'. *Indian Express,* 25 September. http://indianexpress.com/article/india/india-news-india/

pm-narendra-modi-speaks-to-the-people-of-pakistan-lets-go-to-war-against-poverty-unemployment-lets-see-who-wins-3048329/.

Mearsheimer, John J. 1994. 'The False Promise of International Institutions'. *International Security* 19 (3): 5–49.

Mehta, Pratap Bhanu. 2012. 'State and Democracy in India'. *Polish Sociological Review* (178): 203–25.

Menon, Shivshankar. 2007. '"The Challenges Ahead for India's Foreign Policy"—Speech by Foreign Secretary, Shri Shivshankar Menon at the Observer Research Foundation, New Delhi'. *Ministry of External Affairs: Government of India*. Accessed on 11 January 2017. http://mea.gov.in/Speeches-Statements.htm?dtl/1847/The+Challenges+Ahead+for+Indias+Foreign+Policy+Speech+by+Foreign+Secretary+Shri+Shivshankar+.

————. 2012. 'Speech by National Security Advisor, Shivshankar Menon, on "Transforming South Asia" at the Third Asian Relations Conference'. *Ministry of External Affairs: Government of India*. Accessed on 2 January 2017. http://www.mea.gov.in/bilateral-documents.htm?dtl/18872/Speech+by+National+Security+Advisor+on+Transforming+South+Asia+at+the+Third+Asian+Relations+Conference.

————. 2016. *Choices: Inside the Making of Indian Foreign Policy*. New Delhi: Penguin Random House.

Metcalf, Thomas R. 1997. *Ideologies of the Raj* (Revised Edition). London; New York: Cambridge University Press.

Michael, Arndt. 2013. 'Sovereignty vs. Security: SAARC and Its Role in the Regional Security Architecture in South Asia'. *Harvard Asia Quarterly* 15 (2): 37–45.

Miller, David. 2010. 'Why Immigration Controls Are Not Coercive: A Reply to Arash Abizadeh'. *Political Theory* 38 (1): 111–20.

Ministry of External Affairs. 2012. 'India–Afghanistan Relations'. *Ministry of External Affairs: Government of India*. Accessed on 11 May 2017. http://www.mea.gov.in/Portal/ForeignRelation/afghanistan-aug-2012.pdf.

————. 2017. 'Official Spokesperson's Response to a Query on Participation of India in OBOR/BRI Forum'. *Ministry of External Affairs: Government of India*. Accessed on 17 July 2017. http://www.mea.gov.in/media-briefings.htm?dtl/28463/Official_Spokespersons_response_to_a_query_on_participation_of_India_in_OBORBRI_Forum.

Mitra, Subrata K. and Jivanta Schottli. 2007. 'The New Dynamics of Indian Foreign Policy and Its Ambiguities'. *Irish Studies in International Affairs* 18: 19–34. Accessed on 11 April 2017. http://www.jstor.org/stable/254698139.

Mitrany, David. 1948. 'The Functional Approach to World Organization'. *International Affairs* 24 (3): 350–63.

———. 1965. 'The Prospect of European Integration: Federal or Functional'. *Journal of Common Market Studies* 4 (2): 119–49.

———.1966. *A Working Peace System*. Chicago: Quadrangle Books.

———. 1976. *The Functional Theory of Politics*. New York: St. Martin's Press.

Modi, Narendra. 2014. 'Text of Prime Minister's Speech at 2014 SAARC Summit in Nepal'. *Narendra Modi*. Accessed on 27 January 2017. http://www.narendramodi.in/text-of-prime-ministers-speech-at-2014-saarc-summit-in-nepal-6941.

———. 2016. 'Media Statement by Prime Minister during His Visit to Japan'. *Ministry of External Affairs*. Accessed on 18 April 2017. https://www.mea.gov.in/Speeches-Statements.htm?dtl/27595/media+statement+by+prime+minister+during+his+visit+to+japan+november+11+2016.

Moore, Margaret. 2015. *A Political Theory of Territory*. Oxford: Oxford University Press.

Mukherjee, Pranab. 2007. 'Address of the External Affairs Minister, Mr. Pranab Mukherjee, at the Institute of Foreign Affairs and National Security, Republic of Korea on "India's Look East Policy"'. Accessed on 11 November 2016. https://www.mea.gov.in/Speeches-Statements.htm?dtl/1934/address+of+the+external+affairs+minister+mr+pranab+mukherjee+at+the+institute+of+foreign+affairs+and+national+security+republic+of+korea+on+indias+look+east+policy.

Mukherjee, Rahul. 2014. 'India and Global Economic Governance: From Structural Conflict to Embedded Liberalism'. *International Studies Review* 16 (3).

Murayama, Mayumi. 2006. 'Borders, Migration and Sub-Regional Cooperation in Eastern South Asia'. *Economic Political Weekly* 41 (14): 1351–9.

Murthy, Padmaja. 2000. 'Relevance of SAARC'. *Strategic Analysis* 23 (10): 1781–96.

Naidu, G.V.C. 2000. 'Multilateralism and Regional Security: Can the ASEAN Regional Forum Really Make a Difference?'. *Analysis from the East-West Center* (45): 1–8.

———. 2011. 'India and the Asia-Pacific Balance of Power'. *Strategic Analysis* (IDSA) 25 (4): 503–18.

———. 2013. 'India and East Asia: The Look East Policy'. *PERCEPTIONS* XVIII (1) 53–74.

Naing, Shoon. 2016. 'The Pivot toward Closer India-Myanmar Ties'. *Myanmar Times*, 1 September. https://www.mmtimes.com/national-news/22245-the-pivot-toward-closer-india-myanmar-ties.html.

Nasr, S.V.R. 2000. 'The Rise of Sunni Militancy in Pakistan: The Changing Role of Islamism and the Ulama in Society and Politics'. *Modern Asian Studies* 34 (1): 139–80.

Nasr, Vali. 2009. *Forces of Fortune: The Rise of the New Muslim Middle Class and What It Will Mean for Our World*. New York: Free Press.

Nayar, Baldev Raj. 2005. *The Geopolitics of Globalization: The Consequences for Development*. New Delhi: Oxford University Press.

Nayar, Baldev Raj and T.V. Paul. 2003. *India in the World Order: Searching for Major-Powers Status*. New Delhi: Cambridge University Press (in association with) Foundation Books Pvt. Ltd.

NDTV. 2016. 'SAARC Needs To Unleash Collective Strength, Says Sushma Swaraj'. *NDTV*. http://www.ndtv.com/india-news/saarc-needs-to-unleash-collective-strength-says-sushma-swaraj-1288197.

Nehru, Jawaharlal. [1946] 1987. *The Discovery of India*. New Delhi: Jawaharlal Nehru Memorial Fund and Oxford University Press.

————. [1950] 2013. 'Address at the Joint Session of the Pakistan and India Newspaper Editors' Conference'. *Mainstream Weekly*. Accessed on 8 January 2016. http://www.mainstreamweekly.net/article4219.html.

Nevins, J. 2000. 'The Law of the Land: Local-National Dialectic and the Making of the United States–Mexico Boundary'. *Southern California: Historical Geography* 28: 41–60.

Newman, David. 2003. 'Boundaries', in *A Companion to Political Geography*, ed. J. Agnew, K. Mitchell, and G. Toal. Malden: Blackwell Publishing.

————. 2006a. 'Borders and Bordering: Towards an Interdisciplinary Dialogue'. *European Journal of Social Theory* 9 (2): 171–86.

————. 2006b. 'The Lines That Continue to Separate Us: Borders in Our "Borderless" World'. *Progress in Human Geography* 30 (2): 143–61.

————. 2010. 'Territory, Compartments and Borders: Avoiding the Trap of the Territorial Trap'. *Geopolitics* 15 (4): 773–8.

Noorani, A.G. 2006. 'Caroe's Lessons'. *Frontline* 23 (9). Accessed on 2 January 2018. http://www.frontline.in/static/html/fl2309/stories/20060519001908300.htm.

Nye, Joseph S. 2008. 'Public Diplomacy and Soft Power'. *The Annals of the American Academy of Political and Social Science* 616: 94–109.

Nye, Joseph S. Jr. 1971. *Peace in Parts: Integration and Conflict in Regional Organisation*. Boston, MA: Massachusetts University Press.

ÓTuathail, Gearóid and John Agnew. 1992. 'Geopolitics and Discourse: Practical Geopolitical Reasoning in American Foreign Policy'. *Political Geography* 11 (2): 190–204.

Ó Tuathail, Gearóid and Simon Dalby. 1998. *The Geopolitics Reader*. New York: Routledge.

Outlook India. 2004. 'India, ASEAN Sign Historic Partnership Pact'. *Outlook India*. Accessed on 7 October 2016. https://www.outlookindia.com/newswire/story/india-asean-sign-historic-partnership-pact/264536.

Paasi, A. 2013. 'Borders and Border Crossings', in *The Wiley-Blackwell Companion to Cultural Geography*, ed. Nuala C. Johnson, Richard H. Schein, and Jamie Winders, pp. 478–93. New Jersey: Wiley-Blackwell.

Pande, Aparna. 2017. *From Chanakya to Modi: Evolution of India's Foreign Policy*. New Delhi: Harper Collins.

Pantham, Thomas. 1997. 'Indian Secularism and Its Critics: Some Reflections'. *The Review of Politics* 59 (3): 523–40.

Parmar, Sarabjeet Singh. 2012. 'Humanitarian Assistance and Disaster Relief (HADR) in India's National Strategy'. *Journal of Defence Studies, Institute for Defence Studies and Analyses* 6 (1): 91–101. Accessed on 26 December 2016. https://idsa.in/jds/6_1_2012_HumanitarianAssistanceandDisasterRelief (HADR)_SParmar.

Pasha, Mustapha Kamal. 1996. 'Security as Hegemony'. *Alternatives: Global, Local, Political* 21 (3): 283–302.

Patnaik, Prabhat. 1995. 'The Nation-State in an Era of Globalization'. *Economic and Political Weekly* 20 (33).

Paul, T.V., ed. 2005. *The India-Pakistan Conflict: An Enduring Rivalry*. New York: Cambridge University Press.

———. 2010. 'State Capacity and South Asia's Perennial Insecurity Problems', in *South Asia's Weak States: Understanding Regional Insecurity*, ed. T.V. Paul, pp. 3–27. Stanford, CA: Stanford University Press.

———. 2014. *The Warrior State: Pakistan in the Contemporary World*. Oxford: Oxford University Press.

Pentland, Charles. 1975. 'Functionalism and Theories of International Political Integration', in *Functionalism: Theory and Practice in International Relations*, ed. A.J.R. Groom and P. Taylor. London: University of London Press.

Philips, C.H. and Mary Doreen Wainwright. 1970. *The Partition of India: Policies and Perspectives, 1935–1947*. London: Geo Allen and Unwin.

Pillalamarri, Akhilesh. 2014. 'For SAARC to Work, India and Pakistan Must Resolve Differences'. *The Diplomat*, 27 November. http://thediplomat.com/2014/11/for-saarc-to-work-india-and-pakistan-must-resolve-differences/.

PM India. 2014. 'PM's Historic Address to Constituent Assembly of Nepal on 3 August 2014'. *PM India*. Accessed on 2 February 2017. http://www.pmindia.gov.in/en/news_updates/pms-historic-address-to-constituent-assembly-of-nepal/.

Prasad, Kailash K. 2014. 'India Looks Far East: A Growing Presence in the Pacific Islands could have Significant Benefits for India'. *The Diplomat*, 28 April. http://thediplomat.com/2014/04/india-looks-far-east/.

Press Trust of India. 2012. 'Arunachal Pradesh is "integral and important part" of India: Pranab Mukherjee'. *Times of India*, 29 November. Accessed on 5 March 2016. https://timesofindia.indiatimes.com/india/Arunachal-Pradesh-is-integral-and-important-part-of-India-Pranab-Mukherjee/articleshow/26590025cms.

———. 2014a. 'Andaman and Nicobar Can Be Springboard for India's Look East Policy: Pranab'. *Zee News*, 11 January. http://zeenews.india.com/news/nation/andaman-and-nicobar-can-be-springboard-for-india-s-look-east-policy-pranab_903374.html.

———. 2014b. 'Modi Announces USD 1 Bn Concessional Line of Credit to Nepal'. *Deccan Herald*, 3 August. http://www.deccanherald.com/content/423393/modi-announces-usd-1-bn.html.

———. 2015. 'PM Modi Calls for Enhancing Counter-Terror Cooperation with ASEAN'. *Indian Express*. Accessed on 15 January 2017. http://indianexpress.com/article/india/india-news-india/pm-modi-calls-for-enhancing-counter-terror-cooperation-with-asean/.

Raffestin, Claude. 2012. 'Space, Territory, and Territoriality'. *Environment and Planning D: Society and Space* 30 (1): 121–41.

Rais, Rasul B. 1993. 'South Asia and the Global System: Continuity and Change', in *External Compulsions of South Asian Politics*, ed. S.U. Kodikara. New Delhi: SAGE Publications.

Raja Mohan, C. 2001. 'Burying the Indira Doctrine'. *The Hindu*, 24 May. http://www.thehindu.com/2001/05/24/stories/05242523.htm.

———. 2003. *Crossing the Rubicon: The Shaping of India's New Foreign Policy*. New Delhi: Penguin.

———. 2013. 'An Uncertain Trumpet? India's Role in Southeast Asian Security', in *India–ASEAN Defence Relations*, ed. A.K. Das, pp. 8–32. Singapore: S. Rajaratnam School of International Studies.

———. 2016. 'From Looking East to Acting East'. *Carnegie Endowment for International Peace*. Accessed on 23 December 2016. http://carnegieendowment.org/2015/01/26/from-looking-east-to-acting-east-pub-58829.

Rajagopalan, Rajesh and Varun Sahni. 2008. 'India and the Great Powers: Strategic Imperatives, Normative Necessities'. *South Asian Survey* 15 (1).

Ramesh, Jairam. 2005. 'Northeast India in a New Asia'. *Seminar* (550). Accessed on 23 December 2016. http://www.india-seminar.com/2005/550/550%20jairam%20ramesh.htm.

Rana, A.P. 2003. 'SAARC: Evaluating the Bases of Regional Cooperation in South Asia'. *South Asian Survey* 10 (1): 1–39.

Ranade, Jayadeva. 2016. 'PM Modi's Visit Gives Substance to India–Japan Relations'. *The Sunday Guardian*, 12 November. https://www.sunday

guardianlive.com/opinion/7279-pm-modi-s-visit-gives-substance-india-japan-relations.

Ranjan, Prabhash. 2016. 'Coming Closer Together for Trade'. *The Hindu*, 9 September. Accessed on 11 December 2016. http://www.thehindu.com/opinion/op-ed/Coming-closer-together-for-trade/article14628676.ece.

Reid-Henry, Simon. 2010. 'The Territorial Trap Fifteen Years On'. *Geopolitics* 15 (4): 752–6.

Relph, Edward. 1976. *Place and Placelessness*. London: Pion.

Roy Chaudhury, Dipanjan. 2018. 'Australia, Japan and India Trilateral in Delhi on December 12'. *Economic Times*, 12 July. https://economictimes.indiatimes.com/news/defence/australia-japan-and-india-trilateral-in-delhi-on-december-12/articleshow/61840323.cms.

Ruggie, John G. 1993. 'Territoriality and Beyond: Problematizing Modernity in International Relations'. *International Organization* 47 (1): 139–74.

Rumley, Dennis, Timothy Doyle, and Sanjay Chaturvedi. 2013. 'Indo-Pacific as a Strategic Space: Implications of the Australia India Institute—Task Force Report on Indian Ocean Security, Stability and Sustainability in the 21st Century'. *Indo-Pacific Governance Research Centre Policy Brief* 2: 1–7. Accessed on 3 January 2018. https://www.adelaide.edu.au/indo-pacific-governance/research/policy/Rumley_Doyle_Chaturvedi_2013.pdf.

Ruparelia, Sanjay. 2008. 'How the Politics of Recognition Enabled India's Democratic Exceptionalism'. *International Journal of Politics, Culture, and Society* 21 (1/4): 39–56.

Russett, Bruce. 1993a. 'Can a Democratic Peace Be Built?'. *International Interactions* 18 (3): 277–82.

———. 1993b. *Grasping the Democratic Peace: Principles for a Post-Cold War World*. Princeton, NJ: Princeton University Press.

———. 2009. 'Democracy, War and Expansion through Historical Lenses'. *European Journal of International Relations* 5 (9): 9–36.

Russett, Bruce and John R. Oneal. 2001. *Triangulating Peace: Democracy, Interdependence, and International Organizations*. New York: W.W. Norton & Company.

Sack, Robert D. 1986. *Human Territoriality: Its Theory and History*. Cambridge: Cambridge University Press.

Sagar, Rahul. 2014. 'Jiski Lathi, Uski Bhains: The Hindu Nationalist View of International Politics', in *India's Grand Strategy: History, Theory, Cases*, ed. K. Bajpai, S. Basit, and V. Krishnappa. London: Routledge.

Sakhuja, Vijay. 2015. 'India's Yemeni Evacuation'. *Indian Defence Review* 30 (2). Accessed on 22 December 2016. http://www.indiandefencereview.com/news/indias-yemeni-evacuation/.

Samad, Saleem. 1998. 'State of Minorities in Bangladesh: From Secular to Islamic Hegemony'. Country paper presented at the Regional Consultation on Minority Rights in South Asia, South Asian Forum for Human Rights, Kathmandu, Nepal, 20–2 August. Accessed on 15 September 2017. http://groups.yahoo.com/group/muktomona/message/11898.

Samaddar, Ranabir. 1998a. *The Marginal Nations: Transborder Migration from Bangladesh to West Bengal*. New Delhi: SAGE Publications.

————. 1998b. 'The Failed Dialectic of Territoriality and Security, and Imperative of Dialogue'. *International Studies* 35 (1): 107–22.

————. 2001a. 'Friends, Foes and Understanding'. *Economic and Political Weekly* 36 (10).

————. 2001b. *A Biography of the Indian Nation, 1947–1997*. New Delhi: SAGE Publications.

————, ed. 2002. *Space, Territory and State*. Hyderabad: Orient Longman.

————, ed. 2003. *Refugees and the State: Practices of Asylum and Care in India, 1947–2000*. New Delhi: SAGE Publications.

Saran, Shyam. 2005. 'Foreign Secretary Mr. Shyam Saran's Speech on "India and Its Neighbours" at the India International Centre (IIC)'. *Ministry of External Affairs: Government of India*. Accessed on 6 July 2016. http://mea.gov.in/Speeches-Statements.htm?dtl/2483/Foreign+Secretary+Mr+Shyam+Sarans+speech+on+India+and+its+Neighbours+at+the+India+Internatio.

————. 2017. *How India Sees The World: From Kautilya to Modi: Kautilya to the 21st Century*. New Delhi: Juggernaut.

SATP. 2016. 'India Assessment—2016'. *SATP*. Accessed on 11 January 2017. http://www.satp.org/satporgtp/countries/india/index.html.

Scott, David. 2009. 'India's "Extended Neighborhood" Concept: Power Projection for a Rising Power'. *India Review* 8 (2): 107–43.

————. 2012. 'The "Indo-Pacific"—New Regional Formulations and New Maritime Frameworks for US–India Strategic Convergence'. *Asia Pacific Review* 19 (2): 85–109.

Sengupta, Bhabani. 1983. 'The Indian Doctrine'. *India Today*, 6 August.

Shahin, Sultan. 2003. 'India's "Look East" Policy Pays Off'. *Asia Times*, 11 October. http://www.atimes.com/atimes/South_Asia/EJ11Df05.html.

Shastri, Amita and A. Jeyaratnam Wilson. 2001. *The Post-Colonial States of South Asia: Democracy, Development and Identity*. London: Palgrave Macmillan.

Singh, Ajit Kumar. 2013. 'Pakistan: Sinking State'. *South Asia Intelligence Review: Weekly Assessments & Briefings* 11 (36). Accessed on 16 November 2016. http://www.satp.org/satporgtp/sair/Archives/sair11/11_36.htm.

Singh, Jaswant. 1999. *Defending India*. New Delhi: Macmillan India.

———. 2012. 'The Lynchpin of Asia in Great Game'. *Project Syndicate*. Accessed on 15 November 2016. http://www.project-syndicate.org/commentary/the-lynchpin-of-asia.

Singh, L.P. 1999. 'Hearing the Lessons of History', in *Securing India's Future in the New Millennium*, ed. B. Chellaney. Hyderabad: Orient Longman.

Singh, Manmohan. 2005a. 'Northeast 2020'. *Yojana* 49 (12): 3–4.

———. 2005b. 'Speech by Prime Minister Dr. Manmohan Singh at India Today Conclave, New Delhi'. *Ministry of External Affairs: Government of India*. Accessed on 16 January 2017. www.mea.gov.in/Speeches-Statements.htm?dtl/2464.

———. 2012. 'Opening Statement by Prime Minister at Plenary Session of India-ASEAN Commemorative Summit'. Accessed on 23 January 2017. http://www.pib.nic.in/newsite/erelcontent.aspx?relid=91052.

———. 2013. 'Opening Statement by Prime Minister at 11th India–ASEAN Summit in Brunei Darussalam'. *Press Information Bureau, Government of India: Prime Minister's Office*. Accessed on 24 October 2017. http://pib.nic.in/newsite/PrintRelease.aspx?relid=99956.

Singh, P.K. 2015. 'India Pakistan Nuclear Dyad and Regional Nuclear Dynamics'. *Asia Policy* (19): 37–44.

Singh, Ritesh Kumar. 2012. 'Time Intra-SAARC Trade Improved'. *The Hindu: BusinessLine*, 8 January. https://www.thehindubusinessline.com/opinion/time-intra-saarc-trade-improved/article20382905.ece1.

Sinha, Yashwant. 2003. 'Remarks by Shri Yashwant Sinha External Affairs Minister of India at The Plenary Session Second India–ASEAN Business Summit'. *Ministry of External Affairs: Government of India*. Accessed on 17 January 2017. http://mea.gov.in/Speeches-Statements.htm?dtl/4843/Remarks+by+Shri+Yashwant+Sinha+External+Affairs+Minister+of+India+at+The+Plenary+Session+Second+India++ASEAN+Business+Summit.

Sobhan, Rehman. 1998. 'Regional Cooperation in South Asia: A Quest for Identity'. *South Asian Survey* 5 (1): 3–26.

Sparke, M. 2005. *In the Space of Theory: Postfoundational Geographies of the Nation-State*. Minneapolis: University of Minnesota Press.

Stewart, Frances and Taimur Hyat. 2002. 'Conflict in South Asia: Prevalence, Costs and Politics', in *The South Asian Challenge*, ed. K. Haq. New York: Oxford University Press.

Subrahmanyam, K. 2008. 'Nehru's Concept of Indian Defence'. *Strategic Analysis* 32 (6): 1179–90.

Sukumar, Arun Mohan. 2015. 'A Shift from Style to Substance'. *The Hindu*, 16 December. http://www.thehindu.com/opinion/op-ed/modis-foreign-policy-a-shift-from-style-to-substance/article7987958.ece.

Sundar, Nandini. 2012. 'Civil Society and Democratic Change in Asia'. *CETRI*. Accessed on 6 January 2017. http://www.cetri.be/Civil-society-and-democratic?lang=fr.

Swaraj, Sushma. 2014. 'Special Address by External Affairs Minister on "SAARC in a Globalizing World" Organized by South Asian Univeristy at IIC, New Delhi'. *Ministry of External Affairs: Government of India*. Accessed on 7 January 2017. https://www.mea.gov.in/Speeches-Statements.htm?dtl/24439/Special_Address_by_External_Affairs_Minister_on_SAARC_in_a_Globalizing_World_organized_by_South_Asian_Univeristy_at_IIC_New_Delhi.

Talukdar, Sushanta. 2004. 'Looking East'. *Frontline* 21 (20). Accessed on 9 July 2017. https://www.frontline.in/static/html/fl2120/stories/20041008002104200.htm.

Tellis, Ashley J. 2007. 'India in Asian Geopolitics', in *Rising India: Friends and Foes*, ed. Prakash Nanda. New Delhi: Lancer.

Thapliyal, Sangeeta. 2014. 'Modi's Visit to Nepal: An Assessment'. *Mainstream* 52 (34). Accessed on 22 January 2017. http://www.mainstreamweekly.net/article5127.html.

The Tribune. 2002. 'PM to Attend SAARC Summit in Pak'. *Tribune*, 22 August. http://www.tribuneindia.com/2002/20020823/main6.htm.

The World Bank. n.d. 'One South Asia'. *The World Bank*. Accessed on 13 May 2017. http://www.worldbank.org/en/programs/south-asia-regional-integration.

Tuan, Y. 1977. *Space and Place: The Perspective of Experience*. Minneapolis: University of Minnesota.

UNCTAD. 2015. 'World Investment Report 2015: Reforming International Investment Governance'. Geneva: United Nations Publication. Accessed on 11 September 2016. http://unctad.org/en/PublicationsLibrary/wir2015_en.pdf.

Vajpayee, Atal Bihari. 2001. 'India and ASEAN-Shared Perspectives'. Prime Minister Vajpayee's Address to the Institute of Diplomatic and Foreign Relations, Kuala Lumpur'. Accessed on 22 October 2016. http://www.indianembassy.org/special/cabinet/Primeminister/pm_may_16_2001.htm.

————. 2002. 'Prime Minister's Speech at the SAARC Summit in Kathmandu'. *Former Prime Ministers of India*. Accessed on 11 January 2017. http://archivepmo.nic.in/abv/speech-details.php?nodeid=9034.

————. 2003. 'Prime Minister Shri Atal Bihari Vajpayee's Speech at the Chief Minister's Conference on Internal Security'. *Former Prime Ministers of India*.

Accessed on 1 February 2017. http://archivepmo.nic.in/abv/speech-details.php?nodeid=9000.

———. 2004. 'Prime Minister Atal Behari Vajpayee's Statement at the 12th SAARC Summit in Islamabad, Pakistan, on 4 January 2004'. *South Asia Terrorism Portal*. Accessed on 20 January 2017. http://www.satp.org/satporgtp/countries/india/document/papers/SAARC_pak.htm.

van Schendel, Willem. 2002. 'Stateless in South Asia: The Making of the India-Bangladesh Enclaves'. *The Journal of Asian Studies* 61 (1): 115–47.

———. 2005. *The Bengal Borderland: Beyond State and Nation in South Asia.* London: Anthem Press.

Vanaik, Achin. 1990. *The Painful Transition: Bourgeois Democracy in India.* London: Verso.

Varshney, Ashutosh. 1993. 'Contested Meanings: India's National Identity, Hindu Nationalism, and the Politics of Anxiety'. *Daedalus* 122 (3): 227–61.

———. 1995. *Democracy, Development and the Countryside: Urban-Rural Struggles in India.* Cambridge: Cambridge University Press.

Vaughan-Williams, Nic. 2009. *Border Politics: The Limits of Sovereign Power.* George Square: Edinburgh University Press.

Väyrynen, Raimo. 1984. 'Regional Conflict Formations: An Intractable Problem of International Relations?'. *Journal of Peace Research* 21 (4): 337–59.

Wadhwa, Anil. 2014. 'Address by Secretary (East) on 'Security and Defence within the Framework of the Look East Policy' at the International Relations Conference 2014 (Pune, December 14, 2014)'. *Ministry of External Affairs: Government of India.* Accessed on 3 September 2016. http://www.mea.gov.in/Speeches-Statements.htm?dtl/24532/Address_by_Secretary_East_on_Security_and_Defence_within_the_Framework_of_the_Look_East_Policy_at_the_International_Relations_Conference_2014_Pune_Dec.

Wagner, Christian. 2014. 'Security Cooperation in South Asia: Overview, Reasons, Prospects'. SWP Research Paper 2014/RP 06, Stiftung Wissenschaft und Politik, Berlin.

Walker, R.B.J. 1993. *Inside/Outside: International Relations as Political Theory.* Cambridge: Cambridge University Press.

Waltz, Kenneth. [1979] 2010. *Theory of International Politics.* Illinois: Waveland Press.

Walzer, M. 1983. *Spheres of Justice.* New York: Basic Books.

Wendt, Alexander. 1994. 'Collective Identity Formation and the International State'. *American Political Science Review* 88 (2).

Wendt, Alexander. 1999. *Social Theory of International Politics.* New York: Cambridge University Press.

Wendt, Alexander E. 1987. 'The Agent–Structure Problem in International Relations Theory'. *International Organization* 41 (3): 335–70.

Williams, J. 2006. *The Ethics of Territorial Borders: Drawing Lines in the Shifting Sand*. Basingstoke and New York: Palgrave Macmillan.

Wilson, Thomas M. and Hastings Donnan, eds. 1998. *Border Identities: Nation and State at International Frontiers*. Cambridge: Cambridge University Press.

Xiaoping, Yang. 2012. 'The Security Architecture of South Asia: Problems and Prospects'. *India China Institute*. Accessed on 12 October 2016. indiachinainstitute.org/wp-content/uploads/2010/03/Yang-Xiaoping-Security-Architecture-of-SA.pdf.

Index

About the Author

Shibashis Chatterjee is professor, Department of International Relations, Jadavpur University, Kolkata, India. His areas of interest are international relations theory, foreign policy, and political theory. He was a Fulbright-Nehru Visiting Lecturer in 2011, attached to the Department of Political Science at Indiana University, USA, and a Fulbright-Nehru Academic and Professional Excellence Fellow at the University of Yale, USA, in 2016–17. He has published extensively in journals like *India Review*, *Japanese Journal of Political Science*, *International Studies*, *South Asian Survey*, and *Economic* and *Political Weekly*, and contributed numerous research papers to edited volumes.